# Fat Man
# in Argentina

## TOM VERNON

**LARGE PRINT**

Oxford, England

Copyright © Tom Vernon, 1990

First published in Great Britain 1990
by Michael Joseph Ltd
a member of the Penguin Group of Companies

Published in Large Print 1993 by Clio Press,
55 St. Thomas' Street, Oxford OX1 1JG,
by arrangement with Michael Joseph Ltd

The moral right of the author has been asserted.

**British Library Cataloguing in Publication Data**
Vernon, Tom
    Fat Man in Argentina. — New ed
    I. Title
    918.270464

Printed and bound by Hartnolls Ltd, Bodmin, Cornwall
Cover designed by CGS Studios Ltd, Cheltenham

# CONTENTS

**THE NORTH-WEST**

# ACKNOWLEDGEMENTS

I am very grateful to all my companions and friends who contributed to the making of the television programmes, produced by Tomahawk Limited, and to many more Argentines than those whose names appear below or in the text of the book itself. First and foremost, the work of my fellow director/producer, Jenny De Yong, was fundamental to the events of the two bike trips outlined in the foreword, which were planned with the help of research by Chloë Sayer and organization by Roberto Mayer of Patagonian Travel. There would have been no journey at all but for John Willis and Godfrey Thorpe of Channel 4, Nelsa Gidney of WGBH, Euryn Ogwen Williams of S4C, and Julia Vakkuri of Oy Yleisradio A.B., Finland who were instrumental in the commissioning and finance of the venture, encouraged by Carol Haslam and Nigel Houghton of Hawkshead Limited.

Among those in Britain who gave time and advice generously were: Andrew and Michaela Graham-Yooll (who suggested starting at Lujan); Teddy and Gillian Piero; Oscar Grillo; Clare Hargreaves; Ada Coleman; David Wickham; Ian Hibell; Richard Klemperer; Ben Fox; and Barney Miller and others in the Anglo-Argentine Society. Glenn Thompson of F. W. Evans prepared the bicycle, Varig helped with flights for the film crew and Gore-tex with clothing.

Among native Argentines, I most warmly thank Juan Lucas Young, Carmen Stefani Gari and Federico Kirbus for their particularly valuable help. Adriana Zanutigh and Alejandro Massucco were wonderfully agreeable representatives of Argentine officialdom. Among others to whom I am most grateful are: Jorge Cebalos, driver; Anna E. Weinstein of the Jewish Information Centre; Dr Enrique Schoolnik, philanthropist; Ramon Poliearpos Flores, waiter; Aitor Aiboitiz; Claudia of the Argentine National Film Archive; Julian Cooper; Graciella Palotto of the Museo Guiraldes; Juan Jose Draghi, silversmith; Mercedes Zerboni and her family; Eduardo Marino and Ruven C. Falco, agronomists; gauchos at the Festival of Tradition and the Estancia La Barrancosa; scientists of the Institute of Haemorrhagic Fever; a hotel porter of Pergamino; lorrydrivers at Maggiolo; staff of the Estancia La Danesa; Venado Tuerto Polo Club; Tamara Nutting Rodriguez; Beryl Slater and Christina Slater de Díaz; members of the crew of the *Graf Spey*; Raul Cueto, artist.

In Patagonia: Luis Etcheverrigaray, chef; Willy Hassler, taxi driver and writer on Mapuches; Honorio Vera, ox-driver; Jose Calarota-Pino and his St Bernards; chocolate-makers of Bariloche, especially Angel Antolin and Maria Anna Reven of Chocolate Edelweiss; Alejandra Cecilie Ruiz; Nora McKinnen; Rhiannon Aplavon Gough; Ferrocarriles Argentinas, Alistair Grant and railwaymen of the narrow-gauge; an unknown but hospitable road-mender; Rosalia Catriman, Mapuche weaver; Luned Gonzales, schoolmistress; Tegai Roberts of Gaimán Museum; David Drake and Eluned Morgan; Liliana Pantasio; Alicia B. de Fernandez; Gladys Thomas; Sandra Day; Susan Hughes, Norman Caruso of the Dirección Nacional de Vialidad.

In Salta: Karin; Lucrezia of the Tourist Office; Marcelo

of Salta Renta-Autos; Ramiro Penalva, journalist; Christina Pauelo and Maria del Carmen Labata of the Women's Committee; Jacobo Regen, poet; Hugo Julio Garcia, a guitarist who is very kind to strangers.

Finally, my affectionate thanks to Mike, Graham, Paola, Fraser, Jo-Jo, Bella, Jane, Ted, Jimmy, Ann, Emma, Joan, Dee, Carrie, Grant, Tony, Chris, Aad and Diana. And most especially to Sally Vernon, who read the manuscript and rescued me from many bits I particularly liked at the time.

To Sally, again

BRAZIL

BOLIVIA

PARAGUAY

CHILE

ARGENTINA

URU-
GUAY

First Journey

Second Journey

# FOREWORD

This book was written during the research and making of two television films, *Fat Man in Argentina*. They were filmed during the Argentine spring in October and November 1989 in what was fundamentally a re-creation of journeys which had taken place in the April and May before, and which are the journeys described in the book.

The first six-week trip for *Fat Man in Argentina*, therefore, took place in the Argentine autumn, with myself on my favourite bicycle, *The Roman Philosopher*, and my fellow director/producer, Jenny De Yong, in a car. While I cycled, she would drive ahead to research the next place, lining up people to talk to and things to see for that evening and the next morning. We travelled thus across the pampa and across Patagonia, but drove between Córdoba and Bariloche. (I also stayed some weeks on my own account in other parts of Argentina, notably Salta and the north-west.)

For me, the essence of the bicycle is slow travel, close observation, physical contact with the country and unpretentious meetings with the people. I am trying to paint a landscape, not a self-portrait; to seek experience, not endurance. My ordeals in 1700 kilometres of cycling are minor in comparison with those cyclists who are far from home with nothing but what they can carry, for months, even years at a time. All I am doing is paying a country the compliment of not passing too lightly over it.

Though it includes material and events which took place between September and November 1989, the basic setting of this book is in the time of the original journey which it describes. Because different people were involved at different times, I have kept it as an entirely personal account — though I have reason to be very grateful to all my companions.

In the few months between journey and filming, many things changed for Argentina. A new president turned out to offer more hope than many would have believed possible in a honeymoon destined to be followed by a resurgence of extraordinary inflation; relations with Britain advanced from hostility to *rapprochement*; Argentine *militars* (members of the military) facing trial for crimes against civil rights were pardoned, and freely walked the streets again. I happened to make my journey on what the future may see as a cusp of national destiny. As I rode those long, straight highways I was not alone in performing a balancing act. Argentina herself was joining me.

*London and Buenos Aires*
*Winter 1989/90*

# PROLOGUE

# My Father's Pipe

There were three things I knew about Argentina, and the first of these was my father's pipe. He was a man of strong and determined tastes, and when he decided to give up his habitual roll-your-own of Magpie Shag mixed with Digger Shag for a smoke that would be both healthier and more economical, he set out on a course of experimentation which included not only leaves from Ceylon and Darjeeling, but also maté, the Argentine tea.

Maté was finely chopped and an innocent pale green. But ignited, the effect was dramatic, like a bonfire stuffed with fireworks. Festoons and fountains of sparks came out of the smoke which completely enveloped Pa's head, and burnt holes in the armchairs. The smell was choking and abominable. But it was only after the destruction of several pullovers that he admitted defeat, and made tea with the rest of the packet. This was maté *cocido*, though I did not know that then, and in our house we drank it at intervals for the rest of my childhood.

It was about the time that they gave me *Far Away and Long Ago* at school, and this was the second thing I knew about Argentina — a small, blue book on an ink-stained desk at the end of a school day.

Hudson's story of childhood on the pampa is a late afternoon book. He wrote it when he was old and the light he throws on his purple plain has the richness of the magic hour, the film-maker's time of haloed grasses and long shadows. Hudson's Argentina was my Argentina. Cars, aeroplanes, football were nowhere, because he did not write about them: there were no mountains, lakes or jungle, no waves of immigration, no Perón. Even as Hudson wrote, railways had changed his pampa from a place for pioneers to one of business — and many of the limitless grasslands had fences. But not for me. For something of the magic of his childhood hour was upon me, too.

I knew a third thing — a war which was an example of criminal incompetence on the part of two governments, both only too willing to exploit human suffering for electoral advantage. It was one more proof that there is no shortage of personal bravery in the world, only of the judgement to decide when it is right to call upon it.

Years passed. Money poured into the Falklands, which had previously been refused the tiniest grants for the most essential purposes. There was no British embassy in Buenos Aires, nor an Argentine one in London, and Britons who wanted to travel to Argentina had to have visas, just to be awkward. There were no direct flights from Heathrow, just to be awkward. The two countries were like two children who had been cat-calling "horrid" and "beastly", and were not going to play with each other, ever again.

But, given a few years, a state of hostilities over islands, which to one side were so small and to the other so remote, was bound to change: and the background of friendships and former trade links between the two countries made it likely to change sooner rather than later. I thought that it would be right to redress some of the appalling traducements of the Argentines of which Britain had been guilty. Not that

I had any idea what those people in the far south were like: but nobody could be as bad as their image presented in the *Sun* newspaper — other than those cynical enough to paint it.

I was also curious, for by this time I knew more than my father's pipe. The vast and varied geography that went from penguins to parrots in the same land was beginning to draw me. I planned my visit with some apprehension, not only concerned about the reception I might get following the Falklands' conflict but also unable to get out of my mind the thousands who died in the Dirty War. I was not clear how far Argentina had come from that sort of police state, nor how soon it might go back to it again.

Channel Four Television and WGBH of Boston responded warmly to the suggestion of a series: and we began to lay our plans a few months before the newly-elected President Menem proposed his. The thing I did not appreciate at first was how absurd the state of hostility had been. I had to meet the Argentines themselves to recognize that.

# BUENOS AIRES

# CHAPTER
# ONE

# Gaps in a Great City

## *Argentina's Capital*

I came into Buenos Aires in the early morning behind a rattling lorry piled high with celery. The streets were almost empty. Their usual jostling, honking vehicles were still garaged, or asleep by the roadside with pale sunlight streaming over them.

In the wide avenues of the city great trees of unfamiliar shape presided over grass that had forgotten how to be truly green, if it had ever known. The trees were jacarandas, long past the electric blue of their flowering. Others bore straggly but flamboyant petals of luminous pink, though spring was the other side of the year. Towards the bottom, the trunks of the *palo borracho*, "the drunkard's tree", bulged out like a beer belly. Dull green fruit, like large avocados, hung from the boughs — some splitting their skins, with a ball of something like cotton wool fluffing out.

For them, the year was getting old: for me, everything was new. I had never been to another continent before, let alone cycled on it. I had planned two journeys with the aid of maps, books and friendly advice — one east over Patagonia from the mountains to the sea; the other to the west across the *pampa*, as I was already learning to call it, rather than pampas (even in English I prefer the Spanish singular, because it gives a better impression of its limitless and unchanging personality). Now it was limbo time, hanging around in Buenos Aires waiting for off. And the "off" seemed to get further away. Buenos Aires is a magnetic city: it had already attracted a third of the population of Argentina to come and live in it, and was reluctant to let me go and start cycling. Or perhaps I was reluctant, because like all great cities it was a protection, and I really had no idea what to expect in the countryside.

I went to get a press pass at the Ministry of the Exterior. I did not know whether to be flattered that I was being given one or alarmed that it might be needed. The day was balmy at first then became hot. Was it going to stay like this? I asked the Ministry Public Relations man. Yes, he said — nowadays. Ten years ago it would have been different, the winters were cold then; but with the destruction of the Amazonian rain forest the weather is now warm all the year round. And they had changed the water flow in the Amazon, too, which was having its consequences. What with that and three years' inadequate rainfall, the hydroelectrics were running dry.

There were power cuts every day; and engineers had shut down the local nuclear plant on safety grounds, promising another Chernobyl less than a hundred miles from the capital if their advice was ignored. In front of the smart tourist shops in the fashionable streets, a shanty town of generators had grown up — shacks containing monsters of manifolds to pump yet more fumes into the atmosphere. In this Buenos Aires, sweet airs were little in evidence — and, as well as the fumes, strands of fluff from the flowering trees floated in the would-be breeze.

Buenos Aires was big and fast. It had banks like temples,

a ring road like a country estate, elderly buildings curly with rich decoration — but there were hovels in the suburbs and the telephones did not work. The shops were crowded with the most extraordinary leathers and luxurious furs, but the pavements in front of them were full of holes and casual duckboardings over hidden municipal depths. You can tell a lot from a hole in the pavement: from these ones you could tell that there were gaps in the public spirit of Argentina. Let the shoes in the central shops be never so magnificent — and they were, gleaming like ripples — those shoes had to pick their way round the holes left by one gang of workmen for somebody else to clear up. Teetering over planks, scarring themselves on heaps of rubble went the shoes, and never a hesitation: for the shoes are always grand, and the pavements always in holes in Buenos Aires.

There was a crisis. (There is often a crisis.) There was a new finance minister, talk of devaluation and queues outside the banks — and the austral was going down. The days when it had been a crisp new currency on a par with the dollar were long gone. It was now at forty-five to the dollar, having been at forty the day before, and everybody who was sharp enough was making money as it fell. In and out of the banks and the cambios went the middle classes in their fine shoes, shifting money about, those who had it. "Doing the bicycle" they call it — "*hacer la bicycletta*" — a glorious freewheel on creative accounting.

There were others whose ride through life was of a different kind. The people who dug the holes in the pavements were representative of the class of *empleados*, employed people whose prosperity was tied to their wages or salaries. They too played the money market as best they could, but at a disadvantage: their capital was less, and the boss was inclined to prefer them to be working rather than in and out of the *cambio*. Still, even schoolchildren could be seen changing their dollars. *Vivo*, you have to be *vivo* in Argentina — wheel, deal and dodge the holes in the pavement. Why, after floods, it is not unknown for people to fall into those holes in the pavement and drown.

There are often floods: greater Buenos Aires is a city some sixty miles by forty that contains over a third of Argentina's population of thirty million people, but less than half of it has sewerage, and the rest of the drainage seems to match. There is no shortage of public service rhetoric, but somehow it does not fill in the holes.

A great deal of the infrastructure of Buenos Aires — and Argentina in general — dates from its more prosperous period, which may have been as late as the Forties and Fifties, or as early as the turn of the century. Often this is frustrating, as with telephones that manage to combine an extraordinary capriciousness with impenetrable impassivity; and the post, which is a sort of gambling game played with letters. Sometimes it has charm, as in the underground, where the carriages are solid, old fashioned and four-square, a cross between the old Metro and the old London Underground, with little white lampshades. But the tiled murals on the stations are outstanding — beautiful colours, lovely scenes — and when there is a train opposite, its windows frame the scene in such a way that it looks as if the train is passing through fairyland.

The past has created some great public splendours for Buenos Aires, which — in the centre at least — is often a wonderful city. But its present-day spirit seems better expressed by the *colectivos*, the extraordinary system of private buses which began to develop in 1928, following the Wall Street crash, when the Buenos Aires taxis took to offering a fixed fare to a particular place for as many as they could cram into their capacious insides. Today, they are bulbous, gaudy, rattly, uncomfortable Mercedes buses that charge through the streets like mad horses, with the driver dispensing change with one hand as he steers, indicates, gestures and operates front and back doors with the other. If you are young and fit enough to leap on and off like a tango dancer, the *colectivo* works remarkably well — but the devil take anyone who is not *vivo*.

Reeling from my first *colectivo*, I passed down a side street, not far from where General San Martín, architect of freedom, sits proud on his bronze horse in the plaza named after him, pointing the way to nationhood — and down a side street a young woman lay in an alcove with a baby at her breast, unobtrusively but professionally begging. She did not look *vivo*. Nor did she look like the girls ogling the fashions in Florida, the smart shopping street. Some of them were among the most beautiful creatures I have ever seen, with meticulously turbulent hair and bodies like young animals. The girl with the baby just looked tired of life.

I passed a restaurant whose window contained a complete and gigantic camp fire — whole trunk logs, glowing red among its white ashes. Around it, crucified on stainless steel crosses were several sheep, goats and gigantic pieces of cow. A high protein fragrance drifted heavily and mouth-wateringly down the street. I don't think the woman with the baby went there either.

Almost all Argentine towns are laid out on a grid pattern

and have the same street names, which are either patriotic references to heroes and great days from the national history or other countries and towns. In this way you can speedily cross Uruguay, Armenia, Bolivia, Hungria, Indonesia and Boulogne-sur-Mer; take a stroll up Generals César Díaz and Fructuos Rivera, and you wind up in Australia.

I lunched at a pavement café on Córdoba off beer in great round glasses frosty with cold, and *picadas*, which in Spain they would call *tapas*. There were over two dozen tiny dishes, all protein rich, starting with *empanadas*, the pasty of Argentina, much smaller than a Cornish pasty and full of minced meat. Often, they come with *chimichurri*, a savoury sauce of herbs and garlic in oil. Here, the vegetable kingdom was represented by: olives plain green, and black with chilli; Russian salads; crisps, acid pickles and peanuts. There was several times the quantity of meat and cheese: liver sausage, chilli chicken, sausages, frankfurters, Croque Monsieur, cheese and ham sandwich, chunks of cheese, cheese straws, a kind of *boudin blanc* and a hard-boiled egg imprisoned in layers of white meat.

It was all rather bland, textureless and fatty, but the thing that really made it an unsatisfactory meal was the begging. First came a fat miserable woman, then two tots with Indian-black hair, who managed to be miserable at the table but were unable to prevent themselves breaking out in chortles when they had gone past, followed by a doddering old woman with gaps in her teeth and some motor disease, who took her australs with a hand like a claw. A young man laid out a set of tourist maps on the tables and collected them unsold; a small boy did the same with holy pictures, and a brown little girl put a tired red rose before me.

It contrasted sadly with the better-off *porteños*, as the inhabitants of Buenos Aires call themselves — the people of the port. Nowadays, the port has done a remarkable job of pricing itself out of the international shipping market, and captains dread the delays. *Porteños* are more likely to spend their time shifting money across a counter than shipping cargo, and the only time they approach the docks is to visit the pasta restaurants in the vivid Italian and artists' quarter of La Boca, where some of the streets are painted in brilliant yellows, reds and blues, while others remain rickety palaces of corrugated iron. (The area is supposed to be where the ill-fated Spanish expedition of 1536 under Don Pedro de Mendoza christened his landfall Puerto Nuestro Señora Santa Maria de Buen Aire — meaning fair winds for the sailor, rather than a healthy atmosphere on the River Plate. He had to quit in less than two years, with only a third of his original 1600 men having survived disease, famine, incompetence, and the attacks of alienated Indians. However, the delta is advancing about fifty metres a year, from the six tonnes of mud that are deposited every second by the Parana, and not everyone agrees that the monument put up for the fourth centenary in 1936 is in the right place.)

All locals are *porteños* — but some are more *porteño* than others. While the bulk of the inhabitants make the city work dressed in leather jackets, jeans, anoraks and all the other standard international clothes, you will often see a man picking his way through the crowd who is nattily — though not necessarily newly — dressed in a style that perfectly complements the curlicues and grandeurs of the old buildings. In particular, his shoes will shine as I cannot imagine you will find anywhere else in the world, through

9

the attentions of the local shoe-shine men. His is the style of the great days of Buenos Aires, and his wife will have it too. (The style of the young women of Buenos Aires can also be remarkable, but that is something else.)

I met quite another style of citizen when I went to have tea at Quilmes orphanage — a private foundation started by an Englishman, Charles Kirkby, in 1894, after he was pensioned off from the railway. Doing charity work in hospital, he was so distressed by the dying women who asked what would become of their children, that he decided to provide an answer.

Quilmes was where W. H. Hudson had his first family home in the 1850s, among spreading grasslands and birds. I found it an undistinguished suburb well within the edge of the urban sprawl. It was a long, efficient building with a neat garden. Inside it was quiet — the children were still at school — and my footsteps echoed down the high, bare corridors.

Francis Coleman was my host. As well as being a psychiatrist and neurologist, he ran the orphanage, as his mother did before him — half a day on, half a day off, with his wife, Tila. Mother did not seem to me to be the sort of woman who was capable of retiring. Small, with swept-back hair, she had all the power of someone who has spent her life doing important human work well. She was Italian-Argentine: indeed, Argentina Coleman was her name, née Medici, but Francis had kept his father's entitlement to a British passport.

"How was it during the Malvinas War, then, for a man with British connections?" I asked.

He looked like a psychiatrist, with glasses and a goatee,

and he told me that between 1982 and 1983 the proportion of Anglo-Argentines among his patients went up from ten to forty per cent.

"There is no such thing as an Argentine national antagonism towards any British subject at all," he told me, "but all Anglo-Argentines had a hell of a time. I was torn in two pieces — schizophrenic. You're both British and Argentine, and you're really serious about it. You try and do your best with both backgrounds, both sets of principles, both idiosyncracies.

"My ancestors — my father, my grandfather — were British and I was educated along those lines. But Argentina is my country. So I was split down the middle — depressed, miserable.

"We thought we were winning — we thought we were doing the right thing at first, vindicating history and the rest of it. Then we got the BBC news, which was diametrically opposite to the Argentine news. So we didn't know where we were. Half our brains were in the middle of the Atlantic with the British and the rest of ourselves was in Argentina trying to help in whatever way we could. If I'd been called up by the Army, I would have had to go, and I'd have had to do things properly — and I don't think I would have enjoyed it at all."

I said, "I think that both in England and in Argentina we have politicians to prevent this sort of thing from happening, not to encourage it. Neither of us can feel proud of anything in connection with it — it was just a mess and a waste."

"I thought it wasn't worth a toffee. It wasn't worth a war of two thousand dead and all the rest that's tacked on to thousands of people dying. For according to the newspapers it was just for sovereignty — and what is sovereignty, one asks, no?"

We went up to the family flat. The living room contained an electronic organ fire-blackened on one side, and the framed certificates on the walls had burn marks.

"The circuit breakers," said Francis. "German, but they failed to work."

Beneath a painting of waves, the tea-table was spread with a lace cloth edged with pink flowers. The cottage china was an English floral pattern. Tea came: we said grace, the family being Plymouth Brethren. We had little triangles of puff pastry put under the grill with cheese, ham and sugar on top.

"*Mafaldas*," said Argentina.

"We don't eat like this every day," said Francis.

There was salad and ham and egg sandwiches; little cakes with chocolate on top; a large quince cheese tart, latticed with pastry; and tea in a pot.

"No, we certainly don't eat like this every day," Francis said again. "Everybody says, 'Have you been to the States? Have you been to Europe?' Can't afford it. It's very expensive to get out of Argentina. Once you're in and you're part of the country — and not a privileged millionaire — you've had it. There's no possibility of expansion or travelling."

I thought of the smart women and the expensive shops. "One of the things I do notice about Argentina is that there do seem to be a lot of extremely rich and a lot of very poor people."

Francis agreed. "First, politicians are always pocketing the money — everybody says that, the newspapers are full of it. Second, yes, we do know that there are a thousand or so extre-e-emly rich families among the thirty million inhabitants in Argentina. Their ancestors were immigrants who worked very hard in the last century and made a lot of money. It's a bit odd isn't it? There is an unfair distribution of wealth, but I'd say that it's the rich that keep the country alive. It's not the poor people."

Christian, Francis's son, came back from school. He was nearing the top form of St George's College, one of the most celebrated of the British schools of Buenos Aires. There are over thirty of them and they are much in demand, both because they teach in English and because of the demanding standards of their education. Christian wore a school uniform that would have gladdened the heart of a head teacher in Surbiton.

"Mr Sims of Durham is headmaster of St George's College. He says it is far better than Eton," said Francis, with pride.

"I went to a grammar school, myself," I said non-committally, and we went back to the subject of what was beginning to sound more and more like a nation of anarchists.

"I think the word is disorganization," said Francis. "Argentines as individuals are excellent people — very, very capable. But we need powerful leaders. If you study the Argentine history, you will come to the conclusion that, though we are against autocratic governments, somehow or other we are afraid of freedom, afraid of liberty — we don't know what to do with it. We need Daddy coming along to spank us occasionally."

"Is that how it looks to you, Christian?" I asked.

"I think young Argentines are very selfish. They will always do what they think, and would never put other things that are more important before their own concerns."

We went downstairs, back to the high, bare corridors. There was nothing soft or luxurious in the building. The warmth came from the people in it, the children running and jumping round me like affectionate puppies.

Francis introduced me to them.

"Blanca is studying horse-riding at St George's College — that's a little bit of social service they are trying to do." (Aside: "Some of their histories are so traumatic — very, very passionate and very, very violent indeed. We have one girl who remembers her mother pouring petrol over herself and burning to death — and the girl could do nothing about it. She was four years old. She still wakes up at night and screams." I could not say anything: I was only thankful that I did not know which girl it was, for then I would not have known how to look at her either.)

"We have one girl who has just become a lawyer, another who is a chartered accountant, others are graduates in business administration." ("Yet they're from slums. Modestly, we are their mum and dad. Most of them have nobody and nothing in this world apart from this institution and the directors.")

"It must be heart-breaking."

"It is heart-breaking. There's an Argentine expression which I use quite often, 'You've got to be coated in a lot of goose oil.' Things have to slip off you."

"We do it for love," said Argentina, her hands clasped before her. "That's the only thing you can do, is do it for love."

There is a good deal of heart-break in Buenos Aires, both real and affected. Tango, the music of the city, is based on passionate melancholy; it was born in the 1900s in the brothels and cabarets. Later, men would go to dance tango with a professional, since no respectable girl would be allowed to dance it. But dance is only part of this ritual, which also includes both instrumental music and song. As one ageing fan said to me:

"Gardel — you know Gardel, the great tango singer? Gardel died fifty years ago — and still we say, 'Every day he sings better.' The smell of the tango is in the city. I'm not religious at all. But to dance the tango is to be in a church."

So that evening I went to see the tango at the Casablanca on a tourist coach that went round the shows, superintended by an eager-beavering guide like a chipmunk. Her name was Gladys, and the coach-driver's name was Charlie. She gave us a lecture on what we could expect from our various tickets. It was, it seemed, patriotic refreshment. It might be:

1. Two national drinks
2. One national drink
3. Open bar — any number of drinks, but always national drinks.

"Casablanca is open bar," said Gladys, "but you must catch the waiter's eye, and that is sometimes difficult. The show is tango and folklorics."

The coach lurched over the uneven roadways — it was like riding a whale with collywobbles — to a large white colonial-style building with little tables, uncomfortable cane chairs and several hard pew-type constructions in the places where there was no room for the tables. We were in the pews, which allowed you to sit in any posture you liked, so long as it was strictly vertical. Our drinks went where you normally put the Book of Common Prayer. I had difficulty in choosing my national whisky, being equally fascinated by the prospect of "Old Smuggler" and Criadores, "The Breeder's Choice". (Not the only occasion when the agricultural nature of the country influences the alcohol — to Hungary it's "Bull's Blood", and to Argentina a most respectable wine called "Aberdeen Angus".)

In another life the building would have served well for a garage or small slaughterhouse. In ours, a stage had been built across one long side, with a gallery of confused identity on the other. It was half grey masonry with balustrade, one quarter Jacobean staircase and one quarter Spanish wrought iron. The stage had imitation windows either side with flowerpots and plastic flowers to go with them.

Something happened back stage; the curtains billowed. On came the folklorics — with baggy trousers, Spanish dresses and Indian ponchos — and sang with much waving of arms to canned music.

The first tango music began from a white piano, a double bass and a bandoneon and plenty of amplification. The bandoneon is a kind of reduced piano-accordion, or expanded concertina, that makes up in length what it lacks in other dimensions, and is played with a black cloth over the knees, as if in mourning.

The bandoneon player wore a smart grey suit that quickly began to behave in a way that no respectable suit should — jiggling its shoulders provocatively and performing extraordinary manipulations with its legs, putting the bandoneon player's feet in severe danger of permanent entanglement with his chair. He trembled as he pulled his instrument out and gritted his teeth when he pushed it in. He stamped his feet — and generally wore the anguished expression of the player of a squeezing instrument who has absent-mindedly allowed it to become over-intimate with his balls.

The fan had been right. Both the player and the tango singer in her slim white dress and silver shoes enjoyed the great musical privilege of being listened to as if in church. They could pause and linger on a note as they pleased like a psalm which has got severely stuck on some unexpected "begats", and no one would hoot that they had paid good money for this entertainment, and would they get a move on with it.

The genre seemed to have attained the desirable status of perpetual motion. It was a tango about tango, and the singer often sang it to the bandoneon player, who responded by playing to her. This centripetal activity continued until it was time for more folklorics — dancers, Andean flutes and guitars. The audience were encouraged to clap, which they did in the wrong place and had to be shown how. Tango returned in the shape of a white tuxedo with a very loud voice, wide gestures and a big heart that seemed to be giving him trouble, since he clutched it at frequent intervals throughout his song.

The tics of the bandoneon player had now infected the bassist; he twirled and twisted like a mouse on the end of a string. As the miasma of amatory misery thickened, and the player had a particularly painful movement, the expression on the singer's face as he raised the microphone to his lips was of one who has encountered a cockroach in his ice-cream cornet. The socks of the player now assumed great importance, as he shot first one leg and then the other out before him. While he was flashing his ankles in the unfeeling manner, the singer was going through agony as the cockroach refused to go away.

At last, it did, he did — and the folklorics returned with a very energetic and precise stamping of heels on the floor, a knife dance with clangs and a whip dance with cracks. Though the stage setting was apparently rural, the effect of the great outdoors was lessened by the end of the white piano protruding through the curtains.

Try as I might, even remaining awake, I could not feel the wonder of any of these rituals — until the tango dancers came. They were a couple, neither young nor beautiful — unless the marks of life and a hint of world-weariness on lean faces are beautiful. They had no set or pretensions but moved as if their limbs were linked by invisible forces — with a stylized grace increased by the limitations. This was performing art for its own sake, nothing else needed, and it was also personal to them. Precision flashed in a bewildering mixture of limbs — the story of attraction, courtship, evasion, culmination played out like a ritual of black but exotic birds. They did not even bow at the end.

"Well, you don't, do you, in church?" I said to myself.

The tango is a dance elsewhere in the world, but in Buenos Aires it is tango as a song that has been more important, though the dance has had a minor revival in recent times. It is almost urban folk music, with many musicians writing their own material — some of it in *lunfardo*, the patois of Buenos Aires — but its ambience is the café, the tango bar; and it was to the Café Mozart I went in search of a greater humanity than I had seen in the show.

Again the evening began without distinction. A *porteño* was singing — I could tell him by his spotless shoes and thinning hair. The older ones here are like clubmen, somehow disconnected from most of the world. He trolled out Cole Porter-ish stuff to the guitar — rather well, actually. When he had finished, another greying *porteño* in an immaculate blazer came and greeted him. Together, they looked like an airforce reunion for they both had not-quite services haircuts.

Then came the bandoneon player, grinning, who played a piece with such rubato that I thought it a fit expression for the *porteños*, making up in sentimentality and twitches of the shoulders what it lacked in musical substance. It was, however, different from what had gone before; the tango singer, Maria Volonte, who now joined him, was different again. She had a short black miniskirt, a low black mini-top and long hair, loose down her back. She created great commotion among the airforce types, who twitched as much as the bandoneon player at the prospect.

She rolled her eyes, tossed her head, snarled her mouth in beautiful cynicism: she was stoic, despairing, accepting, rejecting. Laughing not too heartily at fate, she sang about a fat girl who couldn't keep out of the *confiteria*, and it sounded like Jean-Paul Sartre on a bad day. She did gymnastics with the microphone, twisted its cable neurotically, clutched it passionately and at one point looked as if she was going to swallow it whole. But the words evidently mattered greatly, for when they were finished, the song came to a stop with little ceremony.

The bandoneon player made his own music in accompaniment with a great deal of improvisation, oscillating between despair and low comedy. He seemed always on the point of stopping, but would be prevented by an attack of accelerandos, runs, trills and little ironic discords. Then off he would go again, until the words were finally over and he came to rest on a particularly plangent chord, his hands like crabs on the keys. He would keep her waiting for a resolution, play with her desire to continue, in a teasing, almost physical, interplay.

The airforce types sang silently along with her and shivered their fists in the most anguished way as she shivered her head. At a lonely table, a *porteño* in suit and cuffs sat looking as miserable as unrequited love over his plate of salad, wiped his mouth with a bitter, enigmatic flourish of the napkin in time to her conclusion.

The show was over. The lights came up and the airforce types were suddenly old men fingering their money and wondering if they had the right change.

As I walked to a restaurant — normal dining lasts until the small hours in Buenos Aires — they were mending the pavement in front of an establishment with a red light in the window. A couple of guys, who I suppose were the pimps, were rather inexpertly ladling cement into a hole. A bare-shouldered woman popped her head out to see what was going on, clasping the door curtains round her to hide whatever she was not wearing. They had a window display of a few native figurines — heavily stylized in the direction of what the macho young men admire as a good pair of *bolsas* — and credit card stickers. It was either a brothel or one of the love hotels which are an institution of Argentine life, in which you rent a room for an hour or two. They are not only for affairs — young people without a place of their own, young married couples with nowhere to escape from the baby and people with any sort of accommodation problem use them.

I ate at a *parrilla* — another institution of Argentine life — a grill restaurant. It was the one with the gigantic barbecue fire in the window that I had noticed earlier. There were two grill chefs — a pasty, phlegmatic one about the height of Frankenstein's monster, and a rapid mover with fine moustachios and dark Latin eyes. He looked a bit like the demon king, coming up in a shower of sparks as a hot coal exploded in a chafing-dish. He was constantly quaffing juice or water, constantly wiping the grill bars. One side of the long grill flamed, the other was calm, and from time to time he raked from the flaming end to the calm. He turned the meat over and cranked the grill up and down occasionally. Most of his time, he did not look at the food at all, but seemed to know by instinct how all the different pieces were doing.

They have the hidden flamboyance of true professionalism. But in no Argentine *parrilla* will you ever get the sense that anyone loves the food they are cooking. Conquers it, yes — with the same machismo with which the diners attack it — but care for it, apply perception to it, no.

There was a frenetic pace of arriving, departing, serving. The Argentine way with a piece of meat is to approach it with great determination, as if it were still on the animal, and might move off before you had finished with it. It was hard on the waiters. There was one who was stooped and hook-nosed, and when he bent over the table he was all bends and hooks; his hands drooped, too — like leaves short of water. Another blotchy-faced man would have been blotchy-faced anywhere. A younger waiter was efficient and good-looking — but what had he to hope for? That he should grow stooped from leaning over tables, blotchy from working late into the night, till his skin crinkles and he is old?

On my own as I was, with nothing to do but watch them, it seemed to me that, in their confined lives, waiters are an expression of the resistance of the spirit. In the face of rudeness, they maintain politeness; in the face of boorishness, they maintain refinement; in the face of drudgery the elegance of a bird carrying worms to its chicks; in the face of penury, style; in subservience, pride.

I saw the customers, myself included, from their viewpoint, and shuddered at lipsticked mouths that gaped like earth-movers, tongues caked with sardine and hard-boiled egg from the last bite. The mayonnaise that is left on the lips and carried bit by bit within as the jaws go round, like cows chewing the cud; the scrubbings with the bread in the juices, the lust for grease, the congealed garbage on the plate — they must bear all this. Like doctors, they are privy to one of our most intimate of orifices — and the only one that writhes and twists and licks itself, and says "*muy bien*" afterwards.

There are more delicate diners in Buenos Aires. I met them in the Botanical Gardens, a delightful place of gravel promenades, the smell of hot, wet leaves rising from the most recent waterings, and an extraordinary number of cats.

Cats were doing their own separate things throughout the gardens, sleeping in the sun, strolling from one unimportant place to another, curled up in holes in the grass, sitting in the botanical specimens in an unscientific manner. I strolled too and encountered an elderly woman feeding a medium-sized dinner party of cats at the back of a shed. Then, several cats later, I came upon a banqueting assembly of perhaps sixty or seventy animals in the corner of a lawn. It was late afternoon, and the low sun, casting long shadows of trees, made the grass even greener.

A middle-aged woman in a safety-pinned tartan skirt that would have been smart had it not been for its recent participation in the feeding of the cats, was putting down sheets of newspaper to serve up what she described rather grandly as pâté — a catfood paste of meat, liver and cereal, and holding a periodic dialogue with a black and white beast in a tree. She was Eva Bernadez de Migueno, and in fifteen years she had not had so much as a weekend off from feeding the strays, of Buenos Aires. A retired social worker, she had gone from social security for people, to social security for cats.

Robert Tibero, another of the five friends who fed and looked after the strays, told me that as Argentina's economy began to crumble, people began to get rid of their pets, leaving cats in the Botanical Gardens, and dogs in the Central Market.

The cats seethed like a tin of maggots — always in motion, even if no more than a flick of the ear, a quick scratch or an alert turn of the head. "They are more nervous in summer. They are all different, each one a different character," said Robert.

One black creature insisted on dining on top of a nearby shed, producing howls from the depths of a mournful stomach until its food was thrown up on to the roof.

"The Little Witch." Robert's voice became almost baby-talk in its affection. "The Little Witch — she's always on the roof." Cats crawled all over him as he talked, leaving fur of many colours, until the worsted of his jacket looked like angora.

"You are good to your animals in England, I know,"

he said to me. "England was the first country to pass a law protecting animals, under Queen Victoria. But do you know the second?"

I did not.

"Argentina in 1882, under President Sarmiento."

I could have done with some protection myself, as I walked to that grand showpiece, the Colón theatre. In front of it, a short young man suddenly grabbed my arm with cries of *"Sucio, sucio!"*, pointing at my bottom. I was not in two minds about his intentions for long, since he took his hand from the back of my shirt with something yellow on his fingers. More cries of *"Mostarza, mostarza!"* ("mustard, mustard!") and a group of young fellows clustered round, one after the other drawing identical wads of toilet paper from their pockets, dabbing at me from every side. I saw that my bag containing my camera had somehow come off my shoulder and was sitting by itself on the bonnet of a car, next to a booklet put down by one of the dabbers. I picked it up, whereupon the dabbers melted away, leaving the booklet behind them, which otherwise, I am sure, would have served as an excuse for picking up my bag as well. Fortunately my money was buttoned up securely in my shirt — for they would surely have had a wallet from my hip pocket. But my back was covered with the mustard they had sprayed on me; nor was it even good mustard. However, there was no sense of alarm in any of this: that was provided by the police.

On the motorway to the airport, the hired car I was in was flagged down by a beaten-up, old red Falcon, with a CB aerial sticky-taped to the boot. Three tough-looking characters in jeans jumped out and announced it was a police check — and so indeed it seemed to be. After a terse exchange of credentials, they left me alone in favour of the other passenger, a Spaniard, whom they questioned very thoroughly and brusquely, went right through his bulging cases, made him roll up his trouser-legs like a knobbly-knees contestant, and discovered the twin wads of $200 bills he carried tucked into his socks. He was a timber merchant who disliked Argentina. "The ones at the top don't want the country to improve," he said. He dislikes it more now.

The plain-clothes men said they were after drugs — and I was touched by the faith with which they thought they might find them by picking up cars at random on a motorway. Still, they were nice enough to me. "Just doing our job," said one of the trio. "No hard feelings?"

"None," I said. "Do you ever find anything?"

"It's getting worse," replied the policeman, evading the question, and they went off.

Generally, in Buenos Aires, I had nothing but pleasant encounters — and one of the most inescapable of these was the brush shop. I knew from the first I would be unable to avoid it. I passed it once with a casual glance, again with a look that pretended to be casual, and at last was drawn into the bristly embrace of its double-front. Argentina is a dusty land, so that it is common to see taxi drivers brushing down their vehicles with a feather duster. There were brushes for cement, badger shaving brushes, a tennis-court brush, a *pita belga* (whatever that was), a window brush, a coconut-matting brush; brushes particular to horses, cars, Persian carpets, wallpaper, grill chefs; pile-raisers, special circular brushes, sauna brushes; and a patent folding coat hanger incorporating a brush.

The star was a grubby blue toothbrush, whose bristles were arranged in three tufts with gaps between — plainly designed for folk with alternate teeth. I could no longer resist, and went in and bought two Argentine common hairbrushes at $50 the pair, so that I could have an excuse to talk to the owner. She was an ebullient woman, one of the generation of Argentines more at home with French than English. Those were the days, when Buenos Aires prided itself on being the Paris of Latin America, and when they stuffed the National Gallery with Rodin's umpteenth version of "The Kiss" and as many French impressionists as they could afford. Her family, however, was Polish: her father had started the brush shop in 1911.

"My father died the *anno passado*," said Elena Eitman de Aranovich. "And he liked Scotch, yes. No Argentine whisky! When I take a trip, he says, 'Black Label!' Horse, no?"

"Horse?" I enquired.

"*Caballito Blanco*. 'White Horse'. Yet he lived until he was 101 — in great cleverness. I have his shop. And I like it. It is a funny shop, eh?"

It was a low hall that retreated into gloom, and the gloom was full of a foliage of feather dusters. The matchboard ceiling was lit by fluorescent circles, like haloes.

"I've never seen so many different sorts of brushes."

"I have brushes for clothes, for shoes, for hair, for tapestry, for the body, to shave. This is handmade nail brushes. Teethbrushes," said Elena, with great satisfaction, and showed me a handmade broom for $50.

"There is a toothbrush in the window . . ." I drew the

one I had seen with the three tufts. "It is for people with teeth missing? Here are the holes."

"Aaaaaay, I think" — she started every other sentence with a war-whoop, like a Red Indian spotting a wagon-load of settlers — "it was an idea from a German. Why?!" War-whoop. "I can't say. He had many strange brushes, but he died, and his son is not interested in brushes. He is a concert pianist — with a grand piano from London. *Il a fermé la compagnie. Il avait beaucoup d'argent, il a la vie de grâce. Les brosses qu'on a laissé dans la fabrique, elles sont vendues, comme ça.*"

It was sad to think that there would be no more toothbrushes specially designed for people without teeth.

"Here is another. Forster — he was a German. It is for his . . ." She made a gesture with her teeth like a rabbit confronted by a moving carrot which was about to escape. "Dentures." Evidently the man had been obsessed with toothlessness. In the avant-garde of brushes, he had blushed unseen.

"Strange designs, but the Argentines like the common," said Elena, as if regretting their lack of intellectual curiosity. Retreating to the back of the shop, among shelves of old cardboard boxes with the splendours of yesteryear's publicity fading on them, she came upon another brush worthy of an ear-splitting yell. It was a pure white feather duster of exquisite lightness. If you had had to dust Sleeping Beauty, it would have been perfect.

"It's strange to see the taxi drivers here titivating their taxis with ostrich-feather dusters," I said.

"Don't they do it in England?" She was aghast. I was suddenly ashamed of belonging to a nation of sluttish taxi drivers. "For why?"

"We haven't got so much dust. All our roads are *pavimento*." Aaaaah. "Also it is *muy, muy humida*."

"There are many Jewish people in England, yes? I am Jewish. It is a hundred years from the first colonization here. We have very many Jews — though I don't say they are so religious as in England." Even as a Gentile and a humanist, I was flattered: it seemed to make up for the taxi drivers.

At the end she gave me a spontaneous present. It was a short, softish brush about the size of a nailbrush but with long black bristles.

"For . . ." she stroked her face with it.

"For stroking the face?"

"For the moustache and the beard. It is imported from Germany."

"Yes, there aren't so many beards here."

"*Ah, l'Argentine est toujours pour l'antiquité*. And under the military government it was forbidden."

"Forbidden? No."

"*Interdit, la barbe ou les cheveux longs*. If you had a beard and long hair, you were a communist. That was the mentality of the militars. If a young man was coloured, he was a communist; if he was a psychologist, he was a communist. *Les choses affreuses*."

Had I seen the mothers of the Plaza de Mayo, who demonstrate every Thursday in memory of their children who disappeared?

"We've forgotten them a bit lately because they've become very political. But they were the first; and they were brave. The police were there with truncheons." She thumped the counter, indignantly.

The Plaza de Mayo is where Buenos Aires really began,

in 1580, with the drawing up of the first town plan as a grid pattern on a piece of hide, and the choosing of the first town council by Juan de Garay, the first successful Spanish colonist. The Town Hall, the Cabildo, still overlooks the square, as does the Casa Rosada, the Presidential Palace, which was coloured pink with cattle blood. Here too, where de Garay planted a tree of justice, the "Mothers of the Plaza de Mayo" sought — and still seek — justice in vain.

The next Thursday afternoon, I arrived in the square at two o'clock; the only mothers apparent were those buying ice-creams for children born in a more fortunate period of Argentine history. *Porteños* demonstrated their footwear on the red gravel walks and took time off from their visits to the bank for a few minutes on the orange benches arranged on the paved circle round the central obelisk. High school students lay on the grass, until a woman with the face of a wardress who really loves her job blew her whistle at them, and made them sit on the benches.

I was tired, and the sun was hot. I settled my elbow on my bag, put my head on my hand and sank to sleep. I would rather have lain on the grass but I feared that the warden would come and whistle at me.

When I woke up, a couple of trestle tables of literature had materialized under the tallest palm tree, together with three public address speakers, each in a tripod of bamboo poles. People met, they talked in groups. Then, without any apparent organization, a phalanx formed itself, and they were walking in a circle, five or six abreast, round the square's central obelisk to the 25th of May, 1810, the first day of Argentina's own government and the start of independence from Spanish rule.

They were in all stages of emotion, some greeting friends,

laughing, chatting. But a few cried — and more than once I saw a comforting hand on an arm. Some cried and laughed at the same time. Some looked shrunken into themselves: many expostulated with each other. Mostly, it seemed to be obstinacy that kept them going: there were men in the procession and young women and whole families. A few carried a photograph of their *desaparecido* slung round their neck.

Juanita de Pargoment told me she had been there since the beginning — twelve and a half years of Thursday afternoons, asking what happened to their children.

"We never received an answer — not from the militars, not from Alfonsin — never. It was no surprise with Alfonsin, and it's no surprise with Menem. You know Menem was in prison? By the militars?"

A younger woman passing by, decided to contribute. "But for a different reason. He wasn't a murderer."

"But he was not in prison like our children. He was living in the province of Chaco, very free. He wanted to forget everything. But a mother whose child was taken away, and she never knew what happened to them, they never can forget."

"People have to forget," said the younger woman. She was upper class, and pretty, and contrasted with Juanita — dumpy, old, sustained only by her will.

"We can't forget."

"I know you can never forget a son, but you have to be able to forgive."

"We can't forget, we can't forgive, we have to continue. Every mother must know what happened to her child."

"But what did those children do? Why were they taken away?"

"They were political dissidents — and that is not a problem so important that they must be taken away, kidnapped, punished and after murdered." The conversation escalated to a pitched battle, and the loudspeakers joined in with a penetrating version of the Last Post. "Go away. Go away," said Juanita, and the younger woman went, with some remark about the duty of a Catholic to forgive.

"I am just one of many cases," Juanita told me. "My boy, a doctor, a psychologist, was taken away at two o'clock in the morning, leaving his wife pregnant; and from that moment, I never, never knew anything about him. And from that day I begin working and wanting to know something. But I never got any information — and many of the mothers are in the same position: their children were taken away in the street, or the office, and they never knew anything more. My son was a political dissident, but he always said that psychologists were clever enough not to need arms to support their views."

At first, I could not place her emotion. It was grief but not only grief; anger, but something more. I could not think what it was at first; but then I understood that I was in the presence of a sense of righteousness — grief, anger, a tale told many times — and a persevering indignation that any human being should be treated so.

"A whole generation they took. And a country that forgets them puts itself in danger. Because everything can be repeated. The mothers are the history of what happened here. We go to the schools, the unions, everybody; they must know it, for the future of the country. When we are here, we feel we are with our children. We are doing something for them. The Thursday that we can't come, we feel that there is something missing inside us."

"Why Thursday?" I asked.

"Because Thursday, April 30, 1977 was the first day when fourteen mothers demonstrated here, in front of the government. And they promised that in the end they would get the knowledge they were seeking. Then came the police and said, 'You can't stay: we are going to arrest you all'. We said, 'We must stay here: we are looking for our children.' They said, 'You must walk.' So we began walking, but in a circle. That was the first time, and that is the meaning of our walking."

"But even though we walked, they came and took the mothers to jail many times. I was in jail three times myself with many others; but they treated us with respect, because we were looking for the children. They said, 'Who told you to come here looking for them?' We said, 'We go everywhere looking for them. You can't prevent us. If you should disappear, be sure that your mother will walk arm in arm with us.' So they couldn't say anything then."

Was it by chance, or did it happen on other Thursdays that a military helicopter flew by at the end?

There was a speech, a little well-drilled chanting. Then the meeting broke up into small groups: as it might be, women with only ordinary cares chatting in the plaza on a sunny afternoon.

Instead of a mother I met a son. Mario Toer was a sociologist, lecturer in Latin American policy in Buenos Aires public university. He was bearded, thoughtful, unassuming: he was also one of the Disappeared. We sat in a restaurant, just as if he was an ordinary academic with an ordinary friend he went to lunch with on Sundays, instead of a man who had lost five and a half years of his life in prison, and whose circle of acquaintance was now smaller by the number of those tortured and murdered by the military, during the Dirty War, the state terror campaign against guerrillas and leftists under the *Proceso*, the military administrations of Generals Videla, Viola and Galtieri, 1977-83.

"Even though our history has violence, the Dirty War went completely beyond our expectation. It was like Germany in the Thirties — nobody expected that in the country of Marx and Engels such things could really happen. It was like that here.

"Not only guerrillas were arrested — others were taken on ideological or political grounds. Then friends of these people were dragged in. Sometimes they were imprisoned, sometimes they just disappeared. Journalists, artists — they would even arrest and investigate some people because they didn't like their dress or their haircut.

"I was put in prison because I had been living in Chile when Allende was overthrown. They put out a dragnet for everyone living in Chile at that time. The main prison in Buenos Aires held people from all over the country. The policy was that you couldn't be with the same people more than three months. And of course there were spies inside too. That was a really hard thing all the time in the jail — to know you couldn't trust anyone.

"Amnesty ran a campaign for me with Camden Council, in London. When the authorities let me out of prison, and I came to London, they gave me a council flat — and a reception."

"So they should," I said. "But an experience like that has to leave its mark."

"Of course. People have now become involved again

but these are some things . . . The important achievement of President Alfonsin is that ideological discrimination finished when he took office. But even in 1984, when Alfonsin won, if you didn't know someone you wouldn't exchange telephone numbers. From 1986 we started to exchange telephone numbers. But even now, we are a little bit more prudent. Because who knows . . .?"

"What are their excuses, the jailers, the policemen?"

"They always say, 'I didn't know. I did my job.' For me it was a big achievement that at least a few of those responsible have been imprisoned. But you couldn't put in prison all those who played a part — there are too many of them. And then, who would be the guards?"

"As always, there was the other side of the coin — the solidarity with others you would not develop in a normal situation. I am still friends with an Italian who disappeared in Córdoba, and sometimes in the street I see somebody whose face I knew from jail. I say 'Hello' and we have a drink. But you know how it is in cities — if you're not next door, you lose touch."

I went north into the prosperous residential districts — Vincente Lopez, Olivos, La Lucila, La Martinez and San Isidro. There were many substantial houses in large grounds, smaller houses well-kept with the gardens and streets crowded with choice trees. Shopping streets included shops where you could buy complete speedboats; there were many restaurants and cafés with shaded tables — and the parasols were new and bright.

I went further towards Tigre through Acassuso and Victoria till we came to San Fernando. It was no longer rich, and on the far side of the Cementerio Virreyes there were slums. The cemetery was arranged like the suburbs I had come through. Near the gate the well-to-do dead lived in marble houses with net curtains, as if they were camping out and would shortly be returning home. In the open part of the cemetery the poorer middle classes had given up owning their own home in favour of occupying their own grave — and, in death as in life, remained detached. Those who had favoured the Italian system of burial, in which the corpse is tucked away in a hole in the wall like a filing cabinet, now rested in three-storey buildings like blocks of flats, only more compressed.

In the corner of the cemetery by the slums was Section Fourteen. There, least privileged of all, was a hole under the wall, three or four metres deep, four or five across. Sad decorations from other parts of the cemetery had blown into it — a few withering flowers, a dirty plastic rose. It had been the grave of eight people who had disappeared.

Mimi Doretti was a slender, attractive brown-eyed woman in her late twenties. You would have taken her for a teacher, a doctor, a civil servant. In fact, her trade was digging up bodies. When they were excavating that grave, she said, the kids from the slums used to come and sit along the wall above them, watching. She was one of the seven full-time members of the Argentine Forensic Anthropology team, which began with part-time work on weekends and holidays, and which, she said, now had eleven members, including the part-timers financed mostly by grants from abroad. We stood by the grave, talking: she told me how she had once thought she might find a career in archaeology and anthropology, perhaps working abroad, but she was drawn into the work of uncovering some of the truth about the Disappeared.

"They were my generation," she said, simply. "And it's the practice to use archaeologists for this kind of work, because otherwise you lose most of the bones."

"The thing I can't understand," I said, "is why the authorities won't let out what facts they know."

"They're afraid of the truth. There's all this policy of reconciliation right now — and it's completely false. None of the people who received this last amnesty have said that they're not going to do it again. In every speech they make, especially the militars, they keep saying that they *are* going to do it again, and that it was the right thing to do. There's not a hint of saying 'We did it wrong', not from anybody. So all this thing of reconciliation is completely false.

"The militars did a lot of things in complete secrecy; but when the bodies appeared, they did a lot of things in the normal way," she told me. "They would put them in a grave, and note it in the cemetery records. There was often a death certificate, with cause of death, height, sex — a lot of information quite in contradiction to all the secrecy."

"It must have been the military habit of mind."

"Either a bureaucratic thing that couldn't stop, or they just didn't care. There was also the sense that it would never be investigated. But that's how we arrived at this place: they left a lot of papers around. Sometimes there are people who saw the bodies coming in — they won't talk openly, but they'll give us the information."

"So did most people at the time not know what was happening, or did they just ignore it?" As I said it, it occurred to me that this is the universal story in times of such injustice. From the death camps down, people just acquiesce.

"I guess it was a combination. A lot of people knew

what was going on, but it was very difficult to know what to do. For one thing, it was extremely dangerous. A lot of those who tried to do something disappeared themselves. But it's true that a lot of people who had the opportunity of doing things just didn't want to know."

"How many was it?"

"We take the number of disappeared as nine thousand, because that's the official number, from the National Commission for the Disappeared. Obviously there are more — I would think about fifteen thousand in all."

"If there were fifteen thousand disappeared, what proportion might have been connected with guerrilla groups?"

"That's very difficult, because there were a lot of supporters of those groups who never had anything to do with guns, or terrorism or anything like that. Two thousand probably? Thirty per cent of those who disappeared were second-rank union leaders — shop stewards and union representatives in factories. They were the biggest group of the disappeared."

"Why did they take those then?"

"They were the people who might be able to make some kind of opposition to the regime. It wasn't only about political control but economic control. Everything was considered subversive — telling people their rights, social workers. It was very common under the previous Peronist government, which was also mad, for middle-class people to work in slums. I did, all of my friends did, for solidarity and to see what we could do. A lot of people who worked in slums were kidnapped and disappeared."

As she spoke, I could sometimes see her fear, hidden underneath, for she knew she was a marked woman —

and, if the militars ever came back, could be a dead one.

"They have the power. That's why when you talk about the future, it's so hard. In the beginning of the human rights trials everybody went out on the streets, in every single town and village in the country they were on the plaza saying, 'Don't give them what they want — be strong.' But Alfonsin couldn't do it. They have the arms. He was afraid of provoking civil war. So then we learned that democracy is kind of weak."

The morgue had a skeleton laid out on a slab, which had been decently covered with brown paper. The skeleton too was brown from its time underground. It might have been an archaeological relic, but for the fact that the skull had been pieced together from many parts, the result of two bullets in the head. The remoteness of the bones and the nearness of the memory made the sensation the more chilling. I did not ask the name.

They were sorting smaller bones, every one numbered, from blue cardboard fruit trays. One man was piecing together another skull. A painstaking process of measurement and the recording of detail was going on, with old wooden boxes of bones arranged on paper trays like apples. Indeed the box label said, "Manzanas Argentinas".

"Is this the only grave here, d'you think, Mimi?"

"We don't know. We think probably not."

In Argentina, the verb "disappeared" has come to have a grammar all its own. "I was disappeared, were you disappeared? They disappeared him, they disappeared her, they disappeared them. Ten thousand people and more were disappeared."

It was really no business of mine, except as a citizen of the world and another human being; but I found that I could not look at an Argentine soldier without half-wondering whether he was a murderer, or a policeman without suspecting the part he had played, or a smartly uniformed officer — and Argentine officers are very smart — without seeing stains on his uniform.

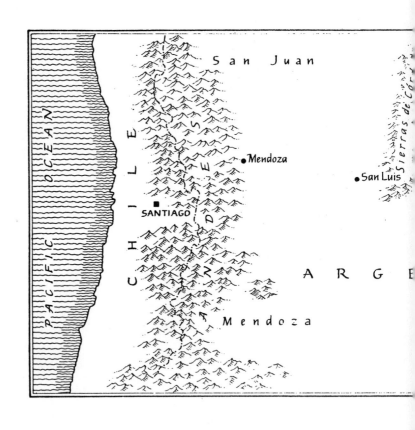

# PAMPA

## *First Journey*

# CHAPTER
# TWO

# Gaucho

## *Lujan to San Antonio de Areco*

I got on to my bicycle in the city of Lujan, which is just west of the capital; I had decided that there was no way that I was going to spend an entire day risking the traffic, swallowing the fumes and navigating the rat-runs of greater Buenos Aires. I came to Lujan as a centre of pilgrimage, though my pilgrimage was to be away from it: in contrast to most people, a number of whom travel on foot or horseback to the twin-spired cathedral to pay their respects to Our Lady of Lujan.

She began holiness as a mail-order Virgin in 1630, as a small image in an anonymous package ordered by an anonymous Portuguese in the Córdoba region, who may have been Don Antonio Farias de Saa. She came from Brazil by sea to Buenos Aires where she transferred to a caravan of covered wagons. After two days on the road they stopped for the night at the River Lujan. Next morning one of the wagons refused to budge. Lightening it had no effect, until one particular small box was removed. Opening it up, the carters found the image, jumped to the conclusion that this was where the Virgin wished to remain and decided that it was probably worse to offend heaven than to make their excuses to the consignee. They took it to the nearest house and in due course chapels, churches and the Gothic cathedral grew up — with all the apparatus of holiness to go with them.

Outside the hushing gloom and glow of the interior of the cathedral, Lujan drowsed, that hot autumn afternoon in April. Stalls like beach huts fringed the plaza — little wood and canvas contraptions laden with knick-knacks for devotion and entertainment. On the stalls where they sold toys, model virgins were virtuous and frilly dolls flashed their dolly knickers unregarded, for the stall-holders were at siesta.

Lujan is a place which has long catered for tourists, religious and otherwise, and is familiar enough with them to drop a yawn in their presence. The cathedral, which was finished in this century, is not at the heart of the town, but on the edge, which is probably why the colonnades are generally full of formality, rather than life. However, it has done its best to make up for any sense of diminished spirituality the pilgrim may feel by installing a modest fun-fair, with the big wheel peeping over the rooftops.

On a busy Sunday it is a different matter, but on an afternoon such as that in which I began my journey there is more life in the mural of Lujan and its people which pupils of the Lujan School of Art have painted on a wall halfway up the approach to the cathedral. It shows the adoration of the Virgin, the famous fun-fair, the great pilgrimage, the pilgrimage of gauchos on horseback, with cattle that have grown wings, as if they were translated to angels — along with the blind man who is always on the square, the nuns, the parrot man, a photographer, the *empanadas* man. Amongst the painted throng is a Negro — incongruous in

44

a country where dark faces are frequent, but a black one uncommon. Argentina did well from the slave trade, but abolished it early; and most slaves were freed by the 1830s, when more than a quarter of Buenos Aires was black. By 1887 the proportion was less than two per cent: yellow fever, army service in dangerous campaigns and general underprivilege are usually given as the cause of a decline which remains mysterious. The Lujan Negro is an attraction in the fun-fair — you punch him to see how strong you are. Many an Argentine child's memories of infant delight are thus associated with putting a fist into a black solar plexus.

The first person I met from the picture was a brown and toothless old drinks seller with his phalanx of glasses ranged on the top of a blue tricycle. He discovered where I came from, said *"Ingles malo"* and spat. On being questioned, he said he was a Syrian, and that the British were responsible for all the trouble in the Middle East through having encouraged the setting up of Israel. Didn't he like Jews? I asked, and from his reaction it appeared that he liked them even less than he liked me. He collected the dues from the souvenir stall I was standing next to, and went his way.

The stall man had a picture of Péron and Eva for sale among the shiny crucifixes. He took out a medal with the Malvinas on it and said something incomprehensible which turned out to be a joke — to the effect that if I took that back to England and showed it around, they would shoot me. He had been in the army at the time of the war. He was young, plump-faced with a moustache and a smile. I was sure that whatever he had said had been jocular, but I couldn't understand what nagging hangnail of memory might have provoked it.

It was not that I was worried, but at the back of my mind was a consciousness that I was going out into the country of a recent enemy, whose prospective president, Menem, was campaigning at that time on the basis of raising the flag for the Malvinas once more. I would have liked to know what that stallholder really thought.

I stood in the square, with its paving regular as a chessboard, in the company of a party of schoolchildren in white coats, required to hold hands as they went from place to place, and General San Martín, one of the architects of South American liberation from Spanish rule. He sat on his charger like a knight; the schoolchildren moved diagonally like pawns over the paving. The only other piece on the board was the photographer. He was a dapper man in late middle age, with a small moustache; and he stood by a wooden camera on a wooden tripod of spindly elegance, hung about with dusters and other tools of his trade. The camera was over a hundred years old, he said, which made it as venerable as the cathedral. The lens was a Zeiss Tessar, and the wooden parts of the machine itself had been rebuilt in formica at some stage of its century-plus of existence.

There are twenty-seven members of the Society of Photographers of Lujan, the one who took my picture being Camera Number Twelve. They do colour pictures at weekends, when the laboratories are open. Otherwise they develop monochromes themselves on the spot in two little tanks hanging down from the back of the camera. Camera Number Twelve directed my pose with the assurance of someone who has been looking at people in front of the same cathedral for the last twenty-two years.

"I am of a family of photographers," said my photographer, as he took out the paper negative, dried it in a book of blotting paper, fixed it to a copying-holder that folded up from the front of the camera and photographed it again to get the positive. It was all done by rule of thumb and a little peering down a kind of stove-pipe that comes out of the top; he washed the print in a can of water hung on the front tripod-leg.

There are four such families, all of Italian origin, and they share the take among them. As I left with my print, I realized that each of the three people I had met had been of a different national origin. At a snack bar up the road I met a fourth — an old Portuguese, first generation Argentine. He was seventy-four, he said, but still working to put his granddaughter through college as a biochemist. His daughter worked in the shop and gave classes in every imaginable variety of chemistry on the side. He was more lines than face and had filmy eyes.

"The British and the Portuguese are like that," he said, putting two fingers side by side. "Very good luck, very."

I bought an ice-cream from him in the shape of a foot (a left foot), and the luck arrived — for when I got to the middle, the stick said I was entitled to another one free — so I turned that one round and had a pair, which felt properly symmetrical. Outside the shop I picked up a mascot — a ten-*centavo* piece, legal tender far back in the mists of time — reflecting that I was not being that much less superstitious than those sixteenth-century carters who decided that a stuck wagon was a miracle. Then I put my own feet in the toe-clips and set off.

My ride began with confusion and hooting from some local driver who seemed to object to the way I was going round the first roundabout. This was odd, but a little girl in a red and yellow frock appeared to know how to do it in the local manner, so I followed her fairy cycle. Unfortunately she turned out to be going in the opposite direction on the wrong side of the road, and after I had gone homewards with her a little way I had to return, having realized my mistake.

Back at the roundabout again, the hooting was continuous. Then I saw legs disappearing under a parked lorry, a bulbous red Mercedes bejewelled with chrome decorations. Obviously something had gone wrong with the horn. The legs twitched, and the hooting stopped. Then, unexpectedly, the horn went "parp-parp" and resumed its ferocious blaring. The legs twitched again, more convulsively, as the mechanic got an earful, close to. I did not realize it then, but that honk was a call to arms, and other trucks throughout the Provincia Buenos Aires were at that moment answering it.

Deciding I had been right the first time, I crossed the bridge over the River Lujan, which is named after one of Mendoza's captains killed by Indians in the Battle of Corpus Christi on 15 June, 1536 — and almost followed him into oblivion as a thundering lorry decided to pass me at the wrong moment.

I had an introduction to a ranch where I could stay the night, Estancia San Francisco de Pilar, and had planned a short ride for the first day — less than 40 kilometres. I cannot say precisely, for once again I had trouble with my mileometer. Only when I rode from Muswell Hill to the Mediterranean had I had one that worked. In Italy, the belt had kept coming off; on the Roman roads of Britain, the batteries had come out, in Norway, the front wheel had buckled in a crash, and with it had gone the mileometer. This time I had ordered the latest gadget and put it in a particularly safe place; but when I came to put the bike together, I could not remember where. Anyway, I did not have it, and it was a great shame as the bracket to put it on was extremely neat.

In a luminous and lengthening afternoon I rode through a verdant landscape — not quite flat, for the road was going uphill. It was a strange mixture of the wild and the kempt, not unlike an emptier version of those parts of the English home counties where there are horses in the meadows and gentlemen farmers. Only a solitary tuft of pampas grass reminded me where I was — and I was lucky to see that, for very little pampas grass actually grows on the pampa, whose soil is too rich for a plant which prefers waste ground. The differences were the birds, which were often more exotic; the trees, which were often more choice; and, though the use of the land was of the same sort of intensity I knew from home, there had evidently been less broadcasting of chemicals, the insect life being extremely abundant: when I stopped at a signpost I spent some time watching a procession of ants carrying brilliant green caterpillars many times their own size.

Autumn was on its way. There were patches of yellow on some of the trees where they had turned. The sun was low, the herbage luxuriant, and sunlight shone through the thistledown and made it silver. There were teasels by the side of the road; a hawk hovered over me.

More big cattle lorries passed extremely dangerously, giving me hardly more than eighteen inches on the side of the road, which for somebody who is approaching that width himself is hardly adequate. It made me wonder whether I would see the end of the journey, and every sound behind was now alarming. I tried hogging the middle of the carriageway, but they simply honked furiously and drove me off the road.

Low-lying patches were still flooded from the rains. There was a kind of golden rod by the side of the road but it seemed more together and vivid than the English version and smelt sweet. Generally the flowers here were more agricultural than hedgerow — something yellow, like a rape or mustard, something white and purple, a cabbagey thing, and a convolvulus, very delicate, which shrivelled the instant it was picked.

A half-moon was growing clear in the sky, the sun still streaming and silvering the fields as I arrived at the green gate of the estancia San Francisco de Pilar and followed a drive of stately grey willows to the house. There was a group of figures over by the stables, for this estancia was one in which Christine and Tony Bullrich bred polo ponies. I approached the woman in the group, and greeted her as my hostess, having no idea what a rich estancia owner might look like — and was patiently led to the house by Irma, the housekeeper.

It was Gorda Maguire who had got me the introduction — a stunning dark-haired woman, like a serene firework, who seemed to know every person of property between one end of Argentina and the other. She had spoken so familiarly of the landowners along my route, and obtained invitations from them with such ease, that for a while I was lulled into thinking that I might be, to some extent, as they were. It was only when I saw a Bullrich street in Buenos Aires, a Bullrich shopping centre of a very exclusive character, and a Bullrich bank to go with it — and came across all these by chance, without knowing what else there might be — that I began to realize that I might be out of my league. What

Christine's relationship was to all these things, I have no idea — for it would have been very rude to ask — but she had greater poise than I am used to. In jeans, talking casually, she looked very young and exceedingly attractive. I know that had I come upon her in a more formal setting, and at the other end of her wardrobe, she would have had the power to make me feel considerably overawed.

The house was deceptively low and spreading, with Moorish tiling on the well on the lawn, a swimming-pool, and a garden with banana palms, exotic flowers and fine trees. Christine said that they were thinking of building another house on the other side of the road. She gave the impression that this one might be rather worn out or small. Perhaps it was because it only had one living-room — though that was big enough for a good-sized dancing class — and galleried, with french windows on to the lawn the length of one side.

It was all rather large. A six-foot log fire was genteelly glowing. A ten-foot mantelpiece was surmounted by ten feet of cups and trophies including a silver horse. A display cabinet contained another ten feet or so of trophies. There was a great deal of horse, namely a picture of a white horse with either the lady of the house or that lady's mother on it; the lady's husband in polo kit (or possibly the father but, whoever he was, as handsome as a polo player ought to be) with a palomino horse; a picture of a nut-brown horse with a tremendous shine on its bottom; a jockey going very fast on a horse; a wooden horse doing a horse laugh; horses on the glasses; horses in the photographs; horse magazines outnumbering the people magazines on the table. Christine herself had a long blond pony-tail.

She rode a great deal, she said. It was part of running the

establishment. Then, somehow, the talk got on to beauty and women. Had I noticed the beautiful women in Buenos Aires? She could say so modestly, for she herself had married into Argentina from Kentucky.

Had I noticed them? Had I not! "Well, yes, now that you mention it," I said. I would have quite liked to add that she was one of them. She went on to say how it was a woman's role to be beautiful and to support her husband. It was plain that in her circle a girl's business was not to be a lawyer or a doctor but to fulfil a more traditional role.

It was when Christine said that she had to get back to Buenos Aires for a party, that I realized that she had probably driven out one and a half hours specially to greet me. It was courtesy indeed.

She went. I looked at some of the horse magazines out of conscientiousness, but was driven to the people magazines before long. On the long coffee table there was a telescope for bird-watching provided for the idle hour, but it was getting dark.

Irma, the housekeeper, pulled down the metal bars before the long windows and showed how you locked yourself in with the other grille. Then she served dinner. There was silver on the table, heavy napkins: carrot soup came and was delicious. Then hiatus. Nothing happened. I drank one glass, another glass. Irma came in and reproachfully showed me to tinkle the little silver bell. As I ate her excellent *tortelloni* in a cream sauce with basil from her own garden, I realized that I had failed as a figure of authority.

I slept in what had been the nursery, in company with a large black and white panda who sat very stiffly all night against the pillow on the other bed, and never closed his button eyes.

*

Next morning there were scrambled eggs for breakfast. I tinkled the silver bell as to the manner born and went out to inspect the estate, since Christine was not there to do it for herself. The stables were smart and clean: I thought for a moment that I had detected an interesting example of peon poverty when I came upon a figure huddled against the bottom of a wall, but it turned out to be only a groom polishing a brass tap till it gleamed and gleamed again. The horses were elsewhere, apart from one magnificent black stallion who stamped his feet, snorted and flashed a contemptuous look when he saw me for having the nerve to inspect him.

In the vegetable garden, Irma was working with her little boy, Pepino; she had a row of enormous basil bushes, which we agreed was the herb of herbs, and a mulberry tree, as well as lemon and orange trees in tubs. The estate accountant passed by and added another national origin to my collection, for he spoke to me in French. The French did not cling together as much as some of the other nationalities he said, though there was a frenchified town at a place called Pigue to the south-west; but did I know there was a Japanese community not far away in Escobar who had a flower festival with chrysanthemums?

The only fault I could find with the estancia was that the phone did not work. It died away in the middle of a conversation, as if someone had faded it out, and never returned in hours of trying. Monsieur Georges, whose father came from Moulins, said it was quite normal. I said, how did anybody ever do any business then? Monsieur Georges said it was quite normal.

I headed for San Antonio de Areco along the Ruta 8,

the main road to the west and north, past a couple of powder-blue policemen running a road-block for everybody else but me. They must have got tired of it, though, for soon the lorries started again — monsters stuffed with steers, whose trailers mooed and wafted a scent of manure down on me, to add insult to injury. I found one way of surviving was to stop, turn round and look them balefully in the headlamps, whereupon they gave me at least six inches more clearance than usual. Unfortunately, this made progress difficult.

Now the pampa became much more farm-like: the clubs and hippicultures disappeared and it became an open land with trees visible miles away in the far distance, and the occasional long avenue to an estancia. The fertility of the pampa is evident — not only in the luxuriance of the grasses or in how quickly the trees grow, but the very air smells rich. I passed through flights of thistledown, as bright and active as small flies in the wind, and many of the butterflies were giant tortoiseshells.

There was a headwind as I went on. It was not strong, but it conflicted considerably with my expectations, which were that, since I could see the horizon, I should quickly be at the horizon. But part of the thing about riding across the pampa is that it is so flat, and the roads are so straight that when you emerge from whatever slight bend the road can muster, you know you are going to have to pedal more or less at the same rate towards the next minor curve or insignificant rise, which may be miles away. I resigned myself to a rhythm of pedalling and dodging lorries.

Indeed, you begin to understand the attitude of the citizens of Buenos Aires who say the pampa is all the same and its little towns too. One measure of the dominance of Buenos Aires over its surrounding districts is that you are seldom out of its company, in the shape of little posts announcing every kilometre you travel from the capital, that say: "94 km — 94 km from civilization, don't you wish you were there?" I thought of W. H. Hudson and rejected the idea. But how strange it must have been for those people who first came to the pampa — that vast expanse of open grassland — much of it coarser in those days, for what I was looking at was introduced. The reason there are also many fine trees is that most of them are somebody's choice — they all have been specially planted. I was grateful for a row of plane trees alongside one long straight section of road: M. Georges' Midi accent was still running in my head, and I wondered if I had some far-flung Frenchman to thank for the shade, hankering after the avenues of the South of France.

I was wary of a military-looking place with grey concrete buildings, a notice forbidding anybody to enter and an Argentine flag in the middle of a small parade-ground. I knew that somewhere not too far distant was a place called Derqui where thirty-two people had been shot and their bodies dynamited by the militars. Was this the sort of camp in which people had once been tortured? There were no soldiers about — only some strange-looking aluminium wagons. I registered that the "Keep Out" sign was headed DNV, and later discovered that these initials meant that what I had been looking at was actually a road-mending depot.

The sun was as hot as a warm summer day in England. Although I had travelled only a few kilometres my lack of training was beginning to show in painful palms, a variously aching body and my shifting awkwardly up and down my saddle.

Solis was a crossroads with a village, one of those

55

wide-open garages that is made to express the loneliness of the long-distance lorry driver, two transport cafés and a Virgin, who lived in a little glass case next to a pride of growling lorries. I was taking her photograph when a local woman came up to ask the time — for in Argentina there are many poorer people who cannot afford a watch, particularly if it carries the phenomenal tax that Argentina slaps on everything *importada*, to encourage local industry. With the other hand, they mulct that same industry of thirty per cent export tax if it is so impertinent as to want to sell anything overseas — which of course, it is thirty per cent less inclined to do. Argentina's tax system is Gothic.

I came to the boundary of the Partido de San Antonio de Areco, which was along the edge of a dowdy river with droopy willows. There was no evidence of fish, and the brown rivers of the humid pampa hardly move, as they have nowhere to go.

Orange-golden butterflies smashed by passing trucks lay every few yards along the road or were blown on to the verge where, caught in the grasses, they would twitch in the wind as if they were still alive — looking so real that other, living butterflies would come and investigate. As I stood among them I counted three dozen at my feet. It was a graveyard of butterflies. Once I saw two lying together, caught in the middle of their mating dance. Time and again I had to swerve to avoid long tawny centipedes or gold-brown fluffy caterpillars crossing the road. I wondered whether the caterpillars were the same sort as the butterflies.

San Antonio de Areco was ushered in by a police inspection — though, as usual, not of me. What the *policia caminiera* are usually looking for is the stolen load or the stolen lorry. It is said that sometimes inexplicable but minor problems arise which may detain the busy private motorist for some hours, in which case the administration of a few well-directed australs is recommended to get you on your way again.

Past grain silos and the Campamento Nazereno, where faithful souls were setting up their tents ready to enjoy a Convention of the Free Bible, I came into San Antonio de Areco. The smells of civilisation became evident — in this case, grilling meat. People were mowing the lawns in front of their single-storey houses, drivers were hooting energetically — yes, this was civilisation all right.

I came to the plaza of San Antonio de Areco just as the children were coming out of school — dressed in little white overalls, as if they were in training to be dentists. It being just after the summer holidays, they wore brand new satchels with an air of ceremony, and there were lots of bouncy children on their own as well as those with proud mums. I sat on a bench in the plaza with its gravel walks, palms and flowering trees — and the all-important flagpole on which to run up the blue and white national flag. The local youth engaged me in conversation on the nature of my bike (*inglés*) and the extraordinarily interesting object on my front forks.

"Yes, it is uncommonly neat, isn't it?" I said. "I had hoped to put my mileometer there." However, it proved impossible to translate the word "mileometer", and the local youth departed bemused.

If you are not observant you may miss a good deal of San Antonio de Areco, whose houses are not very high being mostly single storey. Nor do they show what charms they have, keeping their shutters shut and their doors closed in the heat of the day; nor are they all of them in good repair, but have lost stucco from their walls, and beneath that pointing from the old bricks, which are thin, like Roman bricks, half-way to being tiles.

But if you look into San Antonio de Areco, you will find that on the other side of this patch of ground there is a social club; behind this decrepitude of old bricks, a bar; in the gap between two houses, a new tennis court. Nor can you miss the television aerials and radio masts that tower above these apparently modest dwellings. For San Antonio is an old place and a prosperous place. When it gets to evening the closed doors open; respectable shops appear from nowhere in the peeling fronts; whole streets of smart houses become evident — even a mini-department store. Outside one of those respectable shops I met yet another national group which makes up this extraordinary mixture called Argentina.

"Isabel Dunne, Headmistress of St Mary's," said the new national group by way of introduction. "We're a Catholic school — used to be run by the Irish nuns, the Mercy Irish nuns, but now they're from Paraguay, the nuns."

At the word Irish, I placed the accent; and saw Ireland in her face, though it was her grandparents who last saw Dublin. She had never been there, though she had heard it was very green from those who had — there were many Irish in Areco.

"Indeed," said Isabel Dunne. "And the priests from the two parish churches are Irish-Irish."

"An Irish-Irish I would like to meet."

"Not now, Padre Bertie isn't very well — he has a little

*grippe* today. Bertie Flanagan he is — we call him Bertie. But you can come to the church tomorrow."

And her companion, a tiny voluble woman who ran the Gaucho Museum, and who seemed to be mostly Spanish ancestry with something else included, being named Martha Smith de Basavilbaso, fixed me up with a hotel, and an evening class in gaucho dancing to look at and a recommendation to a restaurant. I was half-way through a plate of tongue with onions, vinaigrette and a bottle of excellent Argentine *tinto*, when she turned up again to say that the evening class was off — having interrupted her dinner so that I could linger over my own.

There is a possibility, I thought to myself, that these are the nicest people in the world. It was a possibility that was often to recur to me.

My hotel was a *residencial*, El Hornero, run by two sisters of uncertain age whose first action on my return was to phone up the police to say that I was there, and whose second was to offer me a mosquito coil. This sinister offering turned out to be only too appropriate: I spent the next hour in single combat with a succession of insects, eventually locking some out in the bathroom, where they remained moaning fitfully, and dispatching some three or four dozen in the bedroom by throwing my notebook at them — doubtless to the irritation of the guests in the adjoining rooms. I got all but one, which was expert in hiding behind the fat old wardrobe, and only came out later on.

It was still dim when a tinkling bell at the church aroused a peepy bird, a squeaky window-blind and a distant cockerel. Someone started a car. A machine wound itself up. Traffic began — there was the first toot of the day. Areco was awake. I went into the hall and was immediately dive-bombed by the mosquitoes that had been awaiting the privilege all night.

I went out to breakfast — El Hornero was adamant about providing nothing but bed, bath and mosquitoes — but on the way was diverted past Mary Clancy, the parish secretary, to find Father Bertie Flanagan in the sacristy of a church about the size of a couple of Dutch barns, which had made a creditable attempt to cover most of itself with gilt, fairground lights, and religious statues in the colours of such things, namely: a peculiarly innocent pale blue, naïve red and an eternally inoffensive eau-de-Nil.

We sat under the eye of a blue and yellow Virgin in a tall stone-floored room with a sonorous clock echoing ticks around the bare walls. Father Bertie himself was comfortable and without sharp edges: he had a round face, round spectacles, and an even temper rolled out of him. He had been in Areco for three years, having spent the previous seven in Africa.

"I like Areco," said Father Bertie, gently Irish. "I came in here and immediately the people of Irish descent invited me into their homes. (There's many an Irish family — Gaynors, Farrells, Lennons, MacCabes and Simons.) There's possibly no place in the world you'll find such openness. The *asado* — the barbecue — is very important here. In the other parish there's an Irish priest and we've had a few bacon and cabbage lunches, but they're a bit heavy in this climate. We spend hours at the *sobre mesa* — the talk at the table. Family life matters a lot as well.

"Argentina could easily be in the first world if they were better organized. It's not a question of ability — they can compete with anybody. But I think you can see the personality when they get on the *ruta* — all the charm and courtesy disappears when they get behind the wheel. But my flock are are not really fanatics — they don't knock down the church doors coming in."

"It's a country that has everything, but the Argentines destroy everything," said Mary Clancy on the way out. "It's a mixture of cultures — and there's everybody bringing up their children in different ways. I've never been to Ireland, but they say it's wet."

"So I believe," I said.

"There's going to be an Irish get-together, you know."

"I wouldn't miss it for all the Guinness in Dublin." I was exaggerating, of course.

Breakfast was in the Café Tokyo, which, though it seemed tiny outside, turned out to be built on the same scale as the church within. A few cheap tables and chairs looked lonely in the emptiness. They had given up hope long since of ever making great progress in cleaning the stone floor — or perhaps, as with the Forth Bridge, they were engaged in sweeping the other corner and would be getting round to my table some time in the spring. However, there was a waiter in a short, white coat, wonderful coffee and fresh sweet croissants of some sophistication. It was a far more pleasant experience than many a well-cleaned, expensive British establishment, chiefly on account of the coffee.

Areco is gauchos. In times past it was their meeting place — and still is during the annual Festival of Tradition, in which they parade through the streets, and have their games. Here is the Guiraldes Gaucho Museum, named after the author of the novel *Don Segundo Sombra*. Don Segundo was a local character who lived long into this century, and he is a candidate for the titles of "Last of the Gauchos", and "Second Most-Celebrated Gaucho" — the most famous being Martin Fierro, the hero of an epic poem much taught in schools.

Gauchos were products of a time. They were half-breeds in days when to be a half-breed was to be rejected; fighters in days when there were battles; nomads in days when the pampa had no fences; profligate hunters in days when there were wild cattle and nandu, a kind of ostrich, in plenty. Today the few ostriches that live wild are in remote areas, and the rest are kept as the hobby of a farmer, or for feather dusters; the most common use of the *boleadoras*, the ropes with weighted balls that were thrown to bring them down, is as a tourist souvenir.

There was great brutality and deprivation in the lives of the gauchos, but also poetry, honour and good fellowship; and if you call someone a gaucho today, it means that he is the type to do anything for anybody. The gaucho is one of the world's great romantic figures — much less known than the North American cowboy, but much more real and complex. Argentines are intensely attached to him.

As the pampa was enclosed the gaucho had no place to go but the ranches of those who enclosed it, and no means of survival but as a hired hand — with the company store and his own fecklessness to make sure he stayed dependent. A substantial part of ranch wages is still often paid in kind, and in the more traditional areas like the Chaco, sometimes still in store tokens.

The gaucho is different now but not dead, as I began to realize that day at the *feria*, a stock market among fields whose animal pens were arranged beneath the shade of lines of trees — not a set of iron and concrete prisons, but a grove. Hooves thumped hollowly on grass as some dozen horsemen marshalled the stock on horseback.

"You see the way he has the knife across the back there? That's typical." I was sharing a fence with Father Bertie, who had come to do something with some cattle with which the parish was connected. The stockman was handsome and lithe, like a horse himself. Not only did he have a silver dagger stuck into his belt across his back, but the belt itself was in the traditional gaucho style — broad, black and heavily ornamented with silver decorations and coins. Long ago, such a belt would be the gaucho's bank — but to find it in a place of work was surprising. Sometimes, the silver even finds its way on to harness. Usually, it is a matter of leather plus a few fittings and decoration, but there are probably about 150 full silver harnesses in Argentina, each worth $30,000 or more.

In the largest corral the gauchos rode up and down like cavalry. Man on horse is always more impressive than man without horse, but some of these had an element of assertive glamour about them that made them stars. It was difficult to see where man began and horse left off: they did not ride, they joined. The gauchos whooped, and the horses whinnied.

I was introduced to the man on my other side, Pakki Lennon, who spoke to me in an Irish accent, as the cattle mooed in the background with an international one. A dealer?

"I have a piece of land," said Pakki Lennon in tones of infinite relaxation.

"It's good land here," said Father Bertie. "There are many important stud farms. The grass is better groomed than elsewhere."

"Did your family come to get away from Ireland because they were poor, or for the railway?" I asked.

"It will be my great-grandfather," Pakki explained. "No, they came with money. They weren't poor."

"They thought there would be more sun here and less rain?" I suggested.

"They were right there, bejabers. And more meat."

That was right too, bejabers. It mooed and fidgeted and flicked with its tail and wondered when this aberration in its existence would be over, and when it would be able to get back to the other meat in the pasture.

"You raise cattle?"

"A few," said Pakki, leaving me wondering whether he meant a few dozen or few hundred thousand. I turned to ask Father Bertie, but he had gone — to do whatever he had to do with his stock. I went too, as the gauchos cantered and wheeled, raising dust clouds into the trees of loudly chattering birds.

Julio Ford was my host for lunch. He was, I think, a kind of municipal gaucho connected with the museum, for it was Martha who got me the invitation. He was also one of the most strikingly beautiful men I have ever seen in my life — descended presumably from an Irishman (for he was a relative of Isabel Dunne), but an Irishman transformed. Great stature, kindliness of countenance — and, again, it was the kindliness that struck me. It was his private party I went to, a complete stranger whom he had been persuaded — possibly dragooned — into inviting, and there was never a trace of resentment. Our meal was held under the trees at the back of the museum, next to a ramshackle shed housing a tractor and a dog-cart. A saddle-horse and an Alsatian on a chain kept company with a dozen or so diners at a long oil-cloth-covered table. A log fire radiated heat beneath an improvised grill in one corner of the compound, and was ministered to with a stoker's shovel and a long stick like a shepherd's crook.

It was an *asado* — "barbecue" is a translation of the word, but the meaning is far more. An asado is a tradition and a ritual. It is the fire, the open-air, the meat (which is usually beef), the wine (which, in spite of it being beef, is often white), the salad and the bread. It is also a period of time and a proper respect given to the company. There is no such thing as a fast asado: the fire must burn, the meat must cook, there must be time to eat and time to converse. It may be ceremonial for a state occasion where the President of Argentina will invite visiting statesmen to it, or it may be a workman pausing for lunch by the roadside; but for all Argentines asado has something of the quality of a communion with the past.

Asado makes its way into the restaurants too: the most common type of which is the *parrilla*, or grill, which is the name of both the establishment and the main dish, and which serves almost everything there is to be served of a steer: *vacio*, from the outside of the ribs; *asado de tira*, the ribs themselves cut into strips lengthways (butchers keep a bandsaw for the purpose); *bife de chorizo* and *bife de lomo*, rump and fillet steaks; *costaletas*, another rib cut; *matambre*, which is rich and fatty; and internal things — especially kidneys and *chinchulines*, which are very internal indeed, being rings of grilled intestine. *Morcilla* is black pudding, and *chorizos*, sausages. It all comes on its own mini-barbecue that keeps it hot at the table — and very necessary too, for even a half-size *parrilla* (which is as much as a strong man can usually manage) takes some time to eat. The standard salad is tomato and chopped lettuce, always dressed with oil, vinegar and salt. White pepper is not uncommon, but black pepper belongs to the better class of restaurant. Argentines are exceedingly unadventurous in terms of flavours. They use almost no onion in cooking, though they take garlic for granted, and do not understand wine cookery or sauces.

Our meal that afternoon was mostly meat, salad, bread and a wine that the more adventurous drank by spurting it into their mouths from leather bottles. Most alarming, however, was the required technique for eating the meat, which was to put a chunk of it on a chunk of bread and slice it straight into your mouth with a dagger over a foot long. However, it was a relief from engaging in conversation, which — with my inadequate Spanish — remained cryptic.

I began by discussing diet. "I think this will make me healthy," I began with my mouth full. "I am like a *gordo*." ("*Si*," said everyone.) "*Mangi*" — I continued — "um, um, *comer*" ("*Se comer, si*") "— *comme ci, comme ça* —" ("?????") "— *les salades, enslada y* —" ("*Carne*") — "*carne, no zoo-car*." (This created considerable approval, "No!" and another, helpfully, "*Vino?*") "*Non, mucho* fat, what is fat? Fat." ("*Si, si.*" Everybody was bored out of their minds at the time this trite observation was taking. "Yes, yes, yes.") "*No, mucho!*" (triumphantly).

"Like a person," said a municipal gaucho, improving his English.

"A gaucho eat meat and no pastas, no? And *toma mucha maté*," said another.

"*Si, si.*" There were many knife and fork, chewing and pouring noises.

"I say what a hard to do," said a laughing woman. "To learn drinking wine with a boot. He say the principal reason is to have a vocation, you say, to love wine."

"*Perro*," said I, "*tambien scrivo, scribo, claro?*" ("—Wryteeng—") "*Uno libro. Tambien.*"

A Uruguayan next to me said a string of Spanish with a question mark. Then Spanish with a question mark again.

"Umm," I replied, non-committally. It was the wrong answer.

"*No*," said the Uruguayan, sternly.

"*No, no, no, no!*" echoed the women in agitation: "*No, no, no, ta, ta, ta, ta.*"

"Um. Um." I said again. There was silence.

"If I want to eat in English," said a woman, firmly.

"Ah-hah." I permitted myself a tentative chuckle, at which the Uruguayan produced a string of Spanish vowels without any consonants.

"Uh-huh. Uh-huh. Uh-huh. *Si.*"

The birds were twittering above. There was a long Spanish conversation, with gestures, about what may have been about a method of cutting up a T-bone steak, or the story of a particularly nasty operation to a dear relative, or something else. I gave up and shut up.

I saw a gathering of gauchos at the Areco Festival of Tradition, which was heralded by a sudden rise in the incidence of horses, gaucho hats, berets and *bombachas* — countryman's trousers whose bagginess is a practical protection against insects and prickles. The style is supposed to have come from Bulgaria via a shipment of army-surplus uniforms bought for use in the Indian wars. They are, in effect, Turkish trousers.

The Day of Tradition is celebrated everywhere in Argentina, but for gauchos Areco's Festival of Tradition, extending over the whole weekend, is special. There gauchos meet together once a year, sing together, hold their games, renew spasmodic friendships — and part. Some come on horseback from thirty or forty kilometres away; whole gaucho families come with tents; bus-loads arrive from long distances. The attraction is the meat. They eat it every day of their lives, yet the ritual of a big asado still pulls them. The slaughter of eighteen cows for the first day and eleven for the second was killing the fatted calf with a vengeance. There were also three thousand *chorizos* to be distributed between them and the expected tourists. The serious *parrilla* chef measures his task not by the kilo, but by the metre. That day it was a mere five metres of asado — but the *parrilla* cook said that he had done thirty metres in his time.

I could see the effects among the older men, where stomachs bulged over traditional belts; for the gaucho eats a good deal of fat with his meat and puts on stomach as he ages, though it seems to have little effect on his toughness.

They had set up the grills in the museum grounds; and the atmosphere was a cross between a village fête and a point-to-point. It was all perfectly casual — the barbecue fire burning and long trestle tables of bare wood, soon stained with grease. The serious business of consuming meat and drinking cheap wine from the bottle having begun, the gauchos decided to delay the first event by a provisional two hours.

Argentina in general is vague about time, but from their every action it was clear that the gauchos were going to make their own running — and most of the time it was going to be more of an amble. I watched a pair of languid piebalds being led across the paddock by horsemen who had the same sort of stroll — easy movement, no hurry. Groups of people who had come on time, hung round waiting for something to start, but the gauchos had got on to singing and improvising passionate verses of good advice and sad experience by way of recitation. The games had to wait. One at least would never take part — a grey veteran who could scarcely find his mouth with his cigarette. The songs went on in tones of impassioned exhortation. One of the *payadores*, the singers, was a woman. The songs had a ritual, bardic quality, and sometimes generated a contest of music or epigram, with people applauding the flourish of a good phrase in *payada*, or improvised song. In one sense, it was obviously a highly practical means of maintaining the community. It made me look at those verses beginning "Come all you young fellows, take a warning by me" in a new light: in a primitive and perilous society, this is not cliché, but moral and community education. It was a people who had never had Church of England hymns to take the belly out of their music. They had question and answer songs, and there was some dancing with heel-tapping. At the end, they got round to telling "green" jokes — which are the Argentine equivalents of "blue" jokes, just as Tuesday 13th is the equivalent of Friday 13th.

When the grass was covered with chewed bones, and the singer had moved off to hold court in the bar opposite, the gauchos got round to starting the *sortilla*, the ring game that I had come to see. (*Sortilla* is the old Spanish word for ring.) By that time most of the original spectators had gone — for the trees were swaying in the strong wind and rain was falling. The gauchos were undeterred. They went out to the dirt road, running between the museum and the old brick bridge over the river, and strung up a rope between a couple of blue-and-white striped posts with a ring, an inch or so across, hanging from the line on a clip. They stood on the backs of their horses in order to adjust the height more easily.

Four coaches with a great flourish of chrome and air-conditioning drew up; the passengers did not get out but remained behind the dark glass windows to observe in comfort. The *Maris*, the local children's trip in the shape of a boat came by, filled with couples dancing to "Funiculi, funicula". The rain was driving now, and the horsemen were huddling under the trees.

The game is extremely simple. You ride up to the ring and ride off with it by putting a short stick, about six inches long, through it. You have two goes, and when somebody fails, they are out. You do it again in one heat after another, and when everybody else is out, or you are the one with an unassailable score — you have won. The only problem is that you have to do it at full gallop.

At the bar the riders were placing bets among themselves. Bicho, in the yellow cape, was the favourite against Topo (Mole) and Mincho (Blind Man); but there were two or three dozen riders in all, trotting up to the starting line with their sticks between their teeth, like pirates.

The horses were often rather small but possessed a phenomenal turn of acceleration, baffling the unofficial dog which raced enthusiastically after them on each attempt, getting more and more bedraggled. It was a hard contest, and a *tour de force* of horsemanship, as the hooves battered through the mud, flinging up the dry earth below. A near miss would make the ring whizz like a Catherine wheel — but there were a surprising number of times when it was carried off.

It was all very formal, under the direction of a marshal in a poncho and red neckerchief. One young man was disqualified for wearing jeans. As the marshal said, "If you can ride the *sortilla* in jeans, it will be the end of Areco." They also got disqualified for bending the arm, losing their hat during the run or standing up so that you could see light between them and the saddle (a rule peculiar to Areco, which is the only seated *sortilla*).

Bicho won, by which time the horses' flanks were wet with rain, the dog thoroughly exhausted — with his tongue hanging out — and everybody else wet through and shivering. In the last twenty years, they told me, the Festival of Tradition parade has been rained off fourteen times and postponed. They go round the town and ask everyone to put the meat and *chorizos* in their freezers for a week.

But in the afternoon of the following day when it had stopped raining, the gauchos were setting up the *sortilla* again.

I entered the gentler world of the middle classes when I met Anselmo Devereux, a broad-shouldered, wide-smiling land-owner, who lived in one of the deceptively modest houses in the centre of town. He introduced me to his wife and his teenage daughter Glenda who came straight up and kissed me.

"She's studying English," said Anselmo. He himself had English grandfathers and Irish grandmothers, and had spoken no Spanish until he was seven and had to learn it at school.

I assumed that her language studies were not the explanation for her behaviour. "It's an interesting custom that you kiss complete strangers when you meet them. Is that because she's young?" I asked.

There was no response. Perhaps they thought that I was asking for the hand of their daughter in marriage and wanted to know if she was old enough.

I persevered. "In France, in some parts, you must kiss people three times."

"Three times?" ruminated Anselmo.

"In other parts twice."

"Here in Argentina, three kisses never. Some old people kisses twice."

Not quite sure what turn the conversation was taking, Glenda left the room before she had to kiss me again.

"Here in the country, kissing is not so common," said Anselmo's wife. "The first time they won't kiss. In Buenos Aires, yes — there they do. Buenos Aires and the country are different altogether."

"It's true, it's true. We go often to Buenos Aires but I don't like it," Anselmo told me. "It's money, money, money. All the money of the country is there — all in one place."

"This government want to put the capital down south in Viedma. They must have dreamt that some night and come out with it the next day. It's impossible — for now it's impossible. Factories, slaughterhouses, freezing plants — all in Buenos Aires. That's why it's got so big. The biggest place where they sell animals in the world is in Lanus, in Buenos Aires. Sixteen, seventeen, eighteen, nineteen thousand animals every day — Monday, Tuesday, Wednesday."

Meat-eating in Argentina is a lust and a cult: people say, "In this climate, if I don't have meat for one day, I feel weak." The average consumption is between about eighty to one hundred and ten kilos a year. Meat is often cheaper than vegetables, and when I was there, you could buy a kilo of the best fillet steak for less than a dollar. If you look at Argentina's economic problems today, and ask what has happened to its former prosperity, one over-simplified but not irrelevant answer is that the Argentines have eaten it.

"Too much meat eaten here," reflected Anselmo, agreeing with me. "In France, you eat a lot of turkeys, no?"

"Turkeys? Yes, I suppose so."

"The big double breast, you call them?"

"Well, yes, they're big."

"France has more money by the export of turkeys than Argentina has from the export of animals," said Anselmo emphatically, proving his point. "We went to a study about rearing turkeys and they told us that. The meat is very cheap here — ten per cent of what it is in Ireland, Father Bertie was saying.

"I'd like to see people eat less meat for the health. The turkey now has nice white meat, no grease. I don't know for why the people don't eat more vegetables. The ground is strong, it's terrible good, and every class of vegetables comes terribly well. A priest came the other day from Peru and he was saying that the best vegetables he ever ate was here."

"Do the doctors here try to encourage people to eat less meat?"

"Aah, they try and take the meat from you." Anselmo was touched to the quick, for all his enthusism for turkeys.

We got into his car and drove into the "camp", which is Argentine-English for the *campo*, or country, back along Ruta 8 in search of history in the shape of an old inn, La Posta de Figeroa, and the *pulpería* Los Ombues, which is unique in the province of Buenos Aires, being a working village store and bar in the style of the nineteenth century — when a slit throat was not an exceptional cause of death and shopkeepers had to be protected from their customers.

"Probably you have the idea the camp is full of gauchos," said Anselmo as we drove along. "It's not that way now. We keep the few that we have. But now there's tractors and machinery. The fences in the camp are all of them electrics. There's a lot of telephones in the middle of the camp. They don't go, but they're there.

"There was nothing but sheep here till 1930. But the camp was full of people — until they broke down their houses and ranches. The way it operated was that anybody who wanted to work a piece of land would speak with the owner, he would give them four or five years, and then he would set up his ranch and plant his trees there. But in the Forties there were rumours of a change with Perón: the owners began to ask back the camps, so their land would be empty.

"Then the new law came, and the owner of the camp could not take his land back: when the contracts were finishing all the tenant had to do was to send a telegram to say they were staying another five years more. It was like that from 1945-67. The camps were destroyed because they used to grow only cereals — no animals. So our rich camps lost the strength that they had. We don't get what we used to. Before this happened the wheat used to give 4000 or 5000 kilos a hectare. Today, with better seed, anyone who takes 2000 kilos is contented. At last they solved the problem by giving a resettlement payment. That way the people of the camp finished altogether."

"They're very rich and powerful, the landowners here," I said. I was thinking of the days of the *caudillos*, a cross between landowners and robber barons, who virtually ran the country after independence was declared at the beginning of the nineteenth century.

"Not far over there is the Estancia La Estrella. When the English had the railways they used to stop the train for the landowner. 7000 hectares he had — and dungeons. They were *caudillos* there: they would tell you who to vote for, who not to vote for. They'd put you in prison."

At Solis ("belongs to the Healeys"), we drove north towards Zárate, turned west along the road to Andonaegui. It was paved, but only just, and after School Number Ten — for Argentine provinces number their schools rather than giving them names — the landscape became ever more deserted. At last we came to an indeterminate place — a bend of the road in the middle of nowhere. And there stood the *pulpería* Los Ombues.

It was a single-storey building with a neat white front and its name elegantly painted, but you could see its age at the back where there was no stucco and the pointing had worn away so badly from between the old bricks that all that remained between them was their shadow. In front of it were the trees from which it took its name. The *ombú* is the only tree native to the pampa, and is a candidate for the most useless tree on earth: since its inside is wet and layered like a cigar it can be used for neither building nor firewood, and the gaucho traditionally refuses to take his siesta beneath it as the devil's tree and unlucky. Botanically it is more of a weed than a wood, and you can hardly say worse of a tree.

The view from Los Ombues was wide in every direction, though not without clumps of trees, some of them choice, like cypresses. The silence was extraordinary along the road until you came to the two *ombúes* themselves, each a sprawly creature, like an octopus with leaves. If a car went past the engine note lingered in reluctant farewell; the drone of a light plane remained in the sky as persistently as a thin cloud. Mostly there was nothing other than the *pulpería* where the traveller entered an oasis of liquid sound; all the birds of the place seemed to have gathered there, in the trees around the house and a garden full of roses and hollyhocks, with agaves beside the gate.

There were geraniums in pots, and the landlady doing her books at a pleasant table with a vase of flowers, including lilies; beneath this was a verandah with a corrugated iron roof, which took the heat of the sun and radiated it inward to the vast discomfort of those within. She was a plump woman with a laugh and a sparkly turn of phrase to contrast with her slow-moving, grey-haired husband. There was also a young man, a nephew, who washed my glass at a blue and green tiled stone sink. He was not quite straight of body. He stooped on one side as if he had been wounded there and looked at you as if the wound had gone deeper within; but he had sensitive brown eyes and a smile that came easily when he was reassured.

A clucking, scratching hen and a black and bristly

puppy chewing a bone on the lawn were all the other inhabitants of the *pulpería*, but three men were drinking in the bare room in front of the bar — which it was in more senses than one, because the proprietor and his shop were enclosed by wrought iron as if imprisoned, with just enough space between bars through which to pass a glass, and one small central portal for something wider. The bars are what make the traditional *pulpería*, dating from more violent and lawless days. In fact the last owner before the present family was knifed in spite of them: though that, said the landlord, was some eighty-five years ago and, therefore, not a matter of immediate concern.

"The same as it was over 200 years ago," said the proprietor — not so much proudly but as if it was the only possible way it could be. A fly settled on his forehead and he did not bother to brush it off. His father bought it, he said, in the days when there were no wires and poles, no verticals in the landscape.

Behind him, the shop, the *almacén*, was a gloomy trove of packets and bottles, cheese and salami. Laden shelves climbed into an obscurity made all the deeper by the single ray of sun that came through the tiny roof-light and splashed on the counter beside the old weighing-machine.

"Did you sell different things here when you were a boy?"

"We sell more now than before. People don't buy *svecos* any more — shoes with soles of wood. The maize pickers used to use them — they were good for frosty mornings. And people don't drink so much."

He caught my glance at the three drinkers present, who looked about as profitable as a visit by a temperance outing.

"On Sundays fifty or sixty people come — all the neighbours from around. They come at four in the afternoon and leave at two in the morning — have an asado, play cards, drink, play *bochas*."

"I don't know that game," I said.

From a large corrugated shed with a brass padlock the nephew brought out a fruit box of bowls for *bochas*: large composition things in dull red and black, about the size of croquet balls, and a little marker ball like the *cochonette* in boules. *Bochas* is similar to boules in that it is played on earth, and the ball may be thrown; but it has more of the quiet precision of bowls to it than *pétanque*. The *cancha de bochas* was an alley of swept earth, meticulously maintained with a broom and an old stone roller, and had a tree trunk and rough wooden benches along one side for the spectators. From the other side, a black and white heifer put a pink and curious nose over the fence, before deciding that her flowery meadow had more of interest in it. Her attitude had the same sort of common sense as the old man's.

"I was born here," said the proprietor of Los Ombues. "It's my place — until the Moment." I think he meant his last.

"I see that every day your government is selling more of the things it has in its hands," said Anselmo. "Our government has to sell those things as quick as they can. Perón bought the railway from the English in 1944. We all thought it was the best business we ever could have done — and it was the biggest mistake we ever could have made. We thought the English were very sorry, but they were contented. They had too old machinery, too old rails. The Union Telephonica belonged to the English. It used to go, and did well. So the government bought it — and it won't go."

"Perhaps it's not the Argentines' fault — perhaps it's the English?" I suggested.

"No. Before in Buenos Aires city, all the trams and buses belonged to the *municipalidad* — they never went, nobody could go no place. They sold everything — private people, private lines — and you see in Buenos Aires buses and all that goes perfectly.

"You see those buses on Ruta 8 — those are good buses — but if they were in the hands of the government they wouldn't go. You get in a train and you have no glasses in the windows, the cushions are taken off the seats. Telephones — we have no telephones. It's scandalous, scandalous here. Banks open at ten o'clock in the morning, and after that you can't make a call — engaged, engaged, engaged."

I wondered whether the problems with the things that don't work were due to the workers or the management.

"Them all," said Anselmo categorically. "The people that work don't care. If a good employee goes in, he's always going to earn less, because they pay more according to seniority. So, a terrible good worker goes in, but it's no use being a good worker, because they're not going to pay him more, nobody's going to see that he works. It's the management. And the wages the government pays, too. They're too low, government people get nothing."

I asked, "Is there nothing the government can do properly?"

"Nothing."

"Nothing?"

Anselmo's voice sank to an emphatic whisper. "Nothing."

He went on, "The people are terrible good. Don't think that all is bad — there's terrible good things. Hospitality, friendship, warmth. They just get too comfortable because everything is cheap."

We turned on to the first road from Buenos Aires to Rosario. It was old, perhaps, but it was not sunk at all, like an English lane. Presumably it had never borne the sort of traffic densities we know in Europe. But it wound as the modern Argentine roads did not.

Like a lumbering shooting-star in the dusk, we drove back to Areco; ahead was a dark slash in the anonymous plain — a pampa river, slow and narrow, which had cut its way down far enough to warrant a bridge.

"That's where they shot the Bolivian President," said Anselmo. "When they killed the Bolivian President, Torrès, they killed him there. There were two children fishing — they got a fright but they saw his coat."

The road got rougher and the dust floated in to lie upon the dashboard, powdering the seats and hanging in the air around us. The car smelled of it.

There was a noise of cicadas, and a single star shone in the sky.

On the day of the Irish gathering, XX Encuentro Argentino, the coaches were coming in from as far as Córdoba, and in the church they prepared to put on as many lights as were safe. (The last time he bought bulbs, Father Bertie told me, he bought 3500 but having more than two altars lit up at one time would blow the local power supply.)

A plump server in freshly laundered surplice was ordering the bent old verger about, till he almost tumbled down the steps in his eagerness to obey. In the front pews, a white-haired man in spectacles sat by himself, long before any other congregation came in, lonely with his memories. Above him the walls bore funeral tablets with half-Irish names — "In memory of Pablo y Isabel C. Day O'Neill from their daughter Maria Caterina O'Neill."

The church was a grand barn of a place, its ceiling decorated in squares of white and gold, and edged with paintings of the saints. It was all marble to the eye, but when you looked closely at the walls and pillars you could see that they were plaster, which had been mended with cement in several places and in others had worn through to the brick.

In honour of the day, there were orange gladioli and green ferns. A picture of St Patrick had been set up on an easel by the altar. He was complete with one brown, one blue and one reddish snake, and was doing his saintly best not to appear self-satisfied at having got rid of them. Under a picture of somebody saintly showing his martyred leg, with the air of an unrespectable lady pulling up her stockings, were two pews full of little fair-haired girls with Irish caps and gymslips in the Irish colours — emerald, white and orange.

There are Irish chins and Irish noses among the congregation, and many with that raw-boned cast of feature that country Irish sometimes have, along with its counterpart — a forehead and a grin as wide as Wexford. From one of the sleeked-back silver heads near me, a strong smell of haircream wafted across. There were mothballs to my left, against a background of the cool smell of the stone.

Julio Ford, a head taller than anyone else in his black gaucho costume, bore in the Argentine flag and, with two infant gauchos, stood on one side of the altar on behalf of the new country; three girls in orange and green displayed the Irish flag on the other, for the old. Isabel Dunne, wearing her glasses on strings in honour of the occasion and dressed very smartly in patterned black, prayed for a free and just country. Before the altar stood ten priests in white and richly worked stoles, including one that was bright with Indian colours. Since the church organ was in bad repair the "Missa Criolla" was sung by a girl and three men to a guitar and something electronic that played with rather more vibrato than is common.

Father Bertie at the altar spread his arms as wide as the world, giving his sermon from a lectern of a marble pillar and two plump plush cushions. He said that there is an Irish tradition that Columbus visited Galway Bay before he set out for the New World. From the faces around me it was evident that this was by no means an unacceptable set of priorities. Father Bertie was wide himself, especially in his robes, with fine, gold glasses that sat on his face like a sparkle of dew on a rosy apple. Saints, Virgins and Saviours looked down on him in implied benediction, pink and blue as heaven itself. The altar boys, too, were in powder blue. One was the size and shape I used to be when I was in a choir. When he goes, I thought, they'll never fill his cassock again, either.

The congregation stood, and the whiff of haircream wafted again.

Meanwhile, in the Spanish social centre with its curly-façaded front, the organizers were wondering how fifty-two Irish dancers from Buenos Aires were going to get on to the tiny stage, and whether two 100-watt bulbs would be sufficient to light them. Rows of white-clothed tables filled the hall and overflowed into the garden — plates, glasses and napkins were already in place, along with the wine, both red and white. The meat had arrived from the next town — five or six cattle quartered and cooked slowly *al cuero*, in the skin, and served as cold cuts.

They were giving away shamrock favours at the gate, and after the shamrocks, *empanadas*. Two of the priests from the row at the altar wore "I love Ireland" buttons backed with a ribbon in the Argentine colours. "Oh, it's terrible rich land here," they said. "Richest land in the country." Then they started on about the British in Northern Ireland — quite genially, but I had no answer for them and wandered off with my mouth full of *empanada*.

Crowds of friends met each other in the sun, speaking Spanish as a general rule, unless there was a reason to speak English. We ate slab after slab of cold beef with salad, bread and wine — but I noticed that many a bottle remained half-empty, and people preferred fizzy drinks.

At first, Ireland herself seemed to take a back seat. It was Argentina that got them going, when the man on the platform started going round the room asking where people came from — and they shouted and clapped for Pergamino, Arrecifes, Venado Tuerto. The new Irish ambassador got a particularly big hand for saying that his wife was Italian — plainly, many Irishmen's wives were Italian. There were gaucho dances with bandoneon, fiddle and guitar.

From the platform, it was announced that Patricia Dougherty had attained the age of 96, and that a string of other Irish names were also of considerable antiquity. The news was conscientiously well received.

Then on came the Irish dancers, schoolchildren of

extremely disparate heights who walked round the stage with expressions of incredulity and acute scepticism that they should find themselves a public show. They did a good deal of counting under their breath and some of them stopped in the middle; but in the end they wound up by being very bouncy, and they went off red-faced and panting.

The girls of St Mary's came on for the songs, in grey gym-slips, and sang with a good deal of internal movement among them, like a choir of rabbits. The songs were at the more basic end of the Irish repertoire, and even with song sheets the audience began by being diffident about joining in. Then a beautiful girl came on to the platform. She was blonde, very young and possessed a personality that transfigured one of the strangest Irish-Spanish accents ever heard on stage. "If yew wornt to come eentoe thee parrlooor," she sang, making a humdrum old ditty charming. If someone older had sung as she did it would have been sentimental: but for her "When Irish Eyes are Smiling" was fresh and exotic. She made it so for us too, by being half-naïve, half-sophisticate. Not a finger stirred, not a head moved among the audience as she sang the verse, for she had captivated them: but when she came to that tired, eternal chorus, it was then the Irish sang.

"But there was no Guinness," I said to Anselmo, afterwards. "That's terrible terrible."

"Now we cannot get it any more," Anselmo replied. "But we have very good beer." And he performed the unusual feat of roaring with chuckles.

As it happened, I found myself face to face with that singer. She was a guest at a fifteen-year-old's ribbon party, and no longer in grey uniform, but glowing like an innocent night-club queen in strawberry satin. It was a dressy occasion, for in Argentina a girl's fifteenth birthday is when she comes out into the world. Traditionally she wears white, as if she were a bride to Argentine society, but the birthday teeny at this party — a dark-eyed brunette with a flashing smile — wore a white bodice above a grey and white striped mini dress that flounced above legs halfway between schoolgirl and woman.

Mercedes was her name. As she arranged prizes on the bar, the little girl from the kitchen peeped round the door, incredulous that such a thing could ever happen to her: which, very likely, it could not. This was the San Antonio de Areco Country Club, exclusive in its country way — as I had already been made aware, when I walked in, by the stares of three tuxedoed waiters, whose gaze began at my tousled hair and grizzled beard, inclined itself down my anorak and ended at my dusty sandals with ever-increasing disdain — and, by the time it got to my feet, with sheer horror.

My welcome was none the less for that. It was the sort of family that had earned the Irish ambassador his applause: mother was the fourteenth child of an Irish family; father was Italian in origin, though in his suit and gold glasses looking more like an accountant than an estancia owner. I noticed that whereas mother spoke English with an Italian accent, her sister — the fourth child and considerably older — sounded Irish. It occurred to me that perhaps, between those two, I was hearing the process of assimilation of Irish into Argentine.

Mercedes' sixteen-year-old sister had old-gold hair, wide eyes and the poise of an Italian aristocrat. She was taking equitation lessons. Both sisters spoke English well. In fact several of the guests did. A waist-high girl chatted away to me like a British child. They had a wonderful freshness and openness. They came and clustered, all sizes of them, and talked unaffectedly.

The boys were being difficult as usual. Too bashful to come in and face the girls, they were hanging around in groups outside, trying to compensate by being boisterous. It was only partly the boys' fault. The girls had done their best to make themselves as unapproachable as possible by dressing up to the limit of sophistication their parents would allow. One luscious creature had chosen bare-shouldered gold with her skirts drawn up in gathers: nothing she could do could diminish her burgeoning attractions, but the general effect was like an animated cinema curtain.

The boys were lively, not knowing what to do with their energies, making knowing jokes about beer like young men everywhere. The party was dry: "Even a glass of wine is too much for them," said mother. Unlike young men everywhere, however, not one of them had a trace of acne. Whether it was the sun, the meat, the open-air life or the continental complexion, I do not know.

"Come to dance," said the waist-high girl, "this is the best singing in Areco." It was Euro-popsicle music, played by a group called Esmerelda, much celebrated locally — five young men jigging in white suits to strobes and coloured lights.

But the dance that mattered was the waltz, because that was what ritually choreographed Mercedes' future role in a macho society in which a woman's most likely future is in the roles of girlfriend, housewife and mother. She led off with her father, and one by one others tapped her on the shoulder, until she had danced with every man in the room. It may not have been progressive, but it was charming — and the cake more so.

Some people look down on the ribbon cake nowadays. The highest society considers it unsophisticated — and you cannot afford the party to go with it if you are poor. So it remains middle-class. It is not a fruitcake, as it would be in Britain, for fruitcakes are rarely found in Argentina except among the Welsh — and the fruitcake allows no room for the inclusion of the Argentine obsession and national delicacy, *dulce de leche*.

This hideously over-sugared substance is said to have been first made by accident in July 1829, when the tyrant Rosas entertained his friend (and later enemy) Lavalle. Ignorant of the awful example of King Alfred and the cakes, Rosas' cook left milk and sugar on the fire, and it turned to a sticky brown syrup, whose crudity has only been modified since by the addition of vanilla flavouring. For myself, I keep an open mind about the tale — noting that one of the ways of making the sickly substance is to knock a small hole in a tin of condensed milk and condense it further in a saucepan of boiling water. It looks to me more like a frontier recipe — and indeed, nothing but the greatest possible deprivations and hardships could excuse anyone from inventing it.

So, not content with eating it with *flan* (caramel custard), *budin de pan* (bread pudding), ice-cream, *Don Pedro* (a glass of whisky with vanilla ice-cream and nuts and *alfajores* — a whole hierarchy of short pastries with the stuff in the middle), the Argentines often make a party cake by combining the maximum of *dulce de leche* with the minimum of solids such as waffles, biscuits or sponge.

If you are expecting a fruitcake the effect is like going to bed with a princess and waking up with a frog.

*Dulce de leche* or not, the cake at the party was beautiful. It was iced like the Snow Queen's palace, ornamented with pink roses, built on the same scale as a spare wheel — and from the top came white satin ribbons about two feet long. At a signal the girls rushed forward, grabbed a ribbon and pulled. On the ends were favours — and, for the luckiest girl, the ring that foretells a wedding.

"Would you rather have a husband or a job?" I asked the wide-eyed brunette who got it. She said a job, but from the way she looked when she saw the ring I think she might have meant the opposite. She ran around showing it to her friends, looking excited, with a charming *naïveté* that in my own country largely belongs to another age.

"A great air of innocence," I suggested to Father Bertie, who was present, as ever; but he was not to be drawn into saying anything on such matters as being innocent to a writer who, as everyone knows, by definition must be anything but.

"They're lovely children," I said to a mother. She was more prepared to commit herself. "Yes," said mother, "aren't they?"

# CHAPTER
# THREE

# Danger in the Grass

## *Through Pergamino, Venado Tuerto and Canals*

I left San Antonio de Areco with the good wishes of a local cyclist. Did I know Paris, France? His family had come from there. The sun was high, the grasshoppers singing and it was 100 kilometres to Pergamino.

My road led straight over the pampa, and so did the railway. Many of the towns along the route were about to celebrate their centenaries because of it. British engineers, nurtured on the Southern, the Great Western, the London Midland and Scottish, built mile upon mile of single track across the grasslands, dreaming of the complex glories of Crewe and Clapham.

Outside Areco station was an old black steam locomotive in a cage, on rails that led nowhere: Locomotive 561, an 0-6-2 of Ferrocarriles Argentinas, with its paint chipped and scaling, pipes hanging in mid-air without other pipes to connect to, and graffiti in its cab. A yellow flower grew on its piston box. It was the only train I saw on that journey: most people had come to prefer the roads.

Most people were not on bicycles. A big blue bus honked

and drove me off the road. A big drinks lorry honked and drove me off the road. There was a tremendous two-tone honking at my back, and from my retreat on the grass I saw two gigantic tankers taking the whole road space as the one engaged in a lumbering race with the other. Then they almost killed an oncoming motorist.

The road was long, straight and "samey" — though not absolutely flat. There was little to see other than estancias with their long drives lined with trees according to the whim of the owner; the twirling windmills jockeying for the light winds of the warm day; ramps that led nowhere — they were for the cattle to climb up to the lorries that take them to market and slaughterhouse.

I blessed those who had planted clumps of trees by the road, for the sun blazed and my forehead was burnt. In the avenues of eucalyptus the scent of the trees came down to me and freshened the hot air. Where the trees were thick there were the chirrups and coos of many birds; and when the traffic took its siesta only natural sounds were left — a distant neigh, a far-off dog, everywhere the grasshoppers' falsetto scrape.

Sometimes I rode through clouds of yellow butterflies. Lorries coming towards me wore their fluttering corpses like a badge on their radiator grilles. The slipstream fluttered their wings as if they were trapped but still alive. There were still hordes of caterpillars crossing the road — all in the same direction. They were all going south. They crawled their way, and I crawled mine over the plain, and at last — past Duggan, Arrecifes, Todd and Maguire — I came to Pergamino.

In the long gaps between traffic, the scent of grasses was heavy in the fields. As I walked among them, lay upon them, picnicked in them, I did not then understand what I was doing.

"We are now beginning the epidemic season," Dr Maiztegui warned me. "When you pass Venado Tuerto, probably you are safe, but here there are some risks if you are in touch with any rural environment." It struck me that "any rural environment" meant countryside, and that I was cycling through it. I had never heard of a disease which you could get simply by picnicking, taking a snooze by the roadside, walking through weeds, chewing a straw. Yet there was Dr Maiztegui with an entire laboratory and hospital devoted to Argentine haemorrhagic fever.

"If you have any kind of symptom, quickly consult your physician. From onset of symptoms to recovery or death is between ten and fourteen days. It is an extremely acute disease: either they recover or die. Untreated, three or four out of ten are destined to die."

"And what do they die of?" I asked, and wished I hadn't.

"Of haemorrhages."

"Internal?" I asked.

"And external. They may start coughing up blood, or vomiting blood, or passing blood, massive bleeding — possibly very severe central nervous system disease. Finally, I want you to know — just in case. Those who recover, recover without any after-effects."

I was already checking myself for symptoms of its insidious onset: weariness, loss of appetite, slight headache and fever followed by pains in the muscles or joints and lumbar pain; then more headache and possibly nausea. As a cyclist who had been out in the sun, I had at least fifty per cent of what it takes to have haemorrhagic fever.

"I noticed you were coughing," said Dr Maiztegui.

"No, not at all," I said defensively.

"You are now in the humid pampa. Almost everybody living here is prone to develop allergies, mostly respiratory." He coughed. "We can easily differentiate the haemorrhagic fever patients from those who have flu by their lack of respiratory symptoms — for if they have a cough it's very little and very dry."

Nevertheless, it appeared that every year there would be one or two deaths of visitors who became ill when they returned home, and whose doctors did not connect the first mild symptoms with a disease which does not exist in their own area. Otherwise, thanks to Julio Maiztegui's work at his institute, immune plasma makes recovery almost certain nowadays, providing it is given within the first seven or eight days; it is of little help afterwards. Those most at risk are farm workers, who may get it through a cut, or may breathe in an aerosol of the saliva, blood or urine of the rodents that carry it.

"And it's only mice?" I asked.

"Small mice you can get within the palm of your hand." He showed me one: it had a pointed snout with very sharp-looking teeth. "In Spanish it's *comadreja*. It's a marsupial. In this area you can see two or three different species by the sides of the roads."

Haemorrhagic fever is also found in China and Africa; but, since its first epidemics in the late Fifties, the Argentine version, the Junin virus has spread from 16,000 square kilometres to 200,000 — throughout the richest farming area of the country.

"But you see, it's a dreadful thing. Imagine a young man

or woman, healthy and working — and within two weeks they die," said Julio Maiztegui. He had given twenty-two years of his life to the institute of which he was director, wheedling and battling the authorities, and his rewards were just about to arrive. There were public health education advertisements on television; at that moment they were field-testing a vaccine with six thousand volunteers; and he took me through the bare corridors and crated equipment of his new laboratory complex, which was to be a World Health Organization virology centre for Latin America, explaining every detail with the enthusiasm of a boy with a new train set — the filters so fine that not even a virus could get through, the air curtains and pressure gradients that would keep the workers safe.

"There is no such building in all Latin America," he said. "It is almost finished. When you come again, it will be working."

The existing laboratory — built up with so much effort — was in an old tuberculosis hospital, its tall corridors crowded with humming freezers that warmed the air with their waste heat. A scrawled notice on an air-conditioning unit said that it did not work; rain had come in through one ceiling, so that they had had to put a corrugated-iron roof and drainpipe over one working area. Shadows moved behind the pebbled glass of the old doors.

"But this isn't like the new laboratory," I said, "and if all these new bio-safety precautions are necessary, then when you have worked here you have been at risk."

"For twenty-two years."

"You don't worry?"

"The history of the last forty or fifty years' development is that many people from different countries — researchers, technicians, animal care people — have died because of handling these very risky pathogens. People have died here. I was lucky."

He was more than lucky: he was dedicated, like the labourer I saw who was giving blood for plasma — and, having been cured of the fever himself, had come eighty kilometres at his own expense to do so. But when I saw Dr Maiztegui again, five months later, the new building was still a dream and the machinery still in crates.

"One day or another it will be finished," said Maiztegui to me then, "but I don't know if I shall see it, though."

I left Pergamino to the sound of pan-pipes — a knife-grinder on a bicycle calling his trade — and made good time over the long straight roads. Further from the great city, which still announced its existence on every kilometre post, people seemed more friendly — giving me toots, waves, greetings. Even the traffic was kinder: I was only run off the road once.

Past Colón, a well-kept town with a monument to one of the battles of the Indian wars of the 1870s, I came to the Province of Santa Fe, and the kilometre post vanished. I blessed Santa Fe for that — I was tired to death of waiting for the next one to come up — but they soon returned again. Could it be that the whole of Argentina had the distances from Buenos Aires?

The country was ever more open, with crops and pasture, in which there were brown cattle with white birds fluttering among them or walking with them like companions. The traffic, too, was unaccountably less; often I could only hear the hollow humming of my tyres and the country noises. In the silences between the traffic the sounds of the pampa were magical — a self-important cockerel, birdsong, gentle grasshoppers, the quick scuffle in the grass of tiny creatures. (The marsupial that carried haemorrhagic fever, I wondered.) Often I could see a car in the distance, but the roads were so long that I could not hear it. The soft clouds were the colour of grey mullet.

I was making very good progress when I was delayed by Our Lady of the Bottles. At a grass lay-by there was a square concrete hut next to a smaller construction shaped like a beehive. A tiny garden of trees and cacti around it was submerged beneath a litter of bottles, whole and broken. In front of the beehive were more cacti, parched in tins of earth, and innumerable bottles of water. A few straggly saplings had been planted nearby, a rough wooden cross put up, and there were a couple of what looked like dog kennels.

Stepping gingerly for fear of the broken glass I entered the hut. There were more bottles, an improvised altar of bricks and another of wood with a holy picture on it — all covered with candle grease. It was a shrine. On the wall was a picture of a young man with sleeked black hair and a neat nineteenth-century collar, the indian San Ceferino, a candidate for sainthood — and as far as many people are concerned already canonised in effect. The place was full of objects: a bike's front forks, old brakes, a car piston, several old plaster-casts without limbs to go in them, a garden gnome, a horse shoe, a toddler's shoe, a stack of schoolbooks, a steering wheel and motorbike tyre. It was impossible to tell what was rubbish and what votive, but everything must have meant some hope or some despair. On the wall were metal plates inscribed with messages of gratitude and devotion.

Though this was the first I saw, such shrines are common alongside the roads of Argentina, often commemorating some death or accident. They are generally dedicated to the Difunta Correa, whose story is that she died of thirst in the desert while on a journey with her baby, but that the child survived at her breast — hence the bottles of water as an appropriate offering, ranging from rain and tap water to unopened bottles of the best mineral water.

Her shrine was the beehive, which was big enough to stoop into. Above a rough altar was a holy picture depicting the Difunta Correa *in extremis* in the desert, in a blue evening dress with an improbably small infant contentedly at suck. Bottles of water, some containing the skeletons of flowers, filled the floor space, together with a difunta head gasket, a paint roller, a plastic rose, and a picture of Father Christmas. There were letters but the ink was faded by the weather. I went on.

Along the railway, the towns had British names as often as they had Spanish, named after some engineer or the *estanciero* who had provided land for a station — though sometimes the pronunciation has become uncertain with time. So I came by what is spelt Wheelwright (but may be pronounced "Wheelrise") and through Hughes (which is not infrequently "Hooges"). There was a fine estancia just before Hughes, with splendid trees and immense lawns, but the town itself was all low buildings and dusty roads. Beyond it I came on to a straight of more than twenty kilometres.

Counting telegraph poles turned out to be scarcely less boring than not counting telegraph poles. I passed an old man watching his beans grow, and it seemed that that was the general pace of life. The nearest thing to excitement came at La Adelita, where I was chased by a small sand-coloured dachshund until his short legs gave up the struggle against the wide open spaces and he had to sit down.

Stopping at a service station for a drink and a horrid *empanada*, which was the only meat pasty I have ever had heavily laced with sugar, a plump boy took time off his biology homework to serve me. In that bare bar with its few things to sell and a melancholy ice-cream fridge with its plug out of the wall he had set up a laboratory — with jars of beans sprouting, plants in pots, bags of water hung up in the sun. In the progress of his fascination he was also growing himself into an agronomist: to spend his adult life too in a world of soya, sunflowers and maize. It struck me that "greater boredom hath no man than he who waiteth for customers in a place where there aren't any", and I comforted myself with the thought that at least I was moving towards my next destination, Venado Tuerto, and its celebrated polo club — the oldest in Argentina — and long a stronghold of the English community.

"Follow the railway," said Stephen Kenny, the Club Secretary. "Follow the rails to wherever they had a big station and you follow the polo grounds." He smiled a square-jawed, dependable smile. He could have been the Honorary Secretary of something exclusive in Sussex, except that there was something missing from his manner. It dawned on me that he was not putting out the same class signals as his present-day equivalent in England, though his family was an old one by Argentine standards, having arrived in 1842.

What I saw played at the club, standing on the touchline in the drizzle as if it were in England, was not polo, but *pato*. It was traditionally played with working horses — though polo ponies are used more now — and a duck. It was much more fun for the ponies, for the role of the duck, *el pato*, was to be the ball. Even today, a duck may sometimes be used at a country celebration, killed and trussed with leather straps. At the Venado Tuerto match, the "ball" was a cross between a Gladstone bag that has grown legs and a spider which has grown handles. The players, four a side, hook one foot up behind the gaucho saddle, lean down and pick up the *pato*; after which they must offer it as they ride, holding it out at arm's length, so that another rider has the chance to wrest it from their grasp. *Pato* is a game without the social pretensions of polo (even in Argentina, where polo is not the preserve of the extraordinarily rich). One player told me that it is also less fun than polo with its mallet and a rolling ball. But the players looked just as romantic: it was easy to see why rich women run off with them.

"My first memories were polo," Stephen Kenny told me. "The tournaments at the Hurlingham Club in Buenos Aires. Fourteen is when you start. Boys make a lot of money playing polo now, but we never did. At eighteen you can get a $2000 a month contract. We have fifty or sixty very well paid 'pros' who travel all through the year. There are also polo players who are middle-aged and very rich. They've tried all the games. If you have money you can have a good pony and pay people to play with you."

We sat drinking beer in the club bar with "Inky" Glass, a plump, middle-aged member who could have been a stockbroker, and remembered the Forties, when the club had its greatest polo successes. It had been the smart place to come for tournaments and race meetings:

"We had everything." It was like Glyndebourne: a special train would come down from Buenos Aires and pull into a siding; people would change and bathe in the train, and dress for dinner.

"At one time in this club we had a cricket team," Inky Glass told me. "In fact, we could almost field two — we were stronger than Buenos Aires. The English-speaking community is waning — and fast. In the old days, the railways used to send British people out. Now there's a lot of intermarrying, and some people are losing the language. Bilingual schools are expensive and they have to take non-bilingual children.

"The Malvinas War was very distressing — caused a lot of problems in families. If Argentina had just left it alone! The islanders were having their children educated out here: they would have gradually looked more and more towards Argentina. It's really true that Galtieri was drunk when he made that decision. Originally the idea was to invade and get out, but when he saw people in crowds cheering he let everything snowball. I don't agree with war, but once one's country gets into it you've got to back it.

"My son was a naval cadet during the War. Fortunately his ship was in the US at the time. He went into the wardroom of an English naval ship that was lying nearby, and the officers said, 'Get out, you goddamn Argie.'" Though he spoke as a man telling a story over a drink, I could see that he was as deeply hurt as if his son had been rejected by his own country.

"He loved polo," reflected Stephen, pointing to a photo on the wall. It was of the Duke of Edinburgh. "He used to go mad when he came here."

I will not forget Peter Miles, at the *pato* match, bearing

**99**

down upon me like a galleon under full sail; for he was a large man with a fine stomach to support, which he did by keeping a straight back or inclining it slightly to the rear. The upper part of his body thus being balanced made his legs largely irrelevant, so that the general effect was of something substantial moving without really touching the ground. And so it was with the man within, for his mind was so capacious that he would often have some difficulty in deciding which piece of scholarly knowledge to bounce on next.

He called himself an amateur and was one in the best sense of the word — a man who is not a professional this or an expert that, and who, therefore, can explore wide-ranging enthusiasms and think freely. He had been a photographer of wildlife, and was immensely knowledgeable about all manner of trees and plants as well as animals and birds. His particular field of expertise was cattle-breeding — his own herd were Holsteins, chosen for their high yield of lower-fat milk.

"I am curious," said Peter Miles as we stood expansively in his garden, watching a gardener meticulously and peacefully circling the flowerbeds on a horse-drawn lawn mower emblazoned with "Ransomes of Ipswich (by Royal Appointment)".

The garden was their luxury — just big enough for his wife Martha to find it convenient to take an old bicycle from one part of it to another; with lawns, choice plants (including roses brought from England in a suitcase), and special trees — often planted by special people. Sally, Duchess of Westminster had planted a geritsia; and a merchant seaman, who survived thirty-six days in an open boat when his ship was torpedoed, put in an Australian silk oak.

"Prince Philip put in the gingko over there, twenty-five years ago. He said it looked like a riding whip, and that every tree he planted died." Sure enough, it wilted, so they took a cutting; and the original tree recovered, so they now have two.

There were English oaks, and a grand *ombú*. "Cut into it and you'll find it's just like a rolled cigar — there's no wood there at all. It's only good for shade, and some people say it's useful as a vermifuge, or for putting into someone's tea if you don't like them — it gives them tremendous stomach pains, or something."

He pointed to a tree I saw everywhere in Argentina, with pale blue-grey flowers and modest yellow fruit that sometimes remain during flowering, or lie in drifts below. "That's the chinaberry tree — the paradise tree from the Middle East, planted as seed by my grandfather. Before the chinaberry came in they only had dung to burn. It was the tree the locusts wouldn't eat.

"In my grandfather's day, locusts used to come every summer, around Christmas: they blotted out the sun for hours. We did our best to protect the fields with coverings of sheet iron. Locusts would crawl up over a house and down the other side. If they stayed the night on a tree their weight would break a great eucalyptus. You couldn't eat eggs when they came, because the hens ate the locusts and that made the eggs taste."

The last time the locusts came, in the Forties, five-foot maize stalks were reduced to four inches in one night. But in the Fifties, Perón bought surplus bombers and dropped DDT on the locusts to exterminate them: since which time the Miles' garden has continued its glorious destiny as a land of plenty.

"I make some rather good fruit gin with these — wild apricots," Peter Miles went on. "And this is a mint my grandfather brought from Devon and said it was the only one to use for making English mint sauce."

The house was rambling rather than grand, higgledy-piggledy rather than luxurious, and full of interesting things. In a country of house servants, the family had none. But they had their past. We saw the old coach house, and the original house his grandfather built with his own hands, now a junk room. I said that it must be wonderful to live where your grandfather lived.

"Well, it ties you. Doesn't make you as versatile as the modern world wants, but I think it's satisfactory. It's a way that you can live poor."

"You are living in two countries at once," I told him.

"I think so. I went to an Argentine public school: I like to think of myself as Argentine. But I can't renounce my cultural background. My grandfather was a County cricketer, I played for the Argentine first division." His mind bounced once more to another idea. "One interesting thing though, you know — the decline of Argentina coincided with the decline of the British Empire."

Peter Miles was almost entirely surrounded by women of considerable character. Sister Susan lived nearby. His wife Martha was of Spanish-Genoese stock, with a personality no less than his — she had been on exploration expeditions when she was younger. Then there were four daughters: Alexandra, who ran the farm; Marina, looking for a job as a museum curator; Marie-Claire, studying political science; Astrid, still at school. The whole family had an easy-going warmth and an encyclopedic curiosity.

I was being treated as a special occasion, so we had tea

on the lawn, as they did increasingly rarely. England had sent out an expeditionary force of drop scones and honey, sandwiches and pastries on doilies, a whole battalion of silver teapots and a table-cloth from Madeira. Argentina was represented by *dulce de leche* and Green Hills tea, for the country grows its own ordinary tea in the north, where it also grows the green tea, *yerba* maté, the Paraguayan holly, which is drunk in every shop, on every farm, in every home across the nation, sucked up through a *bombilla*, a metal filter halfway between a drinking straw and a tea strainer.

The traditional thing to drink maté from is a gourd, which often has elaborately chased silver mountings. For everyday use a metal pot lined with wood is very common, but — Peter Miles told me — the very first pots were ceramic and made in Ireland.

"At one time, maté was used like a drug — pounded in a mortar and sucked up through a double straw into the nose. It contains an alkaloid, matein, but in spite of that the Mormons drink it, though they consider tea and coffee too stimulating," said Peter Miles. "The Jesuits banned it because they said it took up too much time; but people like to waste time in Argentina. I think it's one of the beauties of the country."

Martha went on, "I wouldn't. I won't let the children. Gaucho superstitions, they don't really bother your life; but listening to humble people, you hear about those things — you remember them. When the gaucho sleeps — on the ground with a poncho and his head on his saddle — he puts his hat over his face so as not to go mad with the light of the moon. I shut the window when I see the moon coming round it."

"You don't!" I said: but she did.

"They are disappearing, because those sorts of things have no room in this modern world. In the wilds, in the jungles and the marshes, there is still a sort of gaucho left. The gaucho is in the mentality of people. And a lot of people, because he's a poetic figure. He's a *de luxe* hobo in a way. He's honest, but a fighter — a chap ready to drink and fight too much. He's too proud — and when you're poor you can't be too proud. All his possessions go with him, and life is tough for him. He can't have a love because he hasn't got a house. He needs a very faithful woman to wait while he's away with the horses for months and months, and comes back with little money at the end of it. He is content with freedom — and freedom is expensive. He's full of all sorts of virtues that are not fitted for a woman to share."

I asked, "So, a woman can't be gaucho?"

"The woman is the *china*, the wife of the gaucho. She is gaucho in a different way. She looks after him and she lives with little. Life is harder for her because she has to bring up children. She has to be as proud as the gaucho because otherwise she couldn't understand him. So I think the *china* is more heroic, more poetic than the man, in a way."

"There would be nothing new in that," I said.

I went to see present-day gaucho life on the Estancia La Barrancosa, by invitation of its *estanciero*, Karl Facht. He was a young man of an old Argentine-German family and he seemed to have everything — Nordic blond hair, good looks and efficiency — and a new and beautiful wife, Adriana, who was now in her second year of country life and still managing to continue a successful career as a graphic designer. He also had an extremely large estate, as it was easy to see even at half past four in the morning, which was the time the gauchos saddled up. The main crossroads of the estancia was big enough to be a plaza, dominated by a spreading tree covered with thick spikes of flowers — I could just see their lilac colour in the early gloom. It was a *kiri*, from the north of Argentina — only twelve years old, but the size of centuries' worth of oak.

It had been pouring with rain all night, and the dirt roads were deep in mud. Through the darkness came a man on horseback in a yellow cape, his face so dark that it was like an extra gap in the shadow. He turned in beneath an open barn where there were rows of hitching posts with gaucho saddles slung over them. Other horses were already there, and an old brown dog asleep in the dust, still dry under the roof.

When Karl and I came up with the gaucho, I saw why he had looked so dark: he had Negro in him, and his face was almost purple-black. Following him in among two low buildings with numbered rooms — A6, A5, D1, D2 — we came to a doorway emitting a soft yellow glow — the *materiá*, where the gauchos were drinking maté and having breakfast. There was the sound of sharpening knives and a smell of singeing meat. Above waist height, the room billowed with smoke, which curled up into the rafters around the single, low-powered yellow bulb. It came from the meat sizzling on the grill in the fireplace. Some dozen gauchos stood around cutting off chunks close to their mouths with their long knives and passing round a metal pot of maté with its *bombilla*. I accepted the maté and rejected the meat: though I could see they did not

**105**

understand why I should find it too early in the day for steak, they made no comment among themselves, for they had an uncommon natural courtesy.

Outside, the light was coming up rapidly. A black cat became visible. Birds in the chinaberry trees began the dawn chorus.

A small figure passed us. "That's our butcher," said Karl. "Everyone that lives on the farm gets meat and bread provided, and most of the people who live in the town get the meat as well. The allowance is about thirty kilos of meat a month for a family and the same amount of bread. Their diet is based on meat. Even the caretakers of the different areas who have their own piece of land, they may have pigs, chickens and lambs, but they eat very few vegetables. Most of them are very lazy and they won't make their own vegetable garden. And they won't buy vegetables either — they just eat carbohydrates and meat."

The butcher went off into the gloom and disappeared. Another figure came up to a wagon like a Romany caravan that I had assumed to be an ornament, and harnessed a horse either side of the long front pole: it was the school bus and bread van combined.

Under the open barn the gauchos were saddling up. Though quickly done, it was an involved process: the traditional gaucho saddle has many layers, those underneath protecting the horse, those above making the rider comfortable, and those in the middle giving stability. From the saddle are slung a lasso and a broad whip, designed as much for noise as for hurt.

The rain had stopped. The gauchos rode off into the morning, and we followed in a big pickup. It had a powerful radio transmitter, and a revolver lay on the dashboard next to

Karl's personal organizer, bound in leather with the estancia brand in gold.

"What are we going to do?" I asked as we bumped over the grass.

"Cutting the ears, branding and castrating," replied Karl, cheerfully.

Out on the pampa in the pickup we passed a herd of horses galloping free against the clouds, manes and tails streaming. The gauchos had become a ballet of distant figures on horseback around a scattering of cattle. We hung far back, as the first gathering of the cattle herd is critical. Effortlessly the gauchos shepherded it in, looking as if they were part of the horses they sat on.

The corral where the branding was to be done was on the edges of a small wood with a couple of houses in it. There lived one of the eight caretaking families, each of whom superintended between 1300 and 2500 hectares. The corral itself was deep in mud. We tramped through it, the cattle waded in it. In the middle, a little long-haired dog paddled around wetly on the ridges, in danger of disappearing in the furrows, somehow keeping out of the way of the hooves.

The gauchos whistled, twirled their whips and whooped, "Ay, ay, ayyy." The cattle put out their heads and lowed, mouths wide, in protest at this infringement of their bovine rights. Together they made a noise like the buzzing of a hive of bees.

One gaucho rode through a section of the herd. Like magic, there were the calves on one side and the cows on the other — all but one calf, who was quickly stampeded to his proper place. Karl was impressed.

"That calf's got personality. Wide forehead, broad haunches — he'll be a good bull. He's already mounting his friends. He's a cut above the rest." It was an unkind metaphor. Karl took his knife and slashed off the end of the tail, as a sign to the gauchos that this calf was not for castration. Four or five others out of the hundred and fifty got the same treatment.

It was an extremely unpleasant day in a young calf's life, especially for one of those who was not going to be a bull. First of all he was marshalled into a wooden chute and, as he was pushed along, jabbed several times with large needles, and then pushed into a sort of cage that turned him upside-down. Then things got worse.

The dark gaucho was superintending a fire of tree trunks and branches with ten branding irons in the embers, and a barbecue grill hung up on the fence nearby. He gave the hot irons a quick tap as they came out of the fire to shake the ash off, and two were passed from hand to hand down a line of gauchos so fast that it was remarkable that none of them ended up branding themselves.

The calf was helpless: they branded it either side of the face, with a smell of burning hide, and the calf screaming horribly. Then they opened the side of the cage — which was now the top — and one man pulled the back legs apart. The foreman took hold of the scrotum and tightened the skin, drew a knife across and a ball popped out, white and red. He pulled it, cut it off, did it all again: complete with a pluck on the scrotum to settle things down, it had taken less than ten seconds before the animal was righted again. The balls went into the bloodstained bag hung on a fence-post nearby. The foreman sharpened the short black knife on an oil-stone, whetted it finally on the fence post, turned to me and smiled knowingly. I felt a little worried. He made a gesture with his fingers as of eating.

"This is a real, hundred per cent working farm," said Karl, proudly. "They can do 300 a day. The men, they're so used to it, it's like mechanized. Sometimes they let a calf or two loose and lasso them for practice, and for fun." One of the calves, a bit slow in getting out of the cage, got a gumboot in the face to encourage it.

A stream of Red Angus passed through the chute. Eventually it was all done, and the barbecue grill replaced the branding irons on the fire. The dogs hitherto absolutely impassive, showed a flicker of interest. I must have showed a flicker of apprehension. Karl told me, "Sheep yes, you can slaughter and barbecue immediately, but beef we have to hang three or four days — it's very tough."

We settled ourselves at the corner of the corral where there was the best protection from the biting wind that had sprung up and ate beef. Adriana had brought wine and beer in my honour. The gauchos behaved with the greatest consideration and gentleness: once again, looking at their weather-beaten faces alive with the pleasure of the moment, I marvelled at the contradiction of the small state life and their sensitivity.

"What happens to them when they are old?" I asked Karl.

"Well, most of them have already by then bought themselves a house in the town, with enough space for them to take some chickens with them and some pigs. They move into town and live off the small state pension and what they can produce."

One of the gauchos approached me politely but firmly with something from the barbecue. I thought of the bag on the fence and I knew what it was. Equally politely I chewed and smiled: but the gauchos were smiling more.

**109**

*

From Venado Tuerto I went on my way with a new hat bought at the Killarney hat shop; the shop was run by a little man with a face like one of Santa Claus's helpers, who has another business on the side — the buying and selling of estancias.

I was heading for the Estancia La Danesa, which lay somewhere beyond a small town called Canals. It was a fine day, and the trucks began to toot and wave — perhaps I had become familiar to regular drivers, or perhaps it was the headgear. The traffic was lighter; there was the same profusion of birds, yellow butterflies and caterpillars — still going south.

The road had been straight almost all the way from Venado Tuerto and again looked straight further ahead. The end of the avenue of trees continued so far into the distance that only a vertical hairline of sky showed above me.

At the Maggiolo crossroads I met some of the men who had been the bane of my cycling ever since I began — the truck drivers. They greeted me and said something I didn't understand, so I stopped to try and understand it. In the shade between a couple of the lorries drawn up side by side on the verge was a table covered with flies — there were demijohns on the grass, ice in the truck — which I noticed was empty apart from a golden carpet of grains of maize — and a fire smouldered nearby.

Having greeted me, they insisted on my joining their asado. Where did I come from, what was I doing? Las Malvinas, what do the English people think? How difficult it was to say anything that mattered in a language so imperfectly understood.

Out came wine, roast meat and bread. They proffered a salad bowl of garlic-tasting leaves — I think it was spinach, but the garlic was so powerful I could not tell. There was a fat joker and a thin man who was his audience. "Make you strong," said the one, flexing his biceps. "Plenty weight," said the other punching his belly. They all laughed a great deal, especially when I said, "Do you have an asado like this every day?" I discovered later that there was a truck drivers' strike for higher wages to compensate for the raging inflation. But even with low wages, even on strike, they were jolly, which had a slightly macabre effect owing to the great gaps in their mouths when they smiled — most of them having the bad teeth so common among poorer people in Argentina.

They absolutely refused to let me go. At last I went off grateful for the full bottle or so of white wine I had inside me, and with an apple for my journey. One of them passed me later and took great pleasure in blowing his horn. So, with a fanfare, I entered the province of Córdoba.

I was looking desperately for a change in landscape. Here, the best I could say was that the land was drier, more grassy, with more fields green and short-grassed. Poplars were yellow as iron that is going white-hot in a furnace. And it was strange to see autumn while the heat of English midsummer hung in the air. But I was getting on better with the straight roads — I had stopped expecting them to come to an end and was learning to co-exist with their endlessness.

Such towns as there were along the way did little to interest me: they all had the familiar appearance of low white houses with tall television aerials. Grasshoppers, butterflies and birds were my entertainment through that day, and the grasses. One kind was a pink mist at that season. Another grass turned the stems in its clumps like the hairs on the crown of the head and shone dark green and silver. Artemisias were fragrant by the roadside.

I came past Canals in a blaze of evening glory from the low sun and to the sound of birds. A great red cattle lorry rumbled into the dusky glow behind me, like something celestial, with the sun in its headlamps. After its passing there twisted in the wind of its passage a *bolas* of bog-cotton linked by cobweb, sinuously gliding over the fields. The sun hit the horizon, became for a moment part of the road — where the distant heat haze was still hanging — and quickly disappeared.

So I arrived at the Estancia La Danesa in its nest of lawn and fine eucalyptus, wondering what I would find, for there were certain to be cattle, and they might be slaughtering that day. I need not have worried. Twenty years ago the farm had employed 120 people and killed a calf a week to feed the hands: but with the staff reduced to fourteen or fifteen workers, it was more economical to buy the meat and put it in the freezer.

The family were *tano* — basically Italian — like so many in Argentina, though few *tano* families could have boasted the magnificently carved Renaissance Italian cupboard in the hall. It was a comfortable house, a very large bungalow, with brightly polished old copper, traditional Argentine wood and leather chairs in the dining room and a big picture window on to the lawn. My room was part of a whole complex of guest rooms: only the fact that the bathroom fittings were in the style of more prosperous times past suggested that Argentina might be going through some kind of economic crisis.

Pia Firpo was cheerfully and extensively pregnant, with the lazy ease of a woman who feels herself part of the cycle of life. Diego was tall, with the moustachios of an Edwardian gentleman, a gentle voice and bambino's eyes. He had been running the 2000 hectare farm for several years — the family had four farms, linked by radio with a central office in Buenos Aires. Family companies are common, to get over the problem of the Argentine laws of inheritance which foster the break-up of estates by stipulating that all but twenty per cent of an estate must be divided between the members of the family.

Diego had been trained as an agricultural engineer and he liked modern ways of doing things. But both of them also appreciated the life of the farm that they had been living on for the previous four years. They would take the car to Buenos Aires quite often, remaining for a few days to take in the social and cultural life they missed, but most of the time it was early to bed, early to rise, like farmers everywhere.

"Nowadays young people like us want to go to the farms. It's easier and cheaper, and the life is better," Diego told me, as we sat at dinner — melon and raw ham, beef fillet, courgettes and potatoes followed by chocolate mousse according to the recipe of Dona Lola, the Argentine Mrs Beeton. I was the only one who drank the wine. My hosts were happy with soft drinks and water.

It was all served by a white-jacketed retainer, whose impassivity was undisturbed by children running in and out of the room. Diego and Pia's children would go to a local school for three or four years from the age of six:

but then they and Pia would have to live most of the time in Buenos Aires, for education and friends, while Diego spent most of his time at the farm.

"Here you may see some people who are well off but if you start looking more closely the picture is very different," said Diego. "There is no good hospital, no good college, no good communications in Canals.

"We have problems in Argentina. Hospitals don't have medicines, syringes. Corruption is a fact of public life. We have the only oil company in the world that doesn't make a profit. If they find oil on a farm, the farmer pays a bribe because otherwise the state issues a compulsory purchase order. And if you take the train from Canals to Buenos Aires today, it takes longer than in 1946."

The farm had 1500 head of cattle. Its business was to produce bulls — Aberdeen Angus and Brangus — its cross with the Indian breed, Cebu which adapts well to poorer country.

"In Argentina, apart from Brangus, we have Herefords, Angus, Shorthorns, Charolais — but these need very good grasses to be fat, and nowadays more and more of the best land is being given to crops. Now cattle must run to places where the grass is not so good — so you have Brangus."

Their land was all topsoil — no stones, no clay, just a metre of good soil above sand. Water came from an artesian bore 200 metres deep, but there was plenty for the pumping only 7 metres down, having come all the way from the mountains.

"We don't need fertilizers — and don't need irrigation, so our costs are lower. We rotate crops every four to six years. Nor do we use hormones in the breeding — but many do," said Diego, and took me to see what could only be described as the bull room. It was hung about with paintings and photographs of bulls, bulls alone, bulls with people (much less important than the bulls), rolls of honour and bull diplomas, bull history.

"Alex Ogg of Strathdon used to come for three months every year to brush the bulls," said Diego, wistfully. I wondered what he meant: and the next morning I found out.

It was a dewy morning with a touch of frost on the ruts. The grass was silver as we went out to see the farm, down a track like an English farm track — except that when it had coasted a field edge and passed an avenue of eucalyptus, it went off alone across an endless grassland, a road that went everywhere and nowhere.

Diego took me to see the Cebu, a handsome, light grey beast of aristocratic mien, an effect created by the hump just behind the shoulders, giving it the sort of patrician stoop I remembered from Harold Macmillan. Diego got into the pen with it — ostensibly to position it for a photograph, but also, I think, to play with it.

"A few years ago we had one we used like a horse — we rode it," said Diego, cavorting and pushing simultaneously. "The hump is fat like a camel. They are white because that reflects the sun, and they have very tough skin to keep off insects. We breed seventy-five, fifty and thirty per cent Cebu — we're Brangus crazy here.

"Years ago the bulls used to be short and fat and didn't move. So now we put feed at one end of the corral and water at the other, so that they have to walk, because nowadays we need the muscles," Diego went on. "A bed for a bull used to be oat straw and wheat straw. But it's

**115**

too expensive — it needs a lot of changing. Now we use sand. It's wetter, so the hair grows more." I thought that bald men everywhere must be waiting for this news.

"Every evening we spray the best animals so that they are wet and cold — and the hair grows. Here it's quite warm — ten degrees — but in the USA where the temperature may be minus seven, they still do it."

"Isn't it very uncomfortable for them?"

"For them, yes, but not for me."

We saw the prize bull, which had so much meat to accommodate that it had corners. It came with a gaucho attendant, who held it in the most elegant position possible for a bull and constantly poked its feet into the proper place with a stick.

"We train the bull to stand properly. At three months we take it from the cow and train it for three years. This is our best bull, two and a half years old and 1100 kilos. It has to be brushed twice a day, morning and evening."

"So that's what Alex Ogg of Strathdon used to do," I said, glad that he had not come all the way from Scotland for something frivolous.

"One centimetre of hair represents a hundred kilos of muscle. If you brush up the hair it looks better. We cut it specially. If the bull is too fat on the chest we cut it thin. Or perhaps the bull has a problem with stance, so we cut it more to one side but, of course, the judge knows."

The great solid black object looked indifferent to it all — neither showing pleasure at being stroked nor irritation when prodded by the big stick, just moving its feet mincingly back into the right place, as if it were dancing.

"We buy special shampoos and oil for the skin."

"Perfumed as well?" I asked. It seemed they drew the

line there, but given all the trouble and expense to get them to that point, I could hardly see why.

Obligingly, Diego demonstrated with an apprentice prize bull. It had its tail back-combed and blow-dried — after which they tied it in a bun and lacquered it — using human cosmetics, mainly, since the bull cosmetic market is smaller. They painted the hooves with black paint. Then they rubbed it with mayonnaise, a substitute for hair conditioner.

It smelt very strongly of it. In fact, I would go so far as to say that if you have never smelt a bull covered with mayonnaise, you have never smelt mayonnaise at full power.

# CHAPTER
# FOUR

# Has Anyone Seen a German Band?

## *From the Pampa to the Sierras of Córdoba*

I left Estancia La Danesa with a sense of the sierras upon me, but it was to be two days and 250 kilometres before they came, far beyond the bustling town of Río Cuarto. Meanwhile the countryside played tricks with me. There are forty-six micro-climates in the area south of Córdoba, and I must have travelled through a good few of them.

I began on the savannahs, with the Cebu cattle, looking prehistoric with their fat humps, and the black spots of Brangus as far as the eye could see. Then I was convinced that I was heading into desert, as the landscape became much barer.

Artemisias, grasses, teasels were still with me, but pampas grass was more common on waste ground and the trees were scabby. The road was cracked and fissured, the grasses no longer green. Where there had once been water it was dried up and even the bulrushes were brown and fallen; the gates and the posts were like grey bones;

sand came to the surface in patches. The dryness even got into the sky and turned it sullen and sallow at the edges, until it attained an intense but not deep blue in the centre of its dome. Away over the short grasses faded the sound of the wind and the crying of some mournful bird.

In tune with my mood, the wildlife I noticed was predatory — praying mantis by the roadside, a brown and white hawk preying on a dead rat. I came on a broken-down lorry and was alarmed for the unfortunate driver, stranded in the middle of nowhere, with his legs stuck out from beneath the chassis and heavens knows what improvised repairs to do. Would vultures come and prey on him, if they had not done so already? However, when I got closer I saw that there was a large white handkerchief over his face and he was sound asleep.

Next I approached the Andes, which began as a succession of mounds, turned into sand dunes, and went away again shortly afterwards. Crops began again: this was maize country — Piedmontese immigrants came here prepared for the New World with wheat in one pocket and their hard red corn in the other. Even today the strain survives, for it happened to suit the area.

Past Río Cuarto my road swung north and there was a real hill, the longest since I began: I found changing gear a novelty and the climb a puffing joy. At the top there was a view over the pampa, less flat than before, and in the distance — scarcely more than a streak of dust on the horizon — was the outline of the sierras. To dampen my enthusiasm, I was run off the road by a blaring lorry in front, overtaking another and charging down my side of the road like a hippopotamus on heat. Two dogs leapt out of a house, which had abundant pink roses and great purple dahlias, and howled at me, anxious to finish the job — but the fence prevented them. I looked them in the eye with dignity and rode on.

Otherwise the country was more friendly here. One part had enclosed fields, in another the grasses turned a luxuriant golden-green for a stretch — a micro-climate made visible. Houses were well-kept, and the pretty hamlet of Espinillo, with morning glory bright even in the shade and a village school proud of its fiftieth anniversary, had a railway station which was like my childhood — neat, clean and utterly shut up, with a British station clock and Southern Railway gables. The sidings were rusty but there was still a line of brightness on the main track. A phalanx of levers at the end of the platform still had polished handles, but the signals were at stop. Sunny as an Ealing comedy, prim and neat as Victorian England, it was not a station but a monument at the end of a grass track off the road, with poplars waving over it.

By Berrotaran the sierras ahead were a clear outline, and I was taking the hills to my right for granted. At last I came to the point where the way to Córdoba divided into a high road and a low road. I took the high road to the Sierra Grande.

The Sierras de Córdoba are not the Andes themselves, but an offshoot from them, and are quite modest, as mountains go; but to anyone who has cycled the pampa for a fortnight, the wonderfully scrubby brush and the wonderfully humpy ground seemed exotic to a degree I would previously have accorded to the Alps. I wound uphill in a cloud of intensely aromatic scent from the hedgerow. There were thorn bushes by the road and a great dark hawk in the sky. I looked down at my notebook for a moment, looked up again and it had gone.

It must have dived on prey in that instant. Did vultures do that, or was it an eagle?

Everything was harsher. Even the crickets had a more insistent note. The farms were gone, though sometimes there would be a crumbling smallholding or a few poor fields among the scrub. The road switchbacked below crags, whose dignity was only slightly impaired by the election slogans daubed on them, with a smell of meadowsweet. The thorn trees were full of white blossom — not their own, but a rambler rather like old man's beard. More vultures or eagles came and inspected me: I did not know whether to be flattered or alarmed. They really were extraordinarily large; and they could easily have carried off one of the children at the little lone school I passed, where pupils and teacher in white coats were lowering the Argentine flag at the end of the school day. As I went by, I understood what the birds were, for the school was called Los Condores. And over those quite unproductive and magnificently untended hills, I came to Embalse, and settled myself into an agreeable hotel, a three-inch-thick rump steak and a bottle of Cabernet Don David, one of the more sophisticated of the many excellent Argentine wines.

The sun seemed to be late arriving in Embalse, and it took me some time pondering the explanation for this sudden change in the weather, before I realized that it was the mountains getting in the way. The day began with the heavy flapping of an oversize bird into a nearby pine and an extraordinary smell of wet mint. Beyond the telephone and power wires I could see the sun on the topmost sierras.

A town called "Dam" has to have one salient feature, but Embalse has three — all the works of Peronism. The vast hydroelectric scheme and its beautiful lake naturally gave rise to a workers' holiday resort: and in those more naïve days it must have seemed equally natural to set up another monument to Peronist progress a few kilometres down the shore — a nuclear power station.

Embalse had that typical feel of many holiday towns, that they are indifferent to anything but a crowd. There was a long main road with a desultory fringe of cafés and attractions, including a little merry-go-round and a casino; the shop fronts were louder than usual, the restaurants and ice-cream parlours oversize for the place. Rather a lot of buildings were promising to add a storey or two by projecting reinforcing bars from their tops, but the rust on the steel declared the intention to be a long-standing one. Street trees had evidently been an afterthought, for they were still far from maturity, providing just enough shade for a medium-sized dog.

The Hoteles de la Naçion of the Eva Perón Foundation were a different matter entirely — numbered unromantically from one to seventeen, but set in parkland on the shores of the lake, near streets of self-catering bungalows. Elderly people were meandering slowly over the lawns with shopping bags, and plainly wishing that either the lawns were smaller, or there was some means of transport more appropriate to their time of life than the bicycle hire stand. There is a special walk for the midday sun in Argentina — slow, methodical, enduring — and they walked it. Other elderly couples wandered for something to do, with sweaters round their middles in the blazing sun. Brighton and Bognor would have given their eyeteeth for weather such as this, yet it was out of season in Embalse.

All the national hotels were to the same plain design,

which might have been less colourful than the private enterprise buildings along the main road, but was a great deal less tacky. They looked spartan inside, and some showed signs of age — paint peeling off the shutters — and previous repairs — snakes of replastering where cracks had been. But through the trees I could see a couple of white horses grazing like a picture-book on the grassy lake-shore; playgrounds for children; and even topiary in rather good condition — a jug, animals and birds. In the middle of it all was a chapel, which may well have the highest ratio of spire to church of any in the world, being a kind of Latin American Gothic topped with a metal needle several times the height of the building.

While I was attempting to work out just how high it was, one of the aimless elderly couples came up and chatted. Anyone could go to the hotels when they open in high season, they told me; you just applied, but most workers preferred their union hotels because they were more luxurious. Apparently a vacation with the Union of Light and Power was particularly desirable, since it was one of the main unions, along with the metal workers' and the general workers' unions.

It was a perfect day as I rode out past El Camping FitzSimon, wondering whether the name meant that the man who ran it was some scion of a noble house, or whether he had read too many Walter Scott novels. The road wound down to the dam past a cove of tidy yachts and up to overlook the lake.

Nature was failing to clash its colours, as only Nature can — a pink froth of flowering grasses by azure waves with white crests, a great butterfly of the most brilliant orange

I have ever seen, and green-covered slopes. And in all of it, there were no people. I skirted the lake and met hardly a soul: I climbed to a drier sierra and saw nobody.

The road coasted a range of hills that were as gaunt as goats — under the green fleece of scrub you could see their bones. On the other side stretched a smooth valley tens of miles across, leading up to mountains hazy and monotone with distance.

My road ran above the pretty town of Santa Rosa, with its white church and deciduous trees in the valley yellowing among the evergreens. It was very hot and the switchback road was tiring. My skin was blistered and peeling, with a four inch patch of bare epiderm on my left arm. Argentina was being more sensible about the midday sun. I passed a tractor driver asleep at the wheel, a garage man asleep under a tree. So should I be, I thought, but I could not bring myself to be so Latin as to take a siesta: and soon after I arrived at Villa General Belgrano. It had pine trees and alpine woodwork, a Bavarian-looking café, called The Red Stag; a five metre high, plastic rabbit in the main street proclaimed a town not uninfluenced by tourism.

"A Swede crossed my path, so I thought, Why not?" Tamara was telling me her life history. Before she went to Stockholm, she lived in Portugal, with a Portuguese. In Stockholm, her path was crossed by Horaçio, an architect with whom she had now settled down as landlady of the Sherwood English Pub and Fondu House — for she claimed to be a descendant of Robin Hood. Originally she came from Dorset.

"Me too," I said. "Not Stockholm, Portugal or Robin Hood, of course — but yes, I come from Dorset." I could see why her path had been crossed: she was pretty, lively — and combined motherhood with running the pub and singing jazz into the small hours. "I'll have a pint, please: is that English beer?"

"No, I'm trying some home-brew in the cellar, but it isn't ready. This is *chopp*." *Chopp* is the Argentine draught beer, little different from the general run of bottled lager, except that it tends to taste more like old socks. Argentine brewing is monopolistic, with one countrywide brand, Quilmes, which tends to be a slight improvement on the small number of others beers I encountered — Córdoba Dorada, Santa Fé Cerveza Rubia Especial and, in Patagonia, Leon de Oro. Generally they are thin and strong, with the tell-tale tang of malt extract — and get by because they are served extremely cold.

Beer was much in my mind, for Villa General Belgrano is known as a German town, famous for its German beer festival, at which the usual Argentine beer is drunk and pronounced quite exceptional.

"In fact, there are not so many Germans here — only about twelve per cent," Tamara told me, "but the image remains powerful, because they initiate so much. The Red Stag, for instance, is owned by one of seven brothers who have the newsagents', the Munich restaurant, the bungalows — they have a finger in everything."

If you go into The Red Stag about ten o'clock in the morning you are likely to find a small group of men playing cards and speaking German. They are members of the crew of the pocket-battleship SS *Graf Spee*, which was bottled up by the British navy in the River Plate towards the start of the 1939 war and eventually scuttled, leaving the sailors stranded. Some returned to Germany, some stayed

125

in Argentina. They are old now, plain sailormen and genial to the foreigner, even an Englishman like myself: indeed, they have reunions with the British sailors who were their enemies. And if there were telegrams of congratulation to Buenos Aires from Villa General Belgrano when a British ship was sunk in the Falklands War, I am sure that, at the same time, there were more than enough patriotic good wishes going from place to place in Britain too.

People who are respectable in Argentina are occasionally people who have not been respectable elsewhere. Among the many Germans in the hills around Córdoba — and in other parts of Argentina and Latin America, too — there are a small number who are not plain immigrants or simple servicemen, but formerly important Nazis or ex-officers of the SS, and a few who were war criminals. I met none myself, knowingly, but many people, all over Argentina, told me they were still there. In one town — far from Villa General Belgrano and the village often associated with it, La Cumbrecita — there had been a tragic fire not long before in which a whole family had died, including the children. Local people had known that the head of that family had been an SS man and a war criminal; they had also noticed — for it was a small town — that a small squad of strangers arrived just before the incident, and departed immediately afterwards. Even so long after the inhuman event, even in Argentina, even if — like that SS man — he has become the kindly fellow who gives sweets to children, the war criminal has not necessarily escaped scot-free until he himself goes down to his grave in something less than peace.

Such incidents have nothing to do with Argentina, which is not the only country in the world with a small number of nasty criminals among its population; and which — however individuals may cling to their prejudices and wisecracks — knows that the ultimate survival of a hotch-potch of peoples depends on the ability to live and let live.

"We are a town of 5000 people and twenty-two nationalities," said Monsieur Cottereao, a twinkly Frenchman who had come to see me as a representative of the German beer festival. "We are not a united world, but at town gatherings there will be tables of Germans and tables of Jews — separate, but singing the same songs and drinking the same beer."

He had come to Argentina on a visit, stayed for three months, liked the freedom and stayed for good. He had been a publisher in Paris, was an optician in Villa General Belgrano and Director of the Cultural Centre, which was the building behind the plastic rabbit. He wrote poetry in Spanish which had been published in France — translated back into French by someone else.

"*C'est un pays merveilleux — paysages sauvages et inaccessibles, silence total. Le pays le moin Americain de tout America-Latin. On est européen. Pero*, each day I become more Argentine," said M. Cottereao, extolling 300 days of sun a year, with nights that were seldom so hot that you could sleep without a covering.

"There are four *fêtes*, and *spectacles* at Easter," he told me. "La Foire de Noël, La Fête des Gâteaux Viennois, La Foire du Chocolat, and the *bierfest*, which is *turístico*. They are all new institutions: after all, if there are no *fêtes*, it is necessary to invent them."

While it was true that the Cultural Centre was not quite finished in time for the *bierfest*, being all bare concrete sprouting bits of iron reinforcement — even the plastic

127

rabbit had had part of its bottom kicked in, presumably by someone with a prejudice against rabbits — there was no denying that there was a very well-organized festive air in Villa General Belgrano. No seething throng that I saw in Argentina seethed to quite the same extent as New Year's Eve in Trafalgar Square, but the press of humanity at the *bierfest* was almost up to a medium crush on a grey Bank Holiday in Margate. There were crowds, but never enough to get very much in the way of a fast walk from one end to the other. All the action was in the plaza, and that was full; but you strolled in company with people, rather than rubbing up against them. It made me realize how conditioned I was to overcrowding in my own country.

I made initial contact with the Teutonic experience in the shape of a cart drawn by a miniature pony on which was a beer barrel tended by three blonde tots in Bavarian costume who turned their backs when they saw me taking a photograph of them and a golden retriever *au naturel*. In due course, they were supported by the Beer Queen's vintage Ford with yellow and purple rosettes round its windscreen like a drunkard's dream, and the Chocolate Queen's milk-chocolate coloured jeep. Then the Young Friends of Germany from Santa Fé descended from a coach and a German band, struggled up, in lederhosen, which they told me were imported from Germany with a big tax. I was just congratulating them on their devotion to the genuine article when I glanced back and saw that the street was full of costumes and bands as far as I could see. This is typical of Argentina, where events have a way of looking as if they have been called off, and then suddenly materializing on you. We marched to the plaza where we were greeted by a rather fine Scots pipe band which had missed the start.

"I thought this was supposed to be German," I said to a man in a kilt and everything else ceremonial to go with it. "But I just heard the grim words 'international folk dancing', and you would seem to confirm it." It turned out that he was Leslie Thomson from Buenos Aires, and that "international" meant Argentine international. Two of the keenest pipers were from Italian families, he said.

"You find people from one community mingling into another," he said. "We don't have any Japanese yet. I play because it's the sort of thing I can do just by learning. I don't have any real material heritage. There was only one small organized immigration by the Scots, to Monte Grande, but most of them came for the railway or on contract to a farm. They were poor people, with nothing except their blood — and that's what they were proud of. People have Caledonian balls and celebrate Burns' Night, but it's at completely the wrong time of the year for eating haggis, because it's so hot. Again, all sorts of people do Scottish dances — Argentines seem to feel very warm towards the Scots. During the South Atlantic conflict we were able to play in the streets with an absolute minimum of negative comments. For them, it was England at war with Argentina."

I wondered whether it was an advantage or disadvantage to have so many national groups. He thought that it mainly added spice and little characteristics. The days of dominance passing from one group to another seemed to have gone, and what remained was positive. "When you have many groups with defects and virtues mingling together, each national group tries to see the best in itself — and if you insist on that, it becomes a reality."

"So are beer festivals the best of the Germans?"

"The Germans are an example of how to work properly. Other national groups don't take working as seriously as they do, so it's an important contribution. Argentines are extremely fond of mixing their business with pleasure."

Here, pleasure was definitely good business. All round the plaza were stalls, shops and eating places — mostly vaguely Bavarian or Alpine in character, and often leaning for inspiration on the town's other festivals. So, apart from the beer and sausages, there was plenty of chocolate for sale, and a considerable acreage of Viennese gâteaux — Viennese in this context meaning very thick, blowsy with cream, and served in gargantuan pieces. The souvenir shops were doing a roaring trade in Tyrolean hats, which they had dyed in dayglo colours to make them more attractive, and which were even brighter than the wares of the balloon sellers.

The main attraction was a large stage, set up on the central green, from which a handsome young man in an impeccable suit and a quite perfectly attractive young woman in close-fitting leather trousers were uttering a stream of self-congratulatory pleasantries on behalf of the festival and exhortations to me to enjoy myself.

The stage backdrop was a scene of a mythical Alpine town which was plainly intended to represent Villa General Belgrano itself, as it might be beatified in the hereafter with a bit of glitter added. Proudly displayed was the town's heraldry, which some pursuivants might have classified as excessively informal. The crest was a trout rampant in one tierce frightening a horse in another, in a tierce below that, Christmas trees on a ground of brown mountains with a sunflower, or possibly a sun, super.

There were hours of bands and dancers interspersed with commercials, throughout which the comperes never ceased to smile, never ceased to look impeccable — and, it seemed, never paused for breath. Behind the stage was a little alpine cabin for the sound engineers, notably a man with earphones — or possibly ear-muffs — to which he pressed both hands in extreme delight, or possibly agony. You felt the public address system in your most internal of organs: sitting under a loudspeaker, I was forced to roll up bits of my programme and stuff them in my ears.

I had a front-row seat in between the Beer Queen's mother, a vulpine blonde in black, and the disco lighting board, which consisted of a young man flicking switches in time to the music. It was not difficult to do in the case of music which had plenty of time to it in the shape of bass drum and oompah, but got frantic in the Latin-American numbers such as the Ballet Samba from Rio Cuarto — the girls in white satin with sky-blue belts and the men in gaucho costume with what I hope were codpieces. Then the electric meter went round at tremendous speed in tribute to the flicker's efforts. On the main fusebox below it was written "ACHTUNG" in large letters.

Then the comperes came on again with a huge tray of cups and a line of awkward-looking prize-winners, and delivered an impassioned address in which the object was to mention *la cerveza* as many times as convenient in each sentence and with the greatest exultation. Next to me, the switch-flicker was bored, and was blowing bubble gum with the same devotion he had previously applied to his switches. The prizes were presented to the accompaniment of yodelling, after which the Beer Queen left her sceptre with mother, to conserve her royal energies, and the Chocolate Queen came and sat next to me, looking left out.

More hype from the comperes and the Junge Freunde

von Deutschland de Santa Fé came on in their imported lederhosen and Bavarian bodices, as appropriate. The lederhosen had the air of lederhosen everywhere — they looked as if they did not fit, had never fitted and never would fit. The bodices fitted very well, which was delightful. A small folkloric child was detailed to stand at one corner of the stage with his thumbs in his braces, where he remained like a boy in a dunce's cap — uncomfortable but stoic with a shiny brass tuba, only a little dented, waving over him.

The Young Friends did a waltz round the stage, after which they stood panting, discussing in the most informal way what to do next. They decided on a dance in which they bumped bottoms. In a spirit of fair-mindedness, I did my best to work out whether I have been wrong all my life about dances in which you bump bottoms: perhaps they really were very funny, or elegant, or sexually thrilling and valuable for the maintenance of the race. I would have discussed the matter with the Chocolate Queen, but she had taken her seat off somewhere else.

Now the impeccable young man and the perfectly attractive young woman set to work whipping up excitement with the incessant praise of chocolate and beer. You would have thought it a non-starter, especially in a beer festival at which fairly few people were drinking. A few young men were completely but amiably incapable at the beer tents, but everybody else's consumption was modest — and in a good many cases nil. People were getting high on something else, but getting high they were — either on the occasion, or because the comperes told them to.

It began with Isoldo Küchen and his Orchestra, who looked as if they had been designed by the Brothers Grimm. They brought a large keg on to the stage on a sort of portable altar and sang a song about it with a very great many thumpy choruses. And everyone went decorously crazy. People came down the aisle from the audience and began to dance on the bare ground before the stage, kicking up clouds of dust all over the front row. Clapping, jigging, they sang, formed themselves into arches for other dancers to dance through, tossed each other to and fro, until the ground was crowded and a nimbus of dust rising into the flicking lights.

The beer and chocolate queens came on: the audience stood and cheered frantically. A beer barrel was carried forward and tapped; people rushed with tankards held high as it spurted over the crowd. The Beer Queen dutifully attempted to enter into the spirit of things by accepting someone's stein and trying to jump the queue with it, quite unsuccessfully — even from the stage it was practically impossible to get anywhere near the barrel if you did not happen to be already there.

I could not quite understand how an appreciative audience had been so quickly and easily carried at least three-quarters of the way towards becoming a mob and liking it. It was as if they had all been told that they should now go into a frenzy, for there was certainly not the alcohol in most of them to do it. Perhaps it was a wonderfully spontaneous happening: perhaps it was the flip side of an individualistic people — the sort of undiscriminating excitability in a population that makes dictators.

However that may be, the *bierfest* of Villa General Belgrano remains one of the most innocent public events I have ever witnessed — though as evening drew on, rather more young men were beginning to reel around. I decided to make my way back up the dusty road. Trees were haloed in the late sun, shadows beginning to run down the contours of the hills. Above me, a lost orange balloon floated up into the sky, as if carrying a consignment of specially brewed nectar to the gods.

I went back to the Sherwood pub and ordered some more beer. "I'm feeling a bit woozy," I said to Tamara. "I think I've had too many nationalities for one day."

"There's an Irish family talking about opening a fish and chip shop down the road," said Tamara. "Could be the first in Argentina."

The air was clear as I took the road for Alta Gracia: far across the valley, I could see details on the high sierras, a pattern of browns and greys sculpted by sun and shade. The mountains above me were green — and pink with the flowering grasses. Cycling was slow at first, till the switchback changed in my favour and I whooshed downhill to the lake of Los Molinos.

Then, climbing again and rounding a bend, there was a little cluster of buildings, one of which was a long restaurant with a shop at one end full of *hongos* — wild mushrooms — salamis and local preserves. I was some yards past and over the crest, when I realized that I was about to leave behind one of the most beautifully situated eateries in the world. I flogged back up again, and ordered a simple lunch, to be in tune with the clarity of the water and the carefree nowhere of the spot. They brought it to me at a stone table under a tree. I looked out across the blue water to a curving road that would shortly be my way, and ate good bread with cheese, some of that same salami that was hanging in the shop, a tomato salad and red wine.

Peace dropped out of the trees above on to my table,

rolled down the waving pink hills and rested on the water. And, for a moment, I rested with it.

The road led round the lake on a corniche, then broke away to Villa Ciudad de América — a pleasant village with pomegranates rubicund in the gardens and a smell of sawn wood from the timber yard. There were brightly coloured flowers in the long grass, and half a dozen free-grazing horses.

I climbed out of town, and the road began to make hairpins down a stream valley with the salmon-pink grass in the verges. Other streams flowed in, clear among smooth boulders, and there were often willows drooping helplessly above them. I had not thought to come down from the sierras so soon, but I rounded a bend and saw that there was no longer sky between the hills ahead, but distant lowlands, faded by the distance and the sun.

The descent and the winding road continued. It could have been the mountains of France or Italy, but for the strange cries of unfamiliar birds: and it was more beautiful than either, because it was out of the past — somewhere around half a century behind in being exploited. The stream became a wide river, the Anizacate, with sand and boulders. I saw no fish in the clear water, but there were fishing canes for sale along the road.

The way continued downwards to prosperous riverside houses and the long flat road to Alta Gracia, a pleasant place with genial old houses and neat modern houses tumbling together over hill-tops below the sierras, and a fine Spanish church. Beyond, I passed what must be one of the world's tallest monuments to a wife, Miriam Stephenson, killed in a plane crash in the Thirties and commemorated by a hundred foot stone aileron put up by her husband, Baron Bisa.

135

The road gradually acquired the dusty, over-used feel of roads whose only destiny is to lead into big towns. The outskirts of Córdoba were sprawling, dirty and teeming — quite belying what was in the centre. This is the only city in Argentina capable of holding up a candle to the all-suffocating Buenos Aires — with one particularly spacious park and some fine buildings, especially religious ones, doing their best to stand up for the past against the developers.

If an Argentinian meets a man from Córdoba in another part of the country, he is likely to call him "doctor"; for the university was the first in Argentina, and the medical schools are particularly celebrated. I shall always remember Córdoba as the place in which I saw a consultant surgeon go up to ordinary people who were looking lost on a hospital corridor and ask if he could help them. However, I had already suspected that he might be a particularly obliging man, because when rung up and told that Diego Firpo at La Danesa had provided his telephone number, he said, "Who?", sounded puzzled, "Where?" and then said, "Who?" again, several times: from which I concluded that he was willing to chat to any complete stranger around his hospital without the slightest idea of why he should be doing it.

"I'm the one who sings," said Henry Paladini, who was actually the man who had done the first heart transplant in Córdoba. "All the hospital knows me — I sing while operating. I sing very bad. I sing tangos." He went on to say that he had done 105 kidney transplants so far, and I thought to myself that by this time he must have quite a repertoire.

It was then he stopped to ask if he could help three

people on a bench, looking worried over some pieces of paper. They could not buy the drugs they needed because inflation had stopped people dealing in medical supplies, as in other things. (That day the austral dropped from seventy to eighty-four to the dollar.) "We'll supply them from our stocks if necessary," Henry told me, "but you need to keep supplies for emergencies."

He was Swiss-Tuscan-Spanish-British, with the high-pressure-but-healthy look that consultants often have. As well as working at the private hospital, built in 1950 and fairly well-maintained and equipped since, he taught at the university and operated at the public hospital. He also told me about the Italian hospital, which has a grant from the Italian government; the Spanish hospital, supported by the Belgian government; and the emergency hospital. "One of the best centres to provide organs for transplant in the country," said Henry airily, in what I thought was a backhanded compliment.

On the front of the public hospital you could see the outline of the original name, Evita, above the entrance, for it was built under Perón. "If the Peronists win the election it will take that name again," said Henry. The public hospital was obviously short of cash. It had almost three times the number of beds of the private one, but only a few more staff; surgery was only two days a week because of the shortage of facilities — six theatres for 400 beds. I met one woman who had already been in a month waiting for her operation. Equipment was older, and there was less of it — enough intensive care equipment for only ten beds, for instance, a poor proportion. Still, residents worked twenty-four hours every three days, which sounded as if it compared well with Britain — and the hospital worked too.

137

"I did a double valve replacement this morning for a patient from La Paruga," Henry told me, making me wonder whether I could have done something more useful with breakfast time. "They can't do it there or even in Buenos Aires — because in Buenos Aires you have to pay."

Argentine medical care was about twenty-five per cent public, he said, five per cent private and seventy per cent social — from the unions. "Six or seven per cent of national insurance goes to the unions for health, but they do other things with the money, like buy a hotel in the hills for members' vacations — heavily subsidised so that they end up paying perhaps ten per cent of the regular rate. They take the money from the health service: so that when they need an operation, they have to pay extra money. We take care of them, and the government fixes a price for the operation, but it's not enough. So they have to pay."

The atmosphere was not very different from the private hospital, though much less brisk than a British one. People stood around in the corridors chatting amid the smells of hospital lunch — for nothing, even illness, can be suffered to deprive Argentines of their social life. I was surprised to see that, though Catholics had put olive sprigs over their beds, and there were some rather unhappy-looking houseplants, neither hospital had flowers by the beds. Nor had I expected that if I went to hospital I would have to bring three or four blood donors with me and was not supposed to be admitted without them.

"Many things we don't have in the public hospital. But we do have a lot of bureaucracy," said Henry.

"But it's always impressive to see people caring for others." And I said how impressed I was that people could be surgeons.

"Surgery is in the hands and the intellect. That's the European feeling — but not the Argentine. There's no prestige. We used to do heart operations on cows — they were good for applying mechanical hearts. You have to keep the cow upright because if they go down they die. Then I even worked like a garage mechanic under a car."

I said that I had not heard many people talking about their work.

"Whenever the World Cup comes along, everybody knows about football. Say there's something political — everybody's political! Just now, it's politics. Nobody pays attention to what they are doing. Engineers — and everybody — are politicians. I always say to my colleagues, 'Let's talk about medicine not politics.' We don't have a class with a sense of social responsibility. And I think this is a situation the universities have to reform — to create people who can run the country, an elite."

But his own important qualifications were from the United States — not from either the public or private university of Córdoba, of which the earliest was founded in 1613. He told me that Argentine degrees were of too low a standard.

"There's no exam for university — you have to take a special course — and in five or six years you take a degree with easy exams, because of politics. The popularist university dates from Perón. One of the slogans was 'Shoes, not books', because poor people were suffocating from the oligarchy which we had until the Thirties. We have a term *'diri gente'* — to prepare the people. When we can educate the people, we have a country.

"But I remember 1955, my first class in anatomy — I couldn't get there, because there were two thousand other students in the way. That's how it was then — and it's increasing. There are now four thousand medical students in Córdoba."

"But there can't be jobs for all of them," I said.

"No. When you pass your degree here, they say, 'Have you bought the taxi yet?'"

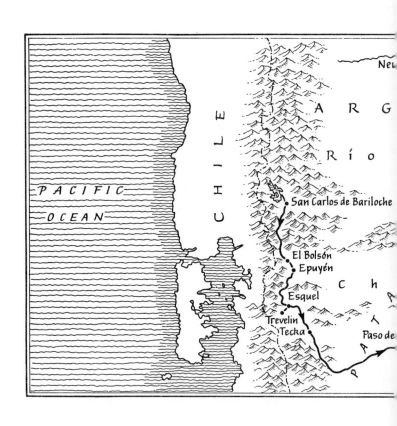

# PATAGONIA

## *Second Journey*

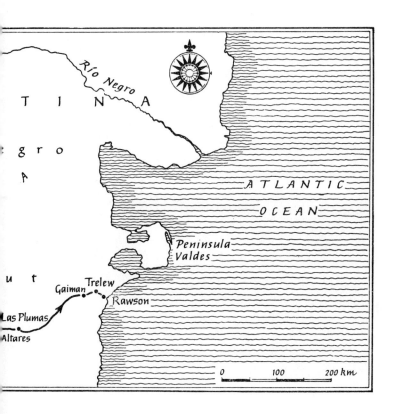

# CHAPTER
# FIVE

# Reflections in the Lake

## *From San Martín de los Andes and Bariloche*

Patagonia is part place, part legend. It was discovered on a legendary voyage; it was given a legendary name, the land of giants; and it is legendary still — a country to which people have come seeking more than really exists on the windswept plains, or even in the fertile valleys of the rivers and mountains. They have followed some vision — a fabled city, sometimes riches, more often a whole life or liberty — and the drive of their fantasy, followed by the necessity of enduring its real consequences, has often made some sort of dream come true. In Mexico and Peru, the *conquistadores* were also driven by the power of imagination — they stole and destroyed; but many of the people of Patagonia came to understand that the riches were in the land, and within themselves. In this, they are the better children of Eldorado.

The expedition of the great explorer Magellan, the first that went round the world, was searching the South Atlantic for the Western Passage in 1520, when it put in at the Bay of St Julián, and brought civilization to a remote coast in the shape of mutiny, murder and execution. At first the land seemed deserted; but when Tehuelche Indians arrived Magellan and his chronicler, Pigafeta, were remarkably impressed by them. They were of great stature, and the traditional story goes that Magellan named them Patagonians from their giant feet (*pata* being Spanish for a foot), though I prefer the theory Bruce Chatwin quotes in his book *In Patagonia*: that the name comes from the giant Patagon in the chivalric romance *Primaleon of Greece*. He then rewarded their friendship by carrying off one of them in irons as an exhibit.

A couple of lesser explorers later, in 1539, Francisco de Camargo was forced to abandon 150 men on his expedition to the region. Legend makes them the founders or discoverers of the mythical Trapalanda, "The City of the Caesars". They were supposed to have been reinforced in later years by survivors of the Indian massacre of the Spanish settlements of Villarrica, Imperial and Osorno, and by the survivors of a shipwreck in the Magellan Strait. Even Jesuits sought the mythical city, anxious to convert any pagan inhabitants to the true faith, and an expedition from Buenos Aires in 1604 penetrated south of the Río Negro in its search.

Another explorer stood on the Road of the Seven Lakes in the mountains near San Carlos de Bariloche 385 years after that. He did not believe in anything mythical, except as a myth, and he knew that any nearby footprints were likely to be size ten and a half, wide fitting. All he knew about Patagonia was that he was now in its mountain region, and that if he looked hard enough under some bridge or other, he might find inscribed the name of Iconomopulos; for he had been chatting about this to Esteban Iconomopulos only the night before, at the restaurant Esteban was running with a friend, who was a trained chef in the ski town of San Martín de los Andes.

"My great-grandfather built the first bridges in Patagonia," Esteban told me. "In the past century Patagonia was a desert — and now the Patagonian provinces are the most powerful in Argentina. You know the history of the pioneers who went to the West in the United States? That's our history now."

"This is the Wild West?" I said to Esteban.

It hardly seemed pioneering. The sofa on which we were roughing it — with the assistance of a bottle of Argentine Moët et Chandon — was puce velvet, and Esteban looked more as if he had come out of a cocktail bar than the high sierras. Both he and his friend were smart, attractive young men with the right sort of pullovers. Around the walls of Rauli, their restaurant, was a contemporary art collection.

In the Forties and after, there was a major migration from the country to Buenos Aires; now there is a drift back to the country again — especially by young people seeking a better quality of life. I was several hundred kilometres into Patagonia, and still in the northernmost province, the prosperous Neuquén: but the young are also moving further south to the provinces of Río Negro, Chubut, Santa Cruz and Tierra del Fuego — for the region of Patagonia stretches two thousand kilometres from the Río Colorado to Cape Horn.

It was a far cry from the Greek island from which Esteban's forefathers had come with an intimate knowledge of boat-building, which they had turned to the construction business. Esteban still sometimes went to the church that they and their friends built in the evenings and weekends as

147

a copy of the church on their island. He remained Orthodox, he said, though his beliefs were more agnostic.

"For me religion is a tradition. Men and women worked during their weekends to build that church, and it's important to remember it. It's in Bamfield, Buenos Aires, where I come from. I went to Balmoral College there — Scots, as you might imagine. Argentina didn't belong to the British Empire, but it often almost seemed as if it did until the 1930s. When Perón became president, he cut all those links to the rest of the world. Argentina was an island for forty years.

"I was born in 1956, at a time when a revolution cut short the Perón administration. In the thirty-three years since, we've had sixteen presidents — and hundreds of ministers. I remember three years between 1973 and 1976, in the time of Isabel Perón, when we had thirty-five different ministers, I think. It was terrible."

Isabel Perón was replaced by the militars. The dollar was cheap, and Esteban went abroad to study greenhouses. But what he learned was something different.

"In Berlin I went to a human rights association. I saw my country — *my* country up on the wall! And I didn't know: I had no information. An Irish woman said to me, 'You come from a land of horror.' 'Where?' I said. And she began to tell me things. Every first Sunday in the month I used to phone my family in Buenos Aires. I told them, 'Be careful, stay quiet,' because I was afraid for them. They didn't understand what I was talking about.

"In London I went to see *Evita*. It was incredible, because I learned new things about my own country. Outside your Houses of Parliament I saw a demonstration against Margaret Thatcher. I said, 'My God!' And a woman answered, 'You don't understand: you don't have a democratic country.' In America I saw a TV broadcast that said there was a concentration camp in Azul. Twenty blocks from my street, a concentration camp! In buildings I used to walk past, people were being tortured — I couldn't believe that it happened, and that I saw nothing. Yet the soldiers would go into the bars, and if someone looked homosexual, they would take him.

"Now I can see that there were a great many clues — but it was a very confused time, with guerrillas, bombs, people dying. When the military came to power, things began to quieten down. But they didn't publicize how they did it.

"In those days, perhaps someone would disappear. After a few weeks someone would say, 'Haven't seen so and so around lately.' Then we would find out she was in gaol. 'In gaol — well she was a bit left-wing. Perhaps she was a communist, perhaps she was really dangerous.' All this time, the military would be going down her address list, and the address lists of the people they took from it.

"Then we had the Malvinas: the world was a big, big circus. Our President totally drunk — drunk! And when they picked the soldiers, they didn't send people from Buenos Aires University. They sent people from the country, people they would be glad to get rid of: poor people from the north-west, Indians, and black half-breeds, communists. They sent them to die.

"This democracy began six years ago with Alfonsin. We have more economic problems now, but for me, this is the first time in all my life when I can look forward to the future. For me, freedom is everything. If I have no money in my pocket, if I have nothing to eat tomorrow — it's no problem, if I have freedom.

"Here in San Martín, the season is a fantasy. People come from Buenos Aires in a conspiracy to ignore reality. Their talk is all about cars, holidays, the good life — anything to forget the real problems. And if you mention them, they look at you — how they look!"

San Martín de los Andes is a small, neat town largely enclosed by shaggy mountains — and from it rises one of the beautiful roads of the world, the Road of Seven Lakes. If you come to it after a journey which has mostly been many hundreds of kilometres of pampa followed by many hundreds of kilometres of near-desert, it is all the more astonishing — not only for the lakes themselves, which are crystal; or the mountains, which are gigantic and snow-capped; but for the coihue tree, the southern beech, *nothofagus dombeyi*. The coihue is everywhere, often hung with knots of sphagnum moss that sit on the branches like a green creature consisting entirely of hair. On the southern slopes of the mountains the trees grow amid exuberant fountains of bamboo.

Among the coihues lived a family of Mapuche Indians, in a vale that was the most perfectly shaped piece of land I have ever seen. Trees and meadow swept down in a curve that was too perfect to be anything but geometrical, and too thrilling to be geometrical at all. A steep track of soft earth led upwards through the woods to their farm — a cluster of corrals, old wooden barns and a wooden cabin that was rather prim and new in comparison with everything else. Overlooking the lake there was a flag-pole for flying the Argentine flag on the national day.

I went with Esteban to meet the master of the house, Amadeo Curruhuinca, who was also chief of a clan of

600 Mapuche families, most of which bore his name. He was stocky — black-haired, but sallow rather than dark, and wore a pullover roughly knitted of heavy wool in natural colours by his wife, Juana. She wore a dark mauve waistcoat as a concession to vanity above a pair of old brown trousers. A cheap digital watch hung on a chain round her neck, evidently a possession of pride. Though weather-beaten, her complexion was yet paler than her husband's, for she had a German father, who was now back in Germany. There were a couple of old people in the farm and several school-age children.

Mapuche, like its equivalent word Araucano, covers a number of tribes of Indians whose origins tended to be in the west, in Chile. (Like everyone else in Patagonia, the Mapuches are immigrants.) Mapuche means "the people of the earth", and the most important constituents of life for the Mapuche are the earth, family union and the preservation of their religion. The name for their gods is "The Owners of the Men", to whom they show themselves for approval at their big festival in February. They have no representation of their gods but themselves, no religious apparatus or temple of any kind: their way of life and social structure are their religion.

Juana had been educated in a Catholic school, and accepted both Catholicism and the Mapuche religion without any sense of conflict. A little worried that I was an unbeliever, she repeated several times that we were all the children of one God — Mapuches, Argentines and British alike, and that we should co-operate rather than fight each other.

I found it difficult to know how to behave with them. I got off to a bad start by asking if I might take a photograph, and snapping one quickly, assuming the answer was yes. As I later found out from a man who had photographed many Mapuches, that whole subject can be exceedingly delicate. One Mapuche whom he admired had been very unhappy about being photographed, so he had given him the pictures. The Mapuche said, "I hope you don't mind, but I'll burn them" — and it was not until ten years later that he returned to have his picture taken, both he and his horse dressed up as grandly as possible for the camera.

Then I was embarrassed because they were much poorer than I was — though, for all I know, they may have been pitying me because I lived in the city with no sheep or goats of my own. I was inhibited, too, by the fact that they were Indians, and it was somehow expected that I would find it difficult to get on with them. But they were friendly, though cautious; and became more so; till at last I made a policy decision that they were people, I was people — and it was to be assumed that we would get on like people.

We seemed to be interested in the same sorts of things. Like any middle-class Englishwoman, Juana showed me her vegetable garden, and pointed out the herbs as of particular interest. Aniseed and rosemary were among them — very good for chest problems, rosemary. Did I have asthma? Oh yes, just what I needed, she said. And here was the kitchen . . . It was a hut in which lunch was being cooked on an open fire of branches within a circle of stones. Juana's daughter lived in the town, in a house with a modern kitchen and bathroom: but when the mother went there, the daughter would make an asado over the open fire in a traditional way. Juana did not approve of gas cooking, because it made moisture, and was bad for the lungs.

The hut contained a meatsafe, which Juana showed me with pride. An entire sheep, skinned, hung in the main cabin, its rib-cage open. I came upon its heart hanging up in the eaves of another hut, with flies crawling on it. A quarter of a lamb hung from a tree before the house, darkening in the sun.

There was no electricity, though they were hoping to have it when they began to use the new building below. I had seen it as I came up — breeze-block hut in the very centre of the beautiful curve of meadow. They had had to haul their water for much of the last three years in the time of drought, but now it came again from the spring — along a hosepipe for the people and a runnel for the animals. The horse trough was a hollowed tree trunk: a peaceful dog lay asleep on the ground below it.

One corral had a brown horse in it, rather knobbly about the pelvis; another was full of goats and sheep together, the morning sun in their coats, poking their heads through the palisade of trunks and branches. Breeding animals and crops was their livelihood, apart from her knitting, she said. They were virtually self-sufficient. She pointed out the cherry trees, whose fruit they sold: and an elder bush from whose berries they made jam.

Before the front door, two old carts, very primitive, were mostly put together with joints rather than nails or screws, though one had some old piece of corrugated iron as sides along the wood rails. The corrugated iron on the roofs and a pickup truck, with its corners much dented, were almost the only objects that could not have been made from something in the landscape. There was nothing affluent, but there was nothing unharmonious.

The English were very clever, that she knew, said

Juana. Cars, aeroplanes, they had invented them all. All modern conveniences had come from the North to Latin America. She welcomed the improvement in relations after the Malvinas War. "We need these things and ideas," she said. "Argentina is a rich country, but the people don't know how to use the natural resources."

We went into the main cabin, where a set of dog-eared files showed that not even a chief of the Mapuches can escape bureaucracy. They had a committee, said Amadeo, and decided things together. We sat at a well-scrubbed table on some very solid home-made chairs and benches decorated with rather grubby weavings. Something savoury was stewing on the hot iron stove, and a kettle singing: on the wall was a guitar.

The chief said he played it, but not so much nowadays, so it was more for the young people. They played gaucho music, because the gaucho was the earth person. "The best music is the guitar," said Juana. "Much better than the accordion." More ethnically, the Mapuches have a horn made from a coihue branch: the *trutruca* is taller than a man, rather like an alpenhorn, and is played at *nguillatún*, the two or three day celebration of the New Year, which is the most important religious and social event in the Mapuche calendar.

They were certainly people of the earth, for it was all round them. In the dell, around the huts, barns and corrals the earth was bare — but it was like walking on dark loam, not dust, there was so much leaf mould in the soil from the great trees standing on the hollows and hills around, the glades below them like lawns.

The last of the Seven Lakes is Nahuel Huapí — Mapuche

for something like "Tiger Island". It stretches almost to Chile, which is not a hundred kilometres away, but it is narrow, so as I cycled round its eastern end to San Carlos de Bariloche, I could see the town across the lake as a white cluster at the foot of snow-capped peaks. It was almost the end of April, and autumn had turned the coihues in the high mountains a dry red and covered the fountains of bamboo with a filigree of frost.

It was a brilliant day. I was among fells of grass and scrub tired out by summer to a listless brown: but wild roses overspread the hillsides with rosehips glowing scarlet against gold leaves. They are not native to the region, but were introduced by those who developed Bariloche, mostly Germans and Swiss, and have grown so extraordinarily that they are now found not by the bush but by the thicket, and often by the kilometre. Bariloche is famous for its flowers and vegetation — particularly for its arrayane trees, which Walt Disney took as his model for the forest in *Bambi*. They have a peeling bark of a rich cinnamon colour, caused by the concentration of tannin; and the biggest grow on an island in the lake, golden-brown trunks meandering up sixty or seventy feet, with tiny dark leaves. They are not only rare but rather sensitive: I passed only one copse of them by the lake-side, but they showed me small white flowers and fruit together.

Even down by the lake there was a nip on fingers and toes and when I went downhill I could feel the increase in speed as an extra chill through my clothes. At a road junction, I passed an open truck loaded with young soldiers. They huddled in their waterproofs with their young faces turned up to the sky as if begging for warmth. I slithered and slipped past them — the road was gravel there — and they all cheered me on, looking happier than before at the unexpected variety I had brought into their lives. I pedalled frantically, in an effort to keep up their delusion that I was some sort of sporting character, until they were lost behind me, and I could relapse into my usual crawl.

Bariloche greeted me with a couple of extremely large St Bernard dogs dwarfing a rather small photographer. He posed us together before the alpine town hall, with me doing my best to look warm, and the St Bernards wearing just the sort of expression you would expect from someone who has to go through life with a barrel tied round his neck. There is a special compulsiveness in the unnatural nature of such photographs. They perfectly express the tourist dream, showing an awkward everyday human being in a setting of fantasy. We may keep such pictures as mementoes, but it is for their surrealism we love them.

There is no more popular tourist town in Argentina than Bariloche, and if a citizen of Buenos Aires knows only two places in the world, the other will be the spot where I was standing with the St Bernards. In its wonderful setting, with long streets running downhill to the waters of the lake, Bariloche has smart shops, tourist shops, cafés, discos, restaurants, hotels — and streets crowded with tour buses.

Bariloche is long on delights — though rather shorter on satisfactions. You can buy smoked trout and salmon from the lake, wild boar, smoked venison, rosehip jam from the golden bushes on the hillsides. And the most popular tourist supermarket in Bariloche was golden too — full of bright yellow boxes and buttercup bags, glass display cabinets spotlit till they shone like diamonds, treasure-chests of nuggets of golden foil: an Eldorado of chocolate — after the scenery and the skiing, it is chocolate that is Bariloche's fame.

I had never seen so much cuteness devoted to chocolate. In the window a mechanical St Bernard stood guard over an enormous cardboard heart full of chocolates, having just emerged from a chocolate dog kennel, and wagged his head and tail in absolute time for ever, or until they changed the display. Bambi shook head and hoof over the bonbons; Little Red Riding Hood headed a cast of Alpine dolls with over-sweet smiles. There were cars in chocolate; chocolate figs, nuts, cherries, grapes; diabetic chocolate; chocolate dachshunds, revolvers, snowmen, Swiss chalets, yachts and boats, robots, men in the moon. And this was only one of the chocolate shops that line the main street, with the chocolate tourists going in and out of them collecting bags of the stuff with great dedication. The truth is, however, that the general run of Bariloche chocolates are usually not very appealing to the non-Argentine palate, being rather coarse, fatty and over-sweet. They have their enthusiasts: I met an ex-undertaker turned chocolatier who was devoting great care to macerating his fruit in spirits for six months at a time, and bemoaning the fact that no one had yet succeeded in reproducing an Argentine After Eight — but the fact remains that Europeans, at least, do not usually ask for a second piece.

With such a dedicated approach to tourism — which indeed is the town's *raison d'être* — there is one surprising omission in the brochures. Bariloche is possibly the only town in the world that can claim to have a monster and yet has not publicized it. They call it Nahuelito, and it is said only to appear in a flat calm. I did not actually see it myself, but I went to see Mrs Hilda Rumboll, who had, fourteen years before.

She was an elderly woman coping with the infirmities of age with great energy; not all of it directed in a straight line. However, her family was noted for its interest in natural history: and her eldest son was a well-known professional in the field.

"That big tree was a tiny tiddly when I came here," Mrs Rumboll informed me, taking the long way round. "We were newcomers here — Bill had retired — it was our second year I think." From the picture window in her house I could see right across the lake. It was seventeen kilometres wide there, she said, and 450 metres deep.

"It was a day with no wind. Over there, at the beginning of the lake, more or less, an enormous wash took place. I've never seen anything like it — it must have been the height of this wall. The monster came in with a terrific rush, and settled. The huge wake was slowing down, and the water was calming — and suddenly there he was, swimming in the water with his head in the air. So I marked him by that tree, rushed straight off and got my husband, and we sat from twelve to fifteen minutes watching the animal. Bill said to me, 'It's a swan or a goose.' I said, 'You're the goose; how can you put a goose seventeen kilometres away and see that?' 'Oh,' he said, 'you're right.'

"Then the water-skiers came out after lunch and started skiing this side of the monster. And the monster still looked magnificent, and high above them by a long way. Well, that really shook us: I began to tremble, I really did. Bill said 'Well look, it's got a goose's back.' I said, 'All right, but it's not a goose.'"

"Did you see any features?" I asked. "Could you see any eyes?"

"I can't see an eye from here to halfway across the lake," said Mrs Rumboll, testily. "The animal is calculated at thirty to thirty-five metres. The head wasn't big in comparison, but the length of neck was frightening. But then, my word! The creature suddenly decided, 'I've had enough of sunshine, I'll go down below again.' So it switched all the way round. Every bit of water was in motion — all round as far as you could see. It disturbed the whole lake. And how can a tail rock the whole of a lake unless it's something pretty hefty?"

"So it was a very active sort of monster?" I suggested.

"Oh, terribly fast — I've never seen anything quicker. But it went down slowly just like the periscope of a submarine, and I didn't see another thing."

"What did people say?" I asked.

"'She's been seen seeing things.' 'She was mad, didn't we tell you?' The television questioned me, and said, 'It's not true. You've been dreaming it.' Maurice, my eldest son, happened to be in the National Parks then, and he got very British. He said, 'My parents do not lie!' I said, 'It may appear tomorrow; it may appear next year; it may appear in a hundred years, and I'll be gone by then — but someone else will see it. That monster exists!' That was my plain answer to him. Of course, they filmed the whole thing, and they filmed my labrador who opens doors and shuts them quite on his own. The television said, 'Did that dog open the door?' 'Yes, why not? Lots of them do.' 'But did he close it after you?' I said, 'Of course, he's got to do that in winter. If he comes in it's bitter cold, so he learned to close it as quick as he could.'"

159

"It's a funny business, investigative journalism," I said. "But did nobody else ever see the monster?"

"This bus-load, they got into such a state. There were thirty odd. People started screaming, 'There's something in the water.' The bus driver stopped, they all got out, and stood on the bank and watched him till he disappeared. He dived, and within a few seconds, he was 700 metres up the lake — there. Twice they saw him, the same bus-load."

Next morning there was no monster, but the wind was raising white horses on the lake, and I donned several layers of clothing against the cold before I set out towards El Bolsón. It was Sunday, and the town was quiet. I passed a few chilly men peering disconsolately into the bonnets of cars, a couple of ragged men, with dark Indian faces, off to some awful job — or worse — to lounge in the cold. Most shops were shut, but in one a woman was mopping her floor to a loud and mawkish ballad from the radio — slurp, slurp, slurp, slurp, together.

I rode out of town in low gear because this was a day when I wasn't going anywhere in a hurry and the road was steeply uphill to the poorest part of town, the Barrio Alto.

When you see a child beggar in Bariloche — not too often, for they are discouraged in the centre of town, not being good for tourism — he will come from the Barrio Alto. A skivvy underpaid in a hotel or the old woman in a red cardigan, who hangs helplessly around the door of the post office, not even daring to ask, but grateful when you give — very likely the Barrio Alto is home to them. And the three kids I saw scrabbling in the rubbish bags in advance of the dustcart — one holding up a light bulb, squinting at it with his head on one side in an effort to decide whether there might be some remote chance of a glow for him — they too will be from that place of blowing dust and stones, high above the lake.

There washing blows in the wind, and the dust blows into the flapping arms and legs, into the pores of the cloth. Somewhere else, in this sun, the washing would be bright: here it is dingy before it is dry. The colours have given up the struggle against poverty and the dust.

Nothing that you have hitherto thought about a house is necessarily true in the Barrio Alto. A window may well not have glass or even flapping polythene — it may be boarded or a hole in the wall. A wall may not be a solid division between the home and the world outside: it may be half-finished or half-demolished — bare breeze block, rusty corrugated iron, shaky timber. From tin roofs, felt roofs, roofs of plastic scraps held down by stones, from these stick up old stove-pipes with smoke curling or no smoke at all. Above and around the wind gusts and howls, and the inhabitants must take what comfort they can from the shining lake (which is the very same the tourists see from their hotels) and the sun sculpting the mountains.

But the Barrio Alto is not hopeless. Homes are growing there. A wooden shack whose only act of construction seems to have been the leaning of one set of old planks against another acquires a fence, the fence acquires a garden, the garden begins to grow trees: there is one wall of breeze block, another, then concrete and bricks appear: the shack becomes a house — poor, but a house. Shacks and people battle together for some slight decency in life, albeit sometimes against all odds.

One such woman was Rosa Elena Carcamo, one of the Chileans who have come to Patagonia in recent years looking for a better life, and who at times have been up to forty per cent of the Patagonian work-force. Rosa's house was a wooden chalet within an open tank of water by the gate. In the small front garden behind a chain-link fence some twelve inches of lilac bush and a bare scattering of new plants were putting up a brave struggle against the wind. A yellow plastic bath shivered on its hook in the outside wall, and smoke from the stovepipe skittered quickly away in the breeze. A kitchen-cum-living-room ran across the front of the chalet. It had electricity and bottled gas for a glowing heater and a cooker. The furniture was a light-wood table and chairs, possibly home-made. Behind the kitchen were two bedrooms, one with a double bed, one with bunk beds for the children.

Rosa's parents were working class, but there had been good education in the more democratic days of Chile — and of the nine children in the family two had gone to university and become professionals. She had come to Argentina to escape the oppressions in her own country. She had had five children, three in Chile, two in the Barrio Alto, where each new mouth to feed is a desperate challenge (though a proof of residence to the authorities as well). She had tried every form of contraception, but something was always going wrong, and she found herself pregnant again — so she had now had herself sterilized.

Her body had spread with the child-bearing and confinement at home, but she must have been in her early thirties at the most. She had a clear, calm face with brown eyes that managed to be both soft and bright at the same time — and as she remembered the bitter hardships of the past, they were sometimes clouded with tears. It was as if she had been deprived of expressing her sufferings for so long that the emotion of pouring them out to a stranger was too much to bear.

When she first came she lived in a very poor place indeed — made out of a bit of concrete, some pieces of wood and holes for the windows covered with polythene. Water had to be fetched from a hollow: she became ill and almost died. She and her husband lived like that for three years, until they could buy their own house — though it was not much bigger than the shack, and by that time they had three children. They had to accept all the adversities, and that life was always going to be that way.

"I know it's silly," she said, "but the one thing I couldn't cope with was not being able to have decent shoes. I would go out for one walk, and the rough roads would break the heels and ruin them. I could take everything but that."

Sometimes another Chilean would get a house, and have a party: they would have a modest asado and wine together, and she could be glad for them. Those were the only happy times.

Life was better now, for children born in Argentina had given her an official status she had lacked before and her husband had a job as a welder and mechanic in Neuquén, though it only allowed him to come home at weekends. I could see a degree of prosperity in the shape of a refrigerator, and a glossy ghetto-blaster on which a little boy was playing at sound recording with a microphone.

"Do you have hope for the future?" I asked her.

"Hope is what gives me the strength to go on," Rosa said. "This is a rich country, and I know that there has to be a change for the better. I don't say anything about the government — that's not my business — but sooner or later someone will come along and say, 'OK, that's enough: now we're going to get things organized, and go forward together.' Chile, Argentina, Brazil, Peru, Bolivia — all of them. More than Chile, more than Argentina, it's Latin America for me."

There are many dogs in the Barrio Alto, and as I moved through it, I made waves of yapping and barking. I am ever more convinced that the character of a people is revealed in its dogs: and Argentine dogs are delightful creatures who make a certain amount of noise, but are otherwise usually quite unaggressive. Like Argentines, they keep late hours, and walking through a poorer suburb at night is like being in a cage full of rabbits, with a sense of constant motion around you as the dogs run up to investigate, and go away again. They have a perky independence, too: and you will often see a small pack of them self-importantly inspecting the town, trotting across the traffic with the greatest equanimity. Everyone seems to manage to cope with this quite well in town, as they cope with the total absence of lights on bicycles, and not infrequent lack of them on anything else. In the country the dogs are apt to try it once too often, so that you see them dead and left by the roadside, along with what Argentines gaily throw out of their car windows, namely non-degradable plastic bags, drinks bottles and used nappies.

Back at the main road to El Bolsón, groups of cyclists were standing around talking. One of them cycled along with me for a while, and I understood from him that of all the roads in the universe the road to El Bolsón was a particular cow. The surface gave out some fifty kilometres distant, on top of which, they were digging up most of it for a new road.

To start with, the surface was perfect: the only problem was the extraordinary and chilling wind. It blew head-on, and I was in low gear going downhill. I got off the bike and spun the wheels to make sure nothing was sticking. It wasn't. I dropped another notch and laboured down to Lago Gutierrez, where the clouds seemed to have got themselves caught on the mountain peaks and were having difficulty dragging themselves off. A chill fell from them to the icy waters of the lake and turned them dark.

The whole valley was in shadow. The chill came in at the feet, the fingers and the top of the head and went right through the body. The only warmth there came in was through the eyes — yellow birches by the lake, and the glorious flame-red rosehips along the shore. The place was almost a suburb by Patagonian standards, with sandy beaches, several houses on the far banks and half a dozen small boats, but to European eyes it was inconceivable that such a beautiful spot should have escaped development. True, there was some on my side — a little shack by which a man was chopping wood. He had made the lake his back garden, setting chairs and a dinner table beneath a tree at the water's edge. With a cranky old 2CV and a boat, his life was complete. No planner had seen him off and he was no eyesore: he shared his life with the passer-by, as the lake shared its beauty.

There was a tooting behind me; a pickup truck passed, bedecked with flags, and then there was a whirring, like killer bees approaching. I was in the middle of a cycle race. Bunches of young men flashed past me, seemingly unaffected by the wind and the cold — some were in shorts and T-shirts, while I was in two anoraks and a heavy pullover. I did my best not to look like one of them, fearing that the finishing line might be round the bend, in which case there might be spectators, crowds, cheering. It would all be extremely embarrassing.

The road continued downwards against the wind, and a few farms later the cyclists and their retinue of cars and pickups started coming back again. As I feared, there was some cheering, which I acknowledged like royalty; then, after the second and third waves of cyclists a frenzy of hootings, flashings of lights and wavings. Even the last stragglers found the energy to lift their heads from their handlebars and smile.

When they had gone, I was utterly alone by the utterly undisturbed Lago Mascardi, lying below a great bare mountain of green rock streaked with white and a few low red trees on its slopes, which descended to ranks of fine coihues along the water and, at the distant end of the lake, a little scatter of white houses which was the town — rather, the hamlet — of Villa Mascardi. The sun had come out, and it was warmer. Above me, white clouds moved among the mountains like whales among islands, and their shadows made new rifts and valleys in the landscape as they passed over.

In the forests above my road, waterfalls sprang from the mountainside with a soundless rush that became a crash on to the stones nearby and a hollow ooomphing noise as they bounced through the pipes under the road on their way to the lake. Ahead, the rolling mountains had a tremendous, lazy spaciousness about them. The whole landscape was a mixture of the spartan and luxuriant.

Past Villa Mascardi, with not a soul to be seen but a van driver making his solitary asado by the roadside, I began to climb up the side of the green and white mountain. I was

166

sheltered, but in the rush of the water on the shore I could hear that the wind was lurking somewhere, and as the road bent round above Lago Guillelmo, it came at my back.

This lake was deserted. Little more than thirty kilometres from Bariloche, I had come to wilderness: no traffic, and everything silent, except for the wind and a few birds. There was not even the barking of a dog.

Now I could actually see the progress of autumn, because half-way up the hillside opposite the foliage changed from green to brown as if by the stroke of a brush. As I went higher, the trees shrank to dwarves. And then suddenly, without any fuss, I came to the end of the paved road. Somebody had put several bullets through the notice saying *"Fin de pavimento"*, for in the remoter parts of Argentina people often use the road signs for target practice.

I climbed up to a bridge over a torrent tossing ice-grey waters. Snow-capped mountains were ahead, but I was almost on a level with the nearer peaks now, the dirt road curving ahead over the highlands of the Pampa del Toro. There was grass, small fields — and behind me the valley was carpeted in the richest brown made up of golds and reds from the turned leaves of the dwarfish trees.

My understanding of the dirt road came gradually. To begin with, it seemed brown and friendly. Then a bus passed, and instead of being enveloped in diesel fumes only, I was showered with a cloud of dust as well and came out of it spluttering, spitting and wiping the grit out of my eyes.

It was slow going, of course. In fact, it was hard going, especially up the hills. Nor was it much fun when you went down, for you had the choice of cravenly putting on the brakes or risking calamity against potholes and jolting the maps out of the handlebar bag. And — going up or down — there was little time for admiring the landscape, since you had to watch constantly for the really big rock which was going to jolt you even more than the smaller rocks that made up the surface, and perhaps buckle a wheel. To encourage this, strips of the road would pretend to be smoother for a while, lulling me into a false sense of security, and then turning immediately and catastrophically into a disaster area of heaps of stones.

I took to resting on the tops of hills and — when nobody was in sight, which was most of the time — getting off and walking up them, just to have a relief from the jolting. But then the road went kilometre upon kilometre down one mountain side; crossed a river; and continued kilometre upon kilometre down another, at last bending round above Río Villegas, a sawmill and a few shacks where the road forks to El Manso and the Chilean border.

It was a pretty tree-covered valley with a crystal-green river, and I had stopped on the bridge to take a photograph of it, when a khaki soldier with a pistol in a very shiny holster came out of a green shack and wagged his finger at me.

"What, not allowed?" I said in a voice of remarkable incredulity, which I hardly had to simulate, since what was in the viewfinder was an outhouse with some wood piled up against it, two green shacks and a radio aerial.

He wagged his finger again. It was forbidden to take photographs. Where were my documents? He had a long face, and I could see that he was a pessimist. Sure enough, where other people's documents filled his life with happiness, mine were fraught with the possibilities of guile. I could see him coming to the conclusion that, with my sort of documents, I was just the kind of character who would go round taking photographs — with all that that implied. It came into my mind that, my country being in a state of diplomatic hiatus with his, I might well be suspected of being a spy on his outhouse.

When he had marshalled all the suspicious circumstances, he invited me to trip up the path to what I now understood to be a police station. It had a glass verandah on the front where he could sit in comfort and watch the road to Chile. Inside, a plump young man lounged on a sofa reading the newspaper, presumably engaged in border control. There was a hard wooden bench for me to sit on, but the room was pleasantly warm. He leafed clumsily through my passport: I took it from him and flicked through it to show him the visa. He questioned me with mutual incomprehension. At last he took his log-book and wrote a several-sentence account of the international incident in a large round script. He shook my hand and wished me a good journey. I expect that, like most such people, all he really needed was a little affection. When I looked back he was sitting there chewing mechanically.

My hands were warm as I took the road upstream — first the green river and then a brown tributary — and along a valley which aspired to the dignity of a few stony meadows, with willows that hung pendulously.

There was a desolation of bare earth beyond. They were building a new road, and had found it necessary to remove half the landscape to do it. Three cows and a horse were contemplating the scene, trying to work out why so much energy could have gone into the removal of the blades of grass which to them had been the only thing worth keeping.

After the village of El Foyel, with its grey wooden houses

and wigwam woodpiles, the road ran through a broad valley under peaks on which I could see the bottom of the snow line. To my right, a bare plain extended to hills and more tremendous mountains, with only the occasional clump of two or three poplars hinting at a dwelling. The few huts along the hills were so discreet as to be almost part of them. Mapuches, for certain, living like British tinkers, except that — instead of scrap iron — the junk scattered about was wood.

On the moorland road over the tops, a little cold rain was falling. My mudguards jammed solid with sand and gravel, so that I sounded like an ambulant grindstone. I took a late lunch, in the valley of the River Foyel, remarkably content with a horrible sandwich and Bariloche chocolate, in the company of a black horse, who was munching rosehips. The river was limpid, but the cold had collected in the dip: on the long climb away, each hundred yards was warmer.

Over the hill, half-way down a set of precipitous hairpins, I heard a high-powered put-putting on the road ahead, and there was a young man riding easy and bare-headed on one of those motorcycles that looks as if it only needs a couple of extra wheels to turn it into a racing car.

There was something not-Argentine in both aspects. We stopped simultaneously. He was a smiling, chortling Belgian — a bricklayer, six months into a tour of South America. He had broken down twice, and the last time had had to take a bus to Santiago for the spare part. He always stopped when he saw a touring cyclist, he said, on principle. The last one had been a Frenchman.

"Where was he going then?" I asked, politely interested.

"I think he was going everywhere. He'd been out for eleven years."

He gave me three films to carry back to Europe for him, too precious to entrust to the Argentine post office, and put-putted off easily up the hill. I carried on less easily down.

But I was on the home stretch. From Los Repollos, where a stream flowed over the road and a couple of lazy pigs rooted in the roadway (but there is school Number 150 and even a small shop), the road follows the river down what must have been a lovely valley before the roadworks came, with its trees and its stony river. Time will repair their desolation, no doubt, but no one will travel the winding road that I did, intertwining with the river.

It was dusk when I came down into a fertile valley with wisps of smoke rising from houses too far off to see, and poplars yellow in the dusk. The darker it became, the more they glowed.

I came on to a paved road. After the many hours of boulders, the surface ran as smoothly as the deepening shadows. There was the smell of autumn leaves and wood smoke, the sound of chopping wood. And in the hollow of the valley I saw the lights of El Bolsón.

# CHAPTER
## SIX

# The Children of
# El Dorado

## *El Bolsón, Esquel and Trevelin*

Ever since a few of the Buenos Aires cast of *Hair* dropped out there for a while in the late Sixties, El Bolsón has enjoyed the reputation of being a hippy colony. In fact, it is a haven of quiet creativity, as even the birds bear witness: it is a place of the *tero*, the bird of contentment and domesticity, which hangs around the houses in monogamous pairs and honks at visitors like a good-tempered guard dog.

El Bolsón means "The Bag", and the bag is a fertile Shangri-La of a valley between tall mountains, through which a river flows. It began as a Spanish community that used to be Chilean until the border changed — then came Germans, Poles, and Syro-Lebanese, who tend to be the more conventional and commercially minded citizens. Peons there always were, and in the Seventies they were joined by another group of outsiders — people from the noisy cities seeking a green El Dorado.

"You don't seem very much like hippies to me," I said to Adriana, who was blonde and *soignée*, and had just finished singing a troubadour song to the accompaniment of recorders, drums and an Arabic lute, played by her husband Marcelo, a respected early musician. He had made the instrument himself and there were specimens of his marquetry on the wall of their living room — a mirror frame, ornaments on a guitar. He had not yet finished building their new music room in a log tower overlooking the valley and their hillside garden of lawns, special trees and a little brook, but it all seemed a good exchange for a flat in Buenos Aires.

Marcelo and Adriana had not only created their home themselves, but had managed to fill it with a feeling of joy in life. There was a neat, well-equipped kitchen and a comfortable living room full of personal, interesting and artistic things. A ceiling light emerged from a dried bush. Home-made birds of straw flew on strings; the twentieth-century hi-fi speakers were hidden behind an Indian weave. Above the guitar, one of Adriana's paintings showed a romantically naïve white horse, with a little house and windmill on a blue plain.

"No, in fact, not like hippies at all," I said, and was answered by one of the other guests, Alejandro. "Once I say to a judge, 'What is a hippy for you? All that comes from outside is a hippy?' He said, 'No, not all. But you are hippy. You are clean, but a hippy.'"

He should have been clean, for his former existence had been as Marketing Director for Avon Cosmetics in Buenos Aires. With his artist wife Susanna, Alejandro had escaped from the city to work for Ford in Bariloche. Then he realized that he was simply going through the same routine in a different place, so he brought Susanna and his children to El Bolsón, and found himself not only without prospects but without status in the eyes of the established community.

"Yes, for those people we are hippies," said Adriana. "When we came they had their farms, their work — not a lot of money, but sufficient. We not. We came with nothing."

In at least one sense that was anything but true. Perhaps they had not had much spare cash left over after buying the house and land, which they would have had to do outright, for mortgages hardly exist in Argentina's unstable economy; but they had brought with them tremendous inner resources of experience and culture — Marcelo's music, Susanna's training at the National School of Art.

"Anyway, you have money now?" I said.

"No, he perhaps, but we not," said Adriana, pointing to Alejandro, and everybody laughed.

It was obvious from everything around him that Alejandro de Canales was a born entrepreneur who had opted for the simple life, but who could hardly hold his commercial abilities in check. His house was further up the hillside, surrounded by its several acres of land. Cultivation came hard to a man whose previous experience was of sitting behind a desk: he knew nothing about it, and he had no tools. His neighbour lent him a horse and plough. He planted raspberries, and by the time I met him there were 10,000 jars of them waiting to go to Buenos Aires, a wheel to turn handmade pots to put them in for the tourist market, a fretwork shop to cut out brightly painted souvenirs and, everywhere, wild flowers drying among silver discs of honesty, sheaves of dried grasses and great purple teasels — even the living room ceiling was hidden by them, like an upside-down meadow.

174

"I used to have seven people in the workshops, but it was too many," said Alejandro, a little apologetically. He had made a policy decision to cut back the number to three to prevent his means of subsistence turning into big business, but he still needed ten hired hands at harvest time. Susanna, too, was successful, with very individual graphics and paintings not only everywhere on the walls but periodically disappearing to her exhibitions in Buenos Aires. Where she was raven-haired, with Indian features and the figure of an earth mother, he was fair and trim. Even after years in gumboots, he had not quite lost the well-kept look of the top executive.

"I don't want money. I want peace," he said. "Silence, rivers, mountains. Last year I went to Buenos Aires and saw my old associates. When they stop rushing, they don't know what to do with themselves. Here I have work till the end of my life."

We stood looking down at El Bolsón below in the valley, a neat white town wreathed in mist. A loud canary sang from inside the house, and a hose trickled musically into the round irrigation pond that doubled as a pool for the children. Everything was productive and organized: they had lavender bushes, quinces, a cow in a small copse of yellowing birches. There was rich, dark loam between the neat rows of raspberry canes, immaculate seedbeds and a Chilean boy on his knees, weeding.

It seemed a picture of horticultural bliss — but it was there that they had buried their books during the military regime, in case they should be thought subversive, and eventually dug them up again to discover that the rats had got into the box and eaten them. Despite continual harassment, only one local man had been taken by the military, but that one happened to have been the man next door.

"The fear was terrible," said Alejandro.

"Do you think it could happen again?" I asked.

"Yes, there is no unity here. Too much immigration has stopped us from being a real community. Chile has had less, and it is more united. We have never suffered sufficiently to bind us together.

"Now with the economy it's the same. We have to go to the bottom to come up. These people need to be hungry to work. But I don't understand how my father was talking about a crisis in 1968 — and we still have it. How can we continue so long in a crisis?

"When I was in cosmetics, it used to be good for business. You sell more in difficult times. We have a saying: 'For bad weather, a good face' — 'Al mal tempo, buena cora'."

Rowan Brian and Mari lived kilometres up a rough road below the mountains in a *chacra*, a small farm, of eleven hectares. He was a potter — a lean man, quick and nervous as a bird, bending in enforced stillness over his wheel in the shadow and celadon of his workshop.

"Stone the crows!" he said in an English upper-middle-class accent, when he heard where I came from. His slang had got stuck in the Seventies, which was when he had left the King's Road and his career in films for a shack in the Andes. Despite his time at Hornsey College of Art, he was no potter then: and he and his wife, Mari, a black North Londoner known to the locals as La Negra, had a hard time when she came out to join him, as she told me.

"I said, 'This is the house?' He said, 'Yes, this is the house.' I was speechless, I couldn't believe it. He said,

'We've painted, we cleaned the place.' There were no words really. There was this smell of rancid sheep everywhere."

"So there was then marital discord?" I suggested delicately.

"Oh, for a number of years. 'Silence', it was called. But the reaction of the child — Abby was full of joy — made me think 'Well, if she's all right it can't be that bad.'" (Abby had her father's lightness and her mother's curls and smiles. She was going to be eighteen next month, already had her own house down the hill and was suckling a baby, with great contentment on both sides of the activity.)

Rowan said, "You really need to be able to drop back two hundred years. Cook on a camp fire in the porch. No electricity, so kerosene lamps and candles. Make your own furniture. The only running water was someone moving fast with the bucket. It was bloody awful: and we were absolutely broke. We all worked as peons for the equivalent of a kilo of lentils a day. Bolsón was tiny then — there was no other option."

"We worked on the hop fields to buy a bag of flour," said Mari. "I was pregnant, and it was really quite hard going. But the good thing is that when the local people see you working like that, with them, they have a lot of respect for you, like you have for them. They know you don't just sit on your arse and the money comes in. That's the best way to open their doors to you.

"One day I said to Rowan, 'I just can't stand being poor — I'm going out to work.' So I started massaging. I usually work at a hotel in town, but once in a while someone will be really crippled with a bad back and come up here."

It was about this time Rowan began potting as a relief from the unprofitable business of growing vegetables for the market. He had some potters' books — by Bernard Leach and Michael Cardew — so he built a wheel and dug clay from the river. They made a day of it, and the family came down to swim and picnic. Then he began to teach himself.

"Cardew talked about flower pots being a basic form, which suited me, because I had no kiln. So I started making flower pots, and by spring I had some to take to market. They were terrible. Heavy, like wet bags of sugar," said the potter, modestly.

"They didn't have flower pots in Argentina?" I asked.

"Oh yes, but none as ugly as those."

Mari defended them. "They weren't ugly! I met the old settlers in town, and they said, 'How beautiful is the pottery that your husband is making.'"

"Beginners' beginner's pots," said Rowan. "They bought them out of kindness. I was really very indebted: it was terribly encouraging."

I walked through the *chacra* with them. There were green tracks, woods and fields, one of which they had recently cleared themselves, pulling out the tree-boles with a tractor, filling in the pits and grassing — but leaving a small clump of woodland in the middle, like a round island. Mari told me that there were quantities of mushrooms to be gathered from the woods in season — including ceps, but no chanterelles.

They had a two-storey wooden farmhouse, but the farmyard's only animals were now cat, dogs and hutches of rabbits; hens scratched, and a glossy cockerel strutted through his domain, very proud of his golden-brown feathers. The muck heap had been replaced by piles of grey clay getting ready to soak in the troughs below the concrete water tank, which had been hoisted up to its commanding position on its log tower in a fishing net borrowed from a neighbour.

In an open workshop in one corner of the yard, a carpenter was meticulously crafting a writing-desk. He was a friend, Alfredo — a young man with a good deal of curly black hair and a beard encircling the very edge of his face, so that he looked like an image from a Byzantine ikon, rather sawdusty. They had now had electricity for four years, and his cabinet-making was assisted by industrial machines — a grey sawbench, a heavy-duty power drill in a tall stand.

For all his machines, he lived in a hut in the woods, with a torn blanket to cover the doorway and nothing in the windows, which were simply holes where the timbers had decided to come to an end. The hut had one tall room with no cupboard, scarcely a shelf, and a rough plank bed. The walls were decorated with the carpenter's clothes hanging at random on nails, an old tennis racquet in a press and a picture of Shylock. The ceiling was smoke-blackened; the floor of dust that rose in clouds with every step; and in the middle, a ring of stones encircled a pyramid of ash. Over the stone hearth hung a chain with a hook for a pot, but there was no pot to put on it. Perhaps it was the bucket of soaking laundry outside by the irrigation ditch, which rippled and gurgled to itself beneath an old green pullover hung out to dry on the branches of a tree.

It was hardly even a shelter. But before it there were pheasant-eye narcissi for the spring, roses for the summer, dandelions and an infant crab apple. The sound of the wind filled the trees round the little house, and in a nearby clearing was a single concession to the delights of civilization — someone had strung up a badminton net.

I thought of the winter winds, and Rowan must have seen my expression. "That's a traditional *fogón* where the peons sleep," he said. "Also used for keeping tack, smoking meat and gathering round to drink maté, tell stories and play cards."

My expression did not change.

"Alfredo enjoys living that way. He asked us to build him a *fogón* to live in, so we built it like that."

"You're all eccentrics," I said.

Rowan answered, "Well, what better way to face a mad world?"

El Bolsón is Argentine individuality in a fortunate mood. The town itself is neat and white — and if there happens to be rather a lot of early Bob Dylan on the café loudspeakers, well, so it can be anywhere. But there is a certain fantasy about the houses as you leave town. There are some which are built as tall triangles; I saw another dwelling of white boarding and glass made in hexagonal section like a threepenny piece standing on end; and in the countryside around, the ramshackle variety of the cabins is often matched by personality in the planting of trees, for you find cedars, eucalyptus or even a date-palm in some gardens.

Just south of the town I passed the provincial border and left Río Negro for Chubut, also named after its river. The sky was blue and it was hot enough for wasps as I rode through the valley; with pine forest and peak to one side, and to the other the effortless curve of golden meadows swooping up the slopes of the far mountain. Halfway up there remained a streak of morning cloud, lower than the idle turns of two tremendous condors, tiny in the distance.

In the windows of houses that advertised home-made jams for sale, faces turned to see me go by. A couple of dogs lazed in the sun under a wall. Tethered at the door, a patient horse wearing the gaucho saddle of a thick pad of sheepskins endured the affection of a couple of schoolchildren in white overalls, who could hardly reach up to pat its nose. Nearby, a family was harvesting potatoes, which were spread out like lines of golden stones over the field. Hops were already gathered, leaving only the wires and poles.

Everything about the land expressed bounteousness: the blackberries were not yet ready, but the bushes hung heavy with dull red fruit; the roadside was crowded with the seed-heads of abundant flowers, spring perpetuating itself; trees took spontaneous root by the roadside among the other plants bursting up through the stones; rosehips glowed everywhere. The sun in the yellowing poplars gave them almost the presence of the human form — indeed, a superhuman form. It struck me that if Moses ever did see a burning bush, perhaps it was an autumn poplar with the sun in its leaves.

The valley narrowed, and I travelled in the company of a river, with rough cabins and winter woodpiles in among the willows, until I came to the boundary of the Epuyén district: here there was a mountain brook and a notice to say that it was Caring for the Future, and had made itself a *zona no nuclear*. I was on my way to see one of the people mainly responsible for that, and for the hour's programme on ecology every week on the local radio station — and also for the fact that there is a Green party with representation on the local council.

It is not difficult to find the house of Lucas and Jillian

Chiappe, but it requires perseverance. Fording the river on the edge of a weir, you turn right under arching sallow trees. There is water over the trail, which then leads along a spit of pebbles and willows that soon has river either side, flowing fast, clear and cold. A stream flows across the path, then another, and then quite a lot of the river itself, which comes up to your knees. The first sign of civilization is timber thrown down over wet hollows, from which comes a smell of wild mint. Facing you is the main stream of the river — which is deep at this point, and grey as glass — and a bridge. Cross the bridge with a stout heart: it may be only a light suspension of elderly boughs held together with wire (it may sway, shiver and crack a little), but everything for the house, from sugar to cement, has to cross it — so even if you are on the heavy side you will probably be all right.

Over the bridge, my footsteps no longer scrabbled among stones, but sounded with a hollow thump. I was on a precarious brown path along a hillside of tall trees, and the musky smell of deep leaf-mould replaced the freshness of the mint. I came to a glade that was a patchwork of grass and round beds of seeds, flowers and vegetables. There was wild rhubarb like a primaeval forest, the crinkly edges of its leaves silvered in the sun. (It is very tart and called "elephant's ear".) And at the end of the path, a higgledy-piggledy house, with a tower that was not quite straight anywhere and a stove-pipe curling out from under the eaves.

"It's not a house, it's a wooden castle," I said to Lucas Chiappe. "I particularly like the stove-pipe — it's so much more interesting than a straight stove-pipe."

The chimney descended to a square wood-burning range

on four curly legs, with a flickering stomach. In fact, natural wood was the keynote of the house, whose interior had a dark, lustrous feeling, like being inside a well-seasoned trunk of walnut. Lucas sat in an armchair which was half-way between an extraordinary log and a living organism, half carved from the block, half grown.

He was dark, with bright eyes in a bearded face that could have belonged below a *conquistador* helmet, but for a peacefulness about it. Jillian was blonde, more serene, and had a fifteen-year-old daughter, Surya; Nahuel, a son of ten years; and a little girl, not yet three — Rocío, whose name means "dew". The other member of the family was Trucho, their oldest dog, who would slowly follow their walks among the trees, as well as his stiff joints allowed. Jillian's sister, Kathy, lived in the dell next door and provided what there was in the way of family transport — an old car that had to be parked at a neighbour's, because it had a big hole in the floor and if you drove it through the streams to the bridge, the river came in.

Lucas and Jillian had married young — he was Argentine, she was from Devon — and they had lived not only in England and Buenos Aires, but in Europe and the United States. With so much travelling, neither seemed to have had much of a career, but they were very competent and intelligent people. Like all the others I had met, their special Eden was the product of considerable organization and hard work — in their case, over thirteen years — and was enriched by a culture they had brought with them from outside, as shelves of dog-eared paperbacks testified.

"We were in the Seventies with the hippy thing on our heads and trying to change the world," said Lucas.

"Travelling, we kept on having our minds opened to different people and different things — and finding that everything was done wrong. This place had a special feeling about it — something more peaceful, more in touch with whatever the planet is. It was the way to becoming the actor and not the spectactor of the thing. So now I won't change the world — I just want to improve my place and my family, that's all."

The first change was before they even bought their twenty-hectare *chacra*. "The guy that sold us the place — to celebrate the sale — he prepared an asado, of course. Everybody was eating but us, and he kept on saying, 'Have some, have some!' When he heard we were vegetarian, he couldn't believe it. So he said, 'Well, have some of this chicken — there's very little meat on it.' It was so thin you see. The place was falling to pieces."

They cut out dead wood, planted vegetable gardens to provide themselves with everything but exotics like bananas and melons. They had two wheatfields — and once again there was a mill in Epuyén, second-hand machinery from up-country to replace the mill closed by a monopoly years before. That and a reaper had been financed by an Italian government aid project to the Third World. That year everyone was sowing wheat.

Electricity and a petrol chain saw made life easier. There was good water from the river. Lucas was taking excellent photographs, ready for publishing in his own books of Patagonian life. Then, one day in the last years of the military government, a group of surveyors came, talking about building a dam across the valley, so that he would lose a few metres of land. Inquiries soon revealed that the provincial government and big construction companies were involved: the dam was a major hydroelectric project, and the Chiappes' house and the farms of everyone else in the area would end up below forty metres of water.

"Even in Paradise problems never end," said Lucas. "But we had a bit of luck because Alfonsin came to power and there were one or two years of real democracy in the beginning. We began an ecological group with a lot of the people who live around here — maybe they didn't have the ecological reason in their head, but if the water came, they couldn't live — and after three years the government said, 'This dam is not so easy,' and put the project on one side.

"It was the beginning of an exercise in democracy for all of us. There was like a rising of pressure groups, a feeling that people could do something. We had elections in '87, formed a party, and won the election by a single vote — so now we are on the council.

"With the experience we had with the *militars*, not many people want to fight. We are very few, and very well known — and that's not so good here in South America, if you know what I mean. But even so, there is a new freedom of speech, an attempt to achieve things. We are only 300,000 people in all Patagonia, so if you do something, a lot of them will care about it."

He had organized cars from all the province in a "motor-protest" against the proposal to build a nuclear waste plant a few hundred kilometres away at Gastre. It seemed bizarre to attempt a traffic jam in a desert, but it was successful.

It occurred to me that, in a new land, the first seed that falls takes root. What if more of the Argentines had been people in search of a new society, instead of adventurers seeking personal profit, or economic refugees bringing the taint of the Old World with them?

"There are people here with the ideals to make something of value," said Lucas. "It happened because a lot of new people came here, all with the same kind of respect for food, the water and the earth. What I believe in is Nature. I think it's the only strong thing that really makes me feel as if I'm in contact with something bigger. You know, when you are alone in the woods you sit down by a tree — or perhaps you embrace it — and you feel the energy. If you have walked through woods, you must know. We do it quite often."

I said, "When you travel through this country on a bicycle, you smell wood and leaves all the time."

"You must come and live here," Lucas told me.

"I don't know what my friends would say if I moved to Patagonia," I answered.

I know that when I go there again, El Bolsón and Epuyén will not be the same. Even if developers have not built the dam they will have finished the paved roads to Bariloche and Esquel, taking away on either side the barriers of ruts and stones that have done much to keep the impatient world away. I only hope that the Chiappes and the other so-called "hippies" will still be there, because Argentina needs them.

(Afterwards, I did try embracing a tree. I don't recommend it. Big or bushy, the process is uncomfortable. For one thing, it's knobbly; for another, you get a tree-shaped streak of dirt down your front; you get ants up your shorts; and people look at you.)

Lucas had described the valleys to me as small holes in the arid *meseta*, but I had not realized how dramatically the land would change when I left Epuyén. A long winding hill was enough to turn the country from green to brown, the trees to grass. At the top, the road branched — to Esquel via the lakes and Cholila (where Butch Cassidy had his ranch), or to Esquel via practically nothing. Even though the road looked shorter, it was probably foolish to choose the nothing.

As I turned the corner and glanced back I could not believe that I had held acquaintanceship with so many impossible-looking mountains for so long. They are frozen power. First, the power of the geological forces is frozen in the stone; then the power of the elements weathers them. Last, the power of vegetation makes itself felt upon the slopes and makes the power of wind and cold visible, where trees or scrub cling to one slope and leave another bare. I was sad to leave their snows behind me.

Ahead the upland was as flat as a table. It was a road on which height seemed to disappear. If you looked directly up into the blue above you could see the dome. Otherwise, even the sky seemed squashed into the earth — as were the mountains ahead on the horizon. There was little against which I could measure my immediate progress: this was a place in which there was no foreground other than a telegraph pole, a wire fence, or a bird that happened to fly close.

I disturbed three vultures taking a competitive breakfast on a rabbit. They flapped up from their prey in agitation, coming back down to it again in greed, making a noise half-way between the gobbling of a turkey and somebody winding up a clockwork train.

Afterwards, there was real silence, but for the gentle creaking of the bicycle and the hollow rumbling of the tyres over the tarmac.

The day was cold and overcast as I covered straight upon straight, each one kilometres long. More and more, the mountains ahead assumed the appearance of fells on a grand scale. One lorry passed me on the road, but otherwise there was not a cow, a sheep, a rider; nothing moved on that plain, except me on my bicycle. Among scattered rocks, grasses grew in coarse tufts golden with dryness. Many plants had given up the struggle against the wind and adopted the shape of least resistance, which was a hemisphere. It gave the entire plain a kind of mottled appearance, like the bed of a dry sea. There were flowers: white, red, magenta, yellow — they were barely millimetres across.

A solo vulture came to look at me and circled overhead. When he was behind me, it gave me a somewhat uncomfortable feeling in the back of the neck. I circled round to look at him. We circled for a while together. The vulture got bored first.

At last I came to the hills. The road bent round under them with plains of better grass, cattle and a solitary flamingo dabbling at an unexpected pool. I crossed dry gullies and even streams: wherever there was water and shelter, willows grew; wherever there was a distant farm, a few poplars stood. Another straight followed, so long that when I saw a black dot in the distance, and assumed it to be a dog, it was minutes before I realized it was a lorry broken down by the roadside. Had I got a spanner to fit this, one of the unfortunate passengers asked? He held up a nut appropriate to a load-bearing section of the Golden Gate Bridge. I regretted that I had not and cycled on. It had become busier; every half-hour or so, something would come by to keep me company.

The road switchbacked. The clouds had come down, and

hail blew into my face. Worse, the road surface disappeared. The unpaved road was almost indescribable: it was engaged in redistributing itself so as to make its surface as much like the surrounding wilderness as possible. To do this it had taken any pebbles which might have filled a pot-hole and arranged them in heaps into which the bicycle wheels ploughed, giving up the ghost of any power that might have been in them.

Rocks lay around on the surface waiting to catch my front wheel and throw me off. Drifts of fine gravel went plink-plonk and screech in the tyres and mudguards. Ruts jarred the frame, the pedals, the seat, and turned anything that might have moved smoothly into a sharp jerk. The handlebars jolted and jittered and thumped. The very worst of all, I decided, was the large stone under the back wheel as I climbed a hill — an extra, unkind obstacle interposing itself between you and your ambition. The chainwheel goes slow, you lurch up it, over the top and crunch on the other side. You have felt every contour of the wretched thing.

And the bike was playing up. It needed its tyres pumped, its bottom bracket tightening, and I had no big spanner. I thumped it with a stone. Then the gear cable came out and had to be put back.

I crossed a little railway line which was no more than narrow-gauge track, flush with the earth. I suppose there must have been sleepers below, but the wind and the sand had tucked them up out of sight long since. The railway did not stay long, but went off on an erratic path of its own. I considered waiting for a train and flagging one down but decided to go on, on the assumption that the next train might not be for some weeks.

It was difficult to believe that I had wilfully got myself

into this appalling situation. The only thing to be said for it was that the hail seemed to have put off the vultures.

By the banks of the Arroyo Lepa I stopped and had lunch. There was a willow tree and a depression in the ground which kept off some of the wind. Unfortunately it also acted as a container for a large amount of rubbish including broken bottles. I attempted to make a fire to keep myself company but the wind blew out the matches. So I settled myself on the cleanest bit of ground I could find and consumed freezing bread and salami.

It was rather cold to enjoy the experience fully, and when the occasional vehicle went past, the dust drifted over, so that it was like eating food on the beach. Also, while I was concentrating on not grinding the sand in my teeth, the only bus I'd seen that day came along going in the right direction, and I missed it.

It was a picnic that was not among the most enjoyable gastronomic experiences of my life. I rose chilled both inside and out, extremely stiff and covered with tomato pips; I picked up the remaining salami, rolling round among the rabbit turds. I donned a heavy pullover immediately, for a strong wind had sprung up, blowing the wrong way. I applied what comfort I could to myself: to wit, a mint from a packet I found in my pocket, and set off. Ahead of me was another plain, and on it one little white house with a few trees. It proved to be a station and was occupied by a small but extremely self-important station dog, which came out and chased me up the road for about half a kilometre or so.

I was now proceeding at something like walking pace, it was going to be dark in two hours, and I was about seventy kilometres from Esquel. Nevertheless, I made a policy decision to be in good heart. The skies had opened up: first there was blue, then sun. I unwrapped another mint.

Around me the desolation was quite frightful. Even the thistles had given up and died. Or, more likely, had committed suicide. A very slow two-wagon lorry passed me, carrying animals, leaving me in a thick cloud of dust with a strong smell of sheep. The gravel got thicker and I came off, fortunately not disastrously. I had no sooner got going again than I had to alight for another level crossing. Thereafter, every few yards the tolerable bit of road I was on would peter out in a heap of stones, and I would have to wheel the bike over to the other side to start again. The tiny railway track kept on recrossing the road as it meandered off by itself. I could see the line curving among the hills, a bright red railway bridge over a gully, incongruous in the midst of emptiness.

Every new stretch of the road I came to seemed to outdo the previous one in bareness. The road wound always uphill, and I had given up hoping it would ever go down. Every bend was an excuse for extra piles of gravel. In the circumstances it was quite remarkable how cheerful I felt. I think it was the tranquillity around me that cheered me up. There was no sense of menace in the sun on the far slopes, or in the desert nearby. There was nothing there to come after me, I thought, by reason of having troubles enough of its own.

The road set off obstinately up the side of a fell, celebrating with extra gravel. My feet sank in it; the tyres slithered and got stuck. Just as the light was going, I got a lift into Esquel. The sunset was exceedingly beautiful behind the mountain peaks, and one of the most beautiful things about it, I thought, was that I was seeing it through a car window. My body felt as if it were held together with string: in the hotel it took an hour and a half of hot baths and a good deal of beer to undo the knots.

Esquel was not a specially attractive town, being mostly fairly standard Argentine "subtopia", arranged in the totally standard Argentine grid pattern, but it had none of the fake alpine of Bariloche and was wonderfully set in the hollow of a mountain. It had a certain feeling of the frontier about it, though otherwise an honest, ordinary place — apart, that is, from a red-brick chapel and a few distinctive red-brick houses with corrugated-iron roofs. If they look Welsh, that is because they are — and it is not unlikely that whoever lives in that house will have Welsh blood in them, and that the dog making a conscientious inspection of the street outside will be a collie mongrel.

As the lady of one of the prettiest houses put it to me, "I am descended from Lewis Jones and also Michael D. Jones." (This is a claim of pride, for both were founding figures of the Welsh settlement in Patagonia, of which Esquel is an outpost.) "They used to change the names, there were so many Jones. We're Aplavon, which means 'son of Jones'. Otherwise I would be Jones Jones Jones, because my mother was Jones, and my father was Jones. In Trevelin there's a family called Jones Kansas, because they came from the States."

I met Walter Cortinez Underwood, a precise, well-organized young man who earned his living in the travel business, often guiding parties into the mountains and forests for weeks at a time. He had escaped the Jones problem, but in name only. His maternal grandmother was Nain Maggie, he told me, who was married to Arthur Jones.

"I have twenty-eight or twenty-nine first cousins on my mum's side," said Walter. "Then, for every one of my grandmother's brothers, there are from twenty to thirty grandchildren. There is no way I can know all of my second cousins. At school, we knew that those who were Jones, Hughes, Williams or Roberts were all related, because the Freeman girls got married to the Hughes, Roberts, Jones and Thomases.

"I see," I said, lying in my teeth.

"All the Freeman family have a particular pattern of freckles on their backs. So when we took our shirts off for gym, you could see the Freemans. There was no difference between those at my school, who were second cousins, and the rest of the children: you just stuck to your brothers and sisters, or to your first cousins. Second cousins? Forget it — it's the whole town."

"And will you be marrying a Jones, a Hughes, a Roberts or a Thomas and perpetuating this state of affairs?" I asked.

"My girlfriend is Syro-Lebanese. She's a belly dancer."

Walter took me to see the railway terminus, which was like one of those peaceful village stops that England closed, apart from a shrine on the platform and a coloured picture of the Pope over the wooden desk of the Scots-Argentine station-master. Chalked on a blackboard was the news that *La Tronchita* was expected at seven o'clock that evening.

Esquel is the bottom end of the line in the Americas. It takes thirty-six hours to get from Buenos Aires to the junction at Ingeniero Jacobacci, on the main line to Bariloche. Then you transfer to *La Tronchita*, the narrow-gauge — which, if the express is late, will wait up to two hours, for there will be no other train for at least two days. (There were originally six wood-fired steam engines, but four have been cannibalized for spares for the other two, which are now converted to oil.) From Jacobacci to Esquel it takes twelve hours — if you are lucky — to cover a distance which, as the crow flies, is less than 200 kilometres. The twists and turns of the extraordinary line add at least a third to this, but the main reason it takes so long is that *La Tronchita*, however picturesque, is often extremely slow — there are times when you can get out and pick flowers or search for interesting pebbles and jump on again without difficulty. There is a post-office wagon and a dining-car, though most travellers prefer to cook their meat and take their maté at the wood-burning stoves in the middle of each carriage. There may be up to ten carriages.

"Up to ten?" I said to Walter. It seemed imprecise.

"Yes, it depends on the load and the time of the year. The train can take more to Jacobacci than it can bring back, because when the hills are steep and the wind against it, it reduces the power of the engine. Sometimes the engine has to stop and wait until the wind has gone."

"This is the train on which I wish to travel," I said.

That afternoon, we got into Walter's old Peugeot, and he drove me, along the awful road of the day before, to the station at Embalse La Cancha, where the train was due at four o'clock. The road was little better in a car than on the bike. We travelled in a cloud of dust, inside and out. But there was oil nearby, Walter told me. An international oil company had asked for seventy per cent of the profits for developing the field, and the government had stuck at less than fifty per cent. So the oil was staying underground. It was the same with the Esquel gold mine, which was closed because the Argentines had objected to a US company coming in.

194

For a long time, there was nothing but the grey-brown road and the golden plain. Then, some distance down a minor road, the horizon was no longer quite regular. It had sprouted an outcrop of a few willows by a white cabin, a signal and a water tower. Our cloud of dust rattled up to the station and found it already occupied by a little aluminium caravan, and a road machine.

There was a roadman to go with it: he was bored because his machine had been out of action for three days. It was a yellow monster, looking like a tractor that had decided to become a low-loader, and beneath was slung the bright, scooped blade that cut the road surface level — incidentally creating the cyclist's purgatory that I had already enjoyed. Charitably I decided to absolve this particular roadman of responsibility.

We were in good time for the train, he said, and the place to wait was in his caravan. It was well equipped with a fridge, a cooker, two bunks and a radio receiver. He put a whistling kettle on the gas and prepared maté.

It was a hot afternoon; the sun streamed through the door. The roadman filled the maté gourd over half-full of the green tea that is the leaf of the Paraguayan holly, and topped it up with boiling water. He drank the first serving himself through the *bombilla*, the metal straw that goes with the gourd, as is maté etiquette — which then decrees that the gourd should be refilled and passed to each person in turn without acknowledgement until you have had enough, when you return it with a "thank you". It is bad manners to wipe the spout of the *bombilla*.

"It's not much of a stimulant, but if I haven't had it for a day I miss it," said Walter.

It seemed to me a thoroughly gracious and excellent

**195**

custom. It was dietary and — like smoking — it gave you something to do with your mouth and hands. It was communal in the same way as marijuana. Like afternoon tea, it was polite and elegant.

"It's after four," I said. "Train's late."

The roadman told me that he had a key to the station, and there was a telephone line to which you could listen to find out what was happening. There was nobody there from the railway, though a stationmaster would be arriving the next day for the winter season to keep a fire lit under the water tower in case it froze in temperatures that went down to twenty-five below. The station house was built of great baulks of quebracho timber from the north of Argentina laid in mortar. It contained a stove and an old black telephone, which, when lifted, was talking to itself in an agitated buzz.

Walter listened. "It's late," he said. "Broke down and had to go back to the engine sheds. It breaks down easily. It's late. But it's coming."

We returned to the caravan. On the rim of the plain there was a dust cloud. Closer to, it resolved itself into a gaucho on horseback and a couple of dogs. The roadman put the kettle back on.

The gaucho on the horse boasted a moustache like a film bandit and did not stay long, as he was coming to the end of a twelve-hour day checking stock and peeling eyes, which is what he called cutting away the surrounding wool to prevent infections. He was of the opinion that, while *La Tronchita* had been known to arrive at Esquel comparatively early — say only one or two hours behind schedule — there had been occasions when it had not got there till one in the morning.

He rode off into what would soon be sunset, for it was now well after five. He was a speck in the distance when there was a noise.

"Train's coming." I said.

We all got up. There was a pause.

"No, it's a truck," said the roadman. We all sat down again. *Peter and the Wolf* began on the radio. The roadman said that this was a good spot for animals, which came to drink at the water bubbling from the tower: guanacos, which are like llamas, and nandus, Patagonian ostriches; skunks — and armadillos in summertime; and one particular grey fox, a tiny animal, which is protected by law.

"With red foxes at six and seven dollars a tail, my brother paid for a pickup truck in one year," said Walter. "A dozen in one night. You play a tape of a vixen on heat, catch them in a spotlight and shoot. They stay still too long." It seemed particularly unfair.

A pre-evening wind came up and ruffled the dry leaves of the willows. The water tank spat and bubbled. *Peter and the Wolf* ended and somebody sang. We went to phone down the direct line again. We cranked the handle on the old black telephone and listened. Walter was optimistic, "They said part of the train had bent but they'd fix it. So it's coming."

We all began to walk round the desert for something to do and converse in shouts over a distance. It seemed that our taste for each other's conversation was beginning to wear thin. It was a quarter to six.

There was a rumbling — it was another pickup truck.

Another rumbling, I rushed for my bag. A car. Another noise, another car. The roadman said that I would see the steam when the train came, and it would blow its whistle.

**197**

It sounded like a delightful and romantic approach, the only problem being that it was not happening.

We moved closer again and talked some more about wars and governments and other foolish things.

At ten past six we went to listen again. I wondered whether the train, if it should come, would ever reach Esquel. Walter made some remark about trains being stuck for weeks in the snow, which I found especially disheartening. The roadman offered us coffee or a nip of brandy and went off to chop wood for his evening fire. The shadows got longer — the sun was approaching the horizon.

Walter had finished listening. "The train went back to Leleque and was fixed and will leave Leleque at about ten to seven — so should be here twenty past, according to what they are saying. Meanwhile, our friend is going to make an asado. For company, you know. That's what makes people in the south of Argentina so friendly — they're lonely."

It was another hour to wait, but Walter was tranquil. "You learn patience in the south of Argentina. Perhaps you have a breakdown — you don't get out and walk in the freezing cold. You stay in the car and wait for the next morning, and somebody to come by and help."

The roadman poured diesel over his pyramid of logs and set a match. The purple distance came nearer: mist began to form in the hollows.

It was just past seven, and the sky had gone mauve, violet, then pastel blue. The roadman came and quenched a long red-hot iron stake, curled at the top like a shepherd's crook, in the pool from the water tower. The point broke off necessitating some discussion and the re-hammering of another one. The fire was burning nicely. A whole side of lamb went on to the stake, meticulously placed by the burning logs.

The roadman said he had been a cook in the road camps for four years. It was a jollier life than being on your own for weeks doing fifty kilometres of road at a time, going back home and having rows because you weren't used to the children making a noise.

"This is country meat, killed in the right way," said the roadman, "not stunned, but the throat cut. A whole lamb takes an hour and a half to two hours, depending on the heat. You must open it up, slash the legs and place it neck down."

It got dark and the lamb got brown, dripping fat into the embers that spurted into flame as it hit. It was ten to eight. Walter went to listen again and returned to say, "By eight it will be here. Since it's broken it's on half power."

I said, "But if I get on it for a journey that normally takes over three hours, and it's on half power, then it will take me seven hours on the train to get to Esquel."

They said, "Well, not quite half power."

The meat smelled more and more appetizing. The conversation turned to the Peronists, of whom the roadman was a supporter because they were for the workers. A chill wind came up at our backs though the fire was warm in front. The lamb had been turned and the skin was blistering. We started up several times, but they were false alarms. The southern stars were bright, flecks of ash flew in the wind. The Tilley lamp flared.

It got to half past eight and my mouth was beginning to water. We conjectured on how many coaches there might be and whether there would be a restaurant car. The meat was now minutely adjusted every few minutes. The light shone redly through the bare spots in the ribs, and it was periodically anointed with *chimichurri* — a dressing made from such things as garlic, chilli powder, oregano, sweet peppers, lots of salt and water, which is more commonly an accompanying sauce.

It was five to nine when the roadman said he thought he heard the phone ring. Walter rushed off to listen. On the horizon something twinkled, but it was only a star. The meat came off the spit and the roadman sprinted into the caravan with it, shouting due to the heat on his fingers. Walter came back — did I want the good news or the bad news? The bad news was that the train had come off the rails: the good news was that another engine was coming from Esquel.

Anyway, it was time for dinner. The roadman had used his few remaining potatoes to make mash and provided napkins torn from a tea towel. The meat was the best lamb I have ever had in my life. We drank wine tasting of muscat, followed by a herb tea called *boldo*. Everything the roadman had, he shared. At the end, he took a plate of bones out into the desert for the grey fox he was feeding. There was no anxiety about missing the train, since the relief engine would have to pass us first. It was not there by ten o'clock.

"Perhaps the relief has been derailed," I said. The general opinion was that this was a ridiculous, if not insulting, suggestion. I began to suspect that a sense of national honour was beginning to colour their predictions.

"It seems to me," I said, "that from the time that the relief engine comes it has to be thirty minutes there, thirty minutes back, plus an hour for mending. At least."

There was a general refrain of, "Only twenty minutes — it must be only ten kilometres up the line."

"An engine on its own goes much faster," said Walter. "And the passengers have been on since six in the morning — they will be even more interesting than usual."

"But if it's derailed they'll never get it back on the track. And the relief engine should have gone past by now."

"It's very light — only fifteen tons," said Walter. "It just needs a couple of extra men. And perhaps the engine is coming from Leleque."

"But in that case it would be at the wrong end of the other train for getting the engine back on the rails. I think it's time for a decision. *A casa*, Perkins! (which is the Argentine equivalent of 'Home, James')."

They were aghast — but I could see the prospect of getting into Esquel at three in the morning and having tomorrow's cycling ruined. I insisted. At last, reluctantly, they conceded. We went to Walter's car. It had a flat tyre. Even by the time the roadman had fixed it, there was no sign of the locomotive. It was quarter to eleven. We rattled back to Esquel.

As I was going out of town the next morning, there was a hooting and puffing above me on the railway track clinging to the edge of the mountain. It was *La Tronchita* coming in at last — oily, beautiful, and almost sixteen hours late.

# CHAPTER
# SEVEN

# The Understanding of El Refugio

## *Tecka, Paso de Indios, Altares and Las Plumas*

Now I turned away from the foothills of the Andes, and began my ride across the Patagonian desert to the sea. From the map, I could see that between Esquel and the area around the next major town, Trelew — a distance of some 600 kilometres — the only paved road boasted hardly a dozen side turnings, three very small towns and one village.

It was a clear, sunny morning, and the wind whistled in the parched grass. A shallow lake to my left was entirely dried up from the droughts of the previous three years, and grass was already beginning to grow on the bottom. A few sheep had taken up residence there, instead of the fish, and were lying on the bottom with their fleece shining in the sun.

I could happily have joined them, for I was experiencing a severe attack of flattening by immensity, with grey-green mountains sweeping to peaks behind me; and there was a vast plain ahead over which the road crawled with scarcely a wriggle. The low hills in the far distance looked as if they came from another planet. There was almost no colour in the landscape — a little pale browny-yellow from some dried grass. Apart from that, the hues of green, grey and yellow were so close to each other that they might as well have all been grey. Over all this circled a condor with all the time in the world.

I have never seen so many birds of prey as I saw that morning: hawks great and slightly smaller would flap heavily up from poles and fences as I passed, making it obvious by their reluctance which of us was the intruder. For them to survive, there had to be a good deal of small life hidden away on the tussocky plain.

As I thought that, across the road came a *piché*, a Patagonian armadillo about the size of a hedgehog, almost mimicking my own progress, for it moved as if on wheels. Intent on its own business it went across the ditch and over the crest of a small rise, creating great interest among the birds.

The large thistles that grew by the road were dead and dry, mummified in every stage of development. In some, the flower buds were still closed, in others down still hung on the shrivelled heads. Twisted bushes had lost their leaves, and the stems were now occupied in contorting themselves into every conceivable posture they could imagine. They had ferocious thorns, big enough to sew with. From the verges, I smelt gusts of astringent artemisia.

Few cars passed, and no lorry, without giving me a wave. In this desert people were too important to ignore. At the far end of the plain, below a range of featureless cliffs, I greeted an even more solitary figure than myself — an old man with a pack on his back, trudging along the way I had come. A car came by, but he made no attempt to beg a lift; he just walked, with miles of emptiness to go.

It was afternoon. My road wound into foothills and down again into a river valley with reddening willows, and the hills above were so smooth they looked as if they had been poured from the sky. There were meadows and the infallible sign of prosperity — a notice saying "Private Property Keep Out". By the roadside was a dead eagle; that was astonishing enough, but I was to pass four more. There was no sign of what killed them, so I took it that they had been poisoned.

Until the plain broadened, the valley had just enough room for the road, a strip of meadow and the river. This was a clear shallow stream, but it ran almost black in the shadow of the trees. With most of the journey done, I sat myself down on a rather muddy knoll under a bank of leaning willows and had a simple lunch.

There was the sound of rippling. The sun came through the willow branches and dappled the river bed. Across the river, the grass did its best to grow a trifle greener along the bank, then stretched drily to the fells. I sat and ate in great tranquillity. The wine was good, and for the amount of traffic that passed, I might as well have been an ancient Roman shepherd as a twentieth-century traveller.

Sitting in the shade as I was, and looking out through the leaves on the sunlit landscape, it was like looking out on to an enchanted country — forever summer and forever golden. Every country gives classical literature its own landscape. In England the everyday story of classical folk is told in fields that are green: in Italy, the grass is browner. In Japan, presumably, Daphnis and Chloë move through a Japanese landscape. I thought that Horace and Virgil would be as well served by the Argentine countryside as by any Italian one.

I poured out the last few drops of wine on to the dry leaves, buckled up my saddlebag and went my way. The effect of this elegiac pastoral was somewhat impaired by the fact that, when I came to get up, I discovered that my muscles had stiffened and I was forced to stand up like a mechanical frog whose batteries were running down.

The road curled round the edge of the valley. I passed a herd of cattle on the move, making a noise just like the cowboy films, a combination of mooing and scrunching; an eagle came winging low over the hillside, and yet another, the light feathers on its wings flashing in the sun.

Across the plain I saw a small cluster of low, white buildings. There is a special magic about the end of a long ride, when the shadows get long and your pedals get slower. All the same, not very far off there is a conclusion: passing three brown schoolgirls out on the road to experiment with a shared illicit cigarette in the middle of nowhere, I arrived at Tecka.

Tecka was hardly more than a village of houses which did their best to be prim in the main street, and were slovenly elsewhere, with peeling paint and crumbling stucco, or no stucco at all. A place of scruffy yards and dust, a squatter in the desert, it managed to look temporary throughout, except for one or two municipal buildings, and a plaza with unsuccessful vegetation but grand and complicated patterns of paths. There was also the Tecka Hotel (closed), a bar (open briefly), and La Petit Residencia-cum-petrol station-cum-butcher.

The Residencia was run by a plump, curly-haired

landlady and boasted an impressive collection of fridges in a white-walled bar full of hard surfaces — terrazzo floor, shiny formica tables and chairs, pine ceiling. Behind this ran a galley kitchen with good stoves and the corridor to a five-bed dormitory and a guest room, which I secured for myself. In the corridor the central heating, a stove, sat and radiated to itself and the washing drying above it.

The prospects for dinner looked good. Three men were sitting at a white table-cloth consuming vast steaks, bread, wine and salad. But it did not seem to be available to such as me.

"*Bollos*," said the landlady in response to my asking what there was to eat.

"*Bollos*?" I was not not sure whether it was a food or a swear-word.

"*Bollos*."

"Well . . ."

"*Bollos*."

"*Muy bien*," I said overcome by her determination. *Bollos* turned out to be a large tray of soggy pizza.

"You don't understand *mucho*," said the landlady, for no particular reason. She was right. However, there was a bottle of *tinto reserva*.

The bar television was on. Argentina was coming close to the presidential elections: there was nothing to watch but the party commercials with middle-aged politicians — and only their upper halves at that, as they ranted and gesticulated as passionately as you can from behind a desk. Outside, a group of children hung round in the cold to watch the magic flicker through the bar windows. A commercial for the radical Angeloz promised them that he would be extremely serious on their behalf. Into the bar came an

Indian-looking family — several large-eyed children, a mother with a young baby in a long shawl and gaucho father. They bought something very small and stayed a long time. A Perónist commercial came on, and Menem promised them a new Argentina. I came to the end of the bottle of *tinta*.

"Time for beddy-byes, and mind the bugs don't bite, eh?" I said to the landlady in English, in tones of extreme gravity. She cast an eye on the bottle, wished me goodnight in Spanish, and ground the coffee-machine so furiously that the lights flickered.

An orange dawn came up over the hills, surly at first then deciding to be splendid. Three white chickens came out to inspect the petrol pumps and inspired me with the concept of two eggs for breakfast. The landlady brought one, and the day began.

After half an hour's climb I found myself in the company of two enormous black and white buzzards and something small and invisible crying alarm in the grass. I was on a bare upland with even barer mountains ahead. The hills close to had outcrops of grey rock and, every so often, a tiny, scrubby patch of grass. The ponds were dried up and white: the whole place was parched.

The road crossed the Sierra de Tecka in a series of switchbacks, with one little house lonely in the middle of all the emptiness. As I came down to the valley, a pair of guanacos were making a hee-hawing noise like donkeys — I was obviously disturbing them. They made off and immediately became invisible among the scrub, so well were they camouflaged.

The River Quichaura, now dry but for a few pools, was

apparently able to support a substantial ranch, with shining tin roofs. I had heard that parts of the Patagonian desert would raise only one sheep for every eleven acres: was this that kind of desert? It seemed not, for over the next sierra, the landscape was even barer. As I made the long descent from its eastern edge I saw my road curling around the edge of the hills to cross a vast plain, the Pampa de Agnia.

The straight came, and was immensely long, but I spun on before the wind springing up behind me. Overhead, the wind was action-painting the sky in many different qualities and textures of grey: some of the clouds were striped by it, some billowed, others seemed to be pressed flat against the sky as if they had been smeared there. The colouring was echoed on the plain by artemisias of various shades of pale greens and greys, almost blues.

There were still the hemispherical bushes that had been with me ever since the road to Esquel — looking from a distance like clumps of grey moss, but full of thorns. *Neneos* were always thought to be good for nothing, though very wind resistant, with a very long taproot and small roots all round: but the plant has its own micro-climate. Within the bush is a humidity in which other seeds can grow. If you are planting a tree in the desert, therefore, plant it in the centre of a *neneo*, which will protect it until the tree grows and it dies. But I could see little chance of reforestation on the Pampa de Agnia: no tree could have grown exposed to that cold wind.

I pedalled a long time with nothing but the dead daisy heads along the roadside for company, till there were buildings ahead — a neat white house and a poorer one, with chickens scratching in the dust and bright washing blowing — and the Argentine Automobile Club filling station, which is the outpost of civilization on the Pampa de Agnia.

It was the loneliest of places: there was only the plain to look out upon, and what had once been a shallow lake, its bed now white with salts, but the filling station made a brave though tiny show with its white walls, yellow roof and twirling windmill with tin sails. The owner had made an optimistic attempt to plant a small garden, over which blew a sepulchral clanking as the wind rattled the rope against the metal flagpole.

I went in for coffee, served by a pale, thin-faced woman with a thin body under a pink nylon housecoat — she was quite young. She came from here, she said: she had lived all her life here. (If anything, that increased the desolation, the idea of a baby born on the Pampa de Agnia.) Sometimes she would go to Trelew to shop. "It's a long way," she said. (So it was, almost the end of my journey, 400 kilometres.) She never saw many people. (I had not seen a car all morning.)

"Isn't it cold?" she said. "Isn't it cold?" she said again.

"Just like England," I replied, "except for the wind." (May the gods of geography forgive me, but the temperature here was the same: the chill that obsessed her was the chill of emptiness.) I bought a bar of chocolate. "Ah," she said, "for the cold."

As I left, the melancholy clanking from the flagpole pursued me, growing fainter and fainter, but unceasing. Out on the flats I could see the wind raising clouds of salt dust.

And the thin woman was right: if I stood still, I could feel the wind biting into me. Then the road veered, and it came at me from the side. I could no longer think clearly, it blustered at me so; it was like constantly being hit around the head with a light towel.

In a dip I passed the sort of architecture necessary to cope with it — a little grey farm with the house and stables built into the inside of the courtyard wall as protection. Inside, a few simple trees had grown: outside, the desert came up to the threshold.

The road turned back, and the wind came behind me again. I felt it pick me up and hurl me forward. On the flat, it would not only take me along without pedalling but accelerate me from a standstill to over twenty kilometres an hour. The slope into the next valley was like going down a mountainside: I gripped the handlebars, not daring to brake, raced past the farm at the bottom and bowled up the next hill in top gear.

It was flat again, and the wind carried me forward at breakneck speed through a landscape of red hills and eroded rocks. There was no question of pedalling — I could not pedal fast enough — and as my speed increased I had to brake as best I could when I came to the corners. The speed was frightening; what I most feared was a rough bit of road which would throw me off, or a gust of wind that would pick me up bodily off the bike. It grew ever stronger: when it came from the side, I had to cant the bike into it as if I was going round a steep curve; and it would blow me incessantly towards the other side of the road, so that I moved at an angle, like a crab. When I stopped, I had to brace myself for fear of being blown over.

Straightening out ahead of me was a tremendous plain, with the road disappearing into the distance under the foot of a great mountain. There were a few low bushes and red hills to my left with the tops dead flat and the edge towards the wind eaten away by it. Everything that could be blown away had been blown away, including large quantities of plants. What little grass there was, hardly dared poke itself above the soil, and clumps could not grow upright. The land was sand and stones, and I could see dust devils whirling.

I passed a small farm with trees bent, and its windmill going so fast that the water was splashing out of the pipe at the top and streaming down the tower. Ahead of me was a lonely muddle of buildings on the plain. I rode with a perpetual screech from the front wheel as the wind shoved the mud flap hard against it. A retinue of pieces of grass — even tussocks and twigs — were blown along with me; fantasmic rivulets of dust writhed over the surface of the road like some kind of demon about to materialize; and so I came to Paso de Indios.

Its few roads were stony, and though the main street was making some efforts to keep up appearances and there was a large white radio dish for communications, there was no disguising the fact that the standard of hotels was going down. The first one I tried either genuinely had no rooms or did not fancy my custom. The second offered three-bed dormitories with candles by the bedside for when they turned the power off at night. Though the sheets were laundered, and the concrete floor as clean as concrete with holes in it can reasonably be, the gents had duckboards, and needed them. There was a cavernous cold tunnel of a bathroom in which a forlorn shower-head had been given such an inferiority complex by the seven-foot bath below that all it could manage was a neurotic trickle.

I ate a tolerable meal at the grill attached to the service station on the main road — cold meats and Russian salad, an escalope, chips and tomato salad, and white wine. The

211

place was run by a smiling young couple who had come to Paso de Indios from Bahia Blanca, on the coast.

"Did you do it deliberately?" I asked the expansive, Italianate proprietor.

"Better than tapping out figures all day in an office," was the reply. "Here I can be with the family." His wife, dark and pretty, brought their eleven-month-old baby to show me.

"But the wind!" I said, referring to the environment, rather than the baby.

"Oh yes, it blows," said the large proprietor. "But sometimes it drops, all of a sudden, and then it's perfectly calm." I did not think that much of a recommendation, but he seemed to be a happy man.

Back at the hotel, there was an echoey, stone-floored bar in which the laconic landlord presided over a gigantic fridge and a shining coffee machine. Some long-past rain had come through in one corner — there were tell-tale brown streaks down the eau-de-nil walls — but there were pool and card tables and a convivial atmosphere among the all-male clientele in berets and *bombachas*. A black and white television added its din to the crack and thump of the pool balls, loud conversation and the delighted screams of the small boy of the house playing pummelling with the grown-ups. Considering the wind and the desolation, it seemed that everybody was remarkably content in Paso de Indios.

After Paso de Indios, the road began to descend towards the valley of the River Chubut, where strange rock formations rose directly from the plain, and the road ran below gigantic cliffs eaten into layers and buttresses by the weather. Suddenly, the valley was quiet and the wind was still — though I could see it, far off, raising dust devils and tossing the autumn willows of the river I had yet to meet.

The whole mountain was rose coloured. Its cliffs were made of wafer upon wafer of strata, so regular that they seemed man-made, and stretching for kilometres at a time. It was this confusion of an artificial with a natural scale that made them appear even grander than they were. Chasms split them from top to bottom, making columns. Fantastic erosions constantly suggested comparisons: such as temples, stalactites, crouching sphinxes, the paws of enormous animals. In that crumbling temple to the power of the weather, I was no more than a dot far, far below the sky.

The valley headed for a gorge, and the river now came close to the road — clear, expansive, winding. As I climbed out of the valley, I looked back; and on the far banks saw a solitary gaucho with horse and dog. Pausing to adjust his saddle of fleeces, the tiny figure cantered away across the plain, raising a small dust cloud behind him.

I was nearing Los Altares, which is so called from a series of buttresses that look like altars: and what I found by the roadside enhanced the solemnity of the place. Two shrines, one the standard wooden kennel housing the Indian saint, San Ceferino; the other, to the patron of parched travellers, Difunta Correa, was no more than a few rough red rocks and broken bottles that had once contained an offering of water. On the sandy verge, with a few small plants growing between its ribs, was the skeleton of a horse, the neck stretched out as if with its last neigh. Further along, opposite a couple of tiny houses on the riverside, was a rusty iron railing enclosing a small family of graves. Even a line of stunted poplars managed to be apocalyptic, for the noise in them was not of wind rustling but of roaring.

The red rocks above me had sunk into sandhills. Now they were replaced by precipices of pale green. At the same time, the cliffs over the river grew to tower above anything I had yet seen. At first, they were rose in colour: then they began turning to a deep purple red. It was not the light but the rock itself; for down by the river the willows were pale golden.

After Los Altares — which is a small village with a shop, a garage and a civilized hotel — the gorge was narrow, and the road wound in and out of the shadow of the mountains, alongside the river rippling over stones. I stopped to talk with a farmer who was leaning on a stockade as I passed and watching his horses running free in the wind and sunshine, haloed in dust. He had been working there since the age of eight, he said. The wind and the dust drove him crazy sometimes, and he dreaded the days when he had to go out in it with the sheep. Otherwise, he said, he liked it.

The river banks had scanty meadows, but as the road struck out across the next plain, they were lost in sand and thornbush. There was not a car on the road, and the plain was only a little less deserted, its only animal life consisting of a few Patagonian sheep — nimble creatures with longish legs, very shy, even of my bicycle. I passed one that had not been shy enough: a roadside casualty whose body had completely disappeared. Something had carried off meat and bones together; all that was left was the skull and the fleece, so that it looked like a dirty old sweater left on the road with someone's head still in it.

It was followed by another roadside grave, decorated with a thornbush and barbed wire put around it. There was an old cross made of two pieces of wood tied together, but the name board had fallen down and the wind and rain or wind and sand had erased whatever had been written on it. There was an iron hoop on the grave as well, which looked as if it had been placed there significantly, but no hint of what it could have meant.

It induced a very macabre frame of mind, which was enhanced at every land boundary, where old tyres, strips of black rubber, rags — flexible junk of all kinds — had been tied up to flap in the wind and frighten the sheep from going along the road and round the fence. Cloths fluttered madly like prayer flags; the whole effect was like some deviant and sinister juju; and under its influence, I found myself mistaking the bleached branches lying along the shores of the river for old bones.

The next valley was called Las Ruinas and not only contained ruins, but enormous spikes of rock, rough as if they had been split with an axe — so that travelling through it was something similar to riding through a mouthful of teeth. Like giant's breath, the wind hissed round them.

Across a stretch of desert scarred by dry gullies, I found myself in the Valley of the Martyrs. The sign telling me so had bullet holes in it, where people had been using it for target practice. Here were two roadside graves, each within its own railing. The larger had polished grey stone with gold lettering in Welsh, and — I discovered later — belonged to a wool merchant who had had a heart attack in the middle of the thirty-day journey from Trelew to Esquel in the last days of the wagons. The smaller grave was for his dog. It had a cross and a white plastic rose, which was more than you could say for the master. (Indeed, the dog had two crosses, for an older wooden one also remained.) I never discovered how the dog happened to meet its end at the same time.

The sand was often many-coloured, like the rocks — brown, ochre, green. Beyond the scrub there was a small herd of guanacos — one, two, three, four, five — going up a sandy ravine among the cliffs. They were extremely delicate and graceful in their movements, but also very assured in their intention to escape from me and my bicycle — unless it was me and my singing, for I had now seen so much of grandiose rocks, sand and low-growing bushes that I had decided to make my own entertainment.

"The Golden Vanity" startled a flock of sheep who ran away at tremendous speed, raising a cloud of dust behind them. Trying to remember which bit went in which version of "Admiral Benbow" took me over the plain; "Gently Johnny My Jingo" along under the next cliffs; and "The Banks of the Sweet Primroses" round a rock of the general appearance of the Coliseum, but about twenty-five times as large — and across the river into Las Plumas.

It was a small place at the foot of formidable hills: on one side of the road the town, on the other a few slum shacks that would not have been out of place in the poorest parts of Africa. Even the river was not what it had been — its 100-kilometre journey from Los Altares had turned it muddy. A lot of the place was mud-coloured and stony, apart from a pretty pink church with children playing nearby, their cries lost in the desert wind that blew the washing-lines so strongly that it got into the jeans and put fat legs in them, fat arms into check shirts. Vultures wheeled darkly over the riverside poplars.

Quite where the hotel might be it was extremely difficult to see. Few places looked as though they would accommodate more than a moderately sized Alsatian — in not too great a degree of comfort. Eventually I found it under the vultures, a rickety television aerial and a double-pronged stove-pipe protruding from the bar roof which was held down with large stones.

The bar of the Hotel Las Plumas was a bare, tawdry room, with a sagging ceiling, bare bulbs hanging on twisted wires and the bar shelves rather empty, but for festoons of sweets in little cellophane wrappers, which made them look rather like icicles. The walls were decorated with a few old photographs of gauchos, and a worn guitar. The bar flap was propped up with a billiard cue — there was, in any case, no table to use it on. The only things in the place of relative charm were a very fine wooden refrigerator with the capacity of several wardrobes and a kitten, which ran backwards and forwards between the bar and the butcher's, which was also part of the establishment.

The landlord, who was also the butcher, gave me a beer and a surly look. There were three or four other men in the bar, all wearing hangdog expressions and staring into space. Conversation was joyless and spasmodic: all the message was in the eyes that stared into the wine, or stared nowhere, but seldom looked into other eyes or at the surroundings. As bored as everyone else, the landlord broke out of the prevailing mood, pounded into the adjoining shop, put on an apron, and became the butcher. He slammed some meat around and chopped a couple of violent chops; but no customers came in, so he took off his apron, came back into the bar and was bored there instead. Then two lively men came in and started playing dice, a piece of

217

animation to which everyone crowded like vultures, with the owner waving the dice box over his head in triumph that something should be happening at last.

It was not enough for me. There was a whole evening before me, and the light had not yet gone, so I got on the bike and went off up the hill towards Horseman's Leap, the famous feature of the area. My expenditure of energy was rewarded by the company of another cyclist — a small boy on a bicycle who asked me where I came from and rode with me until he got tired of it.

Horseman's Leap lies some kilometres off the main road along a cripplingly stony track. The man who leapt was John Evans; he was on a prospecting expedition upriver with three companions in March 1883, when they were attacked by Indians. His friends were captured and cruelly put to death. Evans escaped by jumping a twenty-foot ravine. His horse Malacara — whose name came from a disfiguring blaze on its face — lies buried in Esquel under a tombstone in honour of the exploit, which was the only time that members of the Welsh colony are known to have been killed by Indians. The unanswered question in the affair is why hostility should have flared up in an isolated incident. I heard three opinions: that the Indians were after the white men's gold; that the white men had been interfering with their women; and that the four colonists were all wearing coats which looked like soldiers' uniforms. Since the incident was less than four years after the end of the genocidal "Conquest of the Desert" campaign, the latter may be the most likely.

I passed the sign for a *referencia historica*, which is how Argentina describes such things, and continued uphill: a lorry passed and filled the air with the scent of diesel, which persisted minutes after it had gone. I had come a long way since the Provincia Buenos Aires and its furious smoky cattle lorries. Having been so long in a place where the air was so pure, I had become totally accustomed to the absence of any kind of internal combustion engine.

Making my way through the higher hills up into even higher hills, the ground was red, furrowed with erosion and dotted with small shrubs on which a couple of black horses were doing their best to graze.

The sun was sinking, and the new moon was out as I came by chance to an even stretch of grass by the roadside. It would not have been highly praised as an English lawn, for it was growing between the stones, and every blade of it was parched. But I turned my gaze from the furnace sunset and salmon clouds and thought to myself — not having seen such a thing for a while — that when you are not used to it, there can be a certain wondrousness in quite a small patch of pale grass.

On my return to Las Plumas, it had livened up. There was dancing in the bar, a gypsy-looking woman with curls of jet-black hair twirling and stamping with a skimpy, marionette-like man in a white suit, grimy at the cuffs and lapels. He also wore dark glasses. I thought at first he was blind, but close to at the bar I could see his eyes staring at me through the lenses. They were Chileans, he said: he was eighty-two, his wife thirty-six. They moved like dolls to tangos from a ghetto-blaster behind the bar; dancing with an innocent and undiscriminating gaiety, not caring what or where they were.

My bedroom was across the yard, like the lockless lavatories, of which the gents was unusable, and the ladies indescribable. The bedroom had an oak strip floor which had been neither sanded, polished nor too-aggressively cleaned, as a large drawing of a penis in one corner testified. It was one of the few occasions in my life that I had seen graffiti on the floor. There were two holes through which could be seen the dust below, looking much the same as the dust which was in the courtyard outside.

The walls were pale blue and peeling. The ceiling was partly plaster, partly paint and partly expanded metal where the skimming of plaster had come off. The curtainless windows had shutters in two shades of paint — present and previous. The fact that the light bulb dangled by a big of tangly wire from the metal mesh was in no way dangerous, since the power was turned off until seven o'clock in the morning. The bedclothes were damp, the night was cold, and there was a terrible screaming from some agonized baby during most of it, so I know exactly when they turned it on again.

There was home-made bread and a large chunk of butter and jam for breakfast. Bearing in mind my previous experience with landladies, I asked for one fried egg. This turned out to be a tactical error, as the present landlady said "No!" with great force, and could be heard muttering "Asked for a fried egg! Asked for a fried egg!" on her way out of the dining room, until she could repeat it with the full force of disgust to her family in the kitchen. She then had no change and increased the bill by one quarter to make up for it.

It was my last big cycling day, almost 190 kilometres to Trelew, and the wind had dropped to a whisper of breeze. Above Las Plumas a bare highland stretched to distant horizons, its colour no longer the red out of which I had climbed the night before. Here, the predominant tone was a dusty white, light sand and green — with not even a shadow to disturb its monotone, for the sun was still trying to break through the clouds.

Cocks called as I passed Alto de las Plumas, one of the only three areas of habitation marked on my road before the Chubut valley, the others being Las Chapas, which was on a crossroads and El Refugio, which sounded like a good spot for lunch. Alto de las Plumas was not a hopeful advertisement, consisting of a featureless concrete quadrangle with a few windows and a stove-pipe. It was supported — though only just — by a Nissen hut, a water tank, corrals and a garden shed, which might have been a second little house, since there was no garden.

But high though the upland was, it did not seem to lack fertility. Willow bushes grew as much as a metre high, and the yellow daisies along the verge could achieve almost the status of a miniature chrysanthemum. Dark green shrubs were loaded with small fruit and flocks of sparrows after it. They are not a native bird, having been introduced — to the disgust of many a farmer since — by Sarmiento, who was President at the end of the 1860s.

Among the bushes lives a tiny deer, the *pudu*, which is about the size of a large hare but standing taller on the thinnest of legs. Not that it stands for long: I saw two with strangely blunt heads, round bodies and a bottom almost like the stern of a small boat — black above, and white below the waterline — and they were off in an instant, at a kind of delicate bounce. Excited, I spared the time to put a telephoto lens on the camera, thereby ensuring that all living things on the plain would disappear immediately.

I sped along an endless, undulating straight stretch towards a couple of small humps, the only relief on the horizon. The sun came out, and an early morning lorry showered me with the smell of fresh hay. With the sun, the pastel plain became a mottle of dull green and gold, with grey patches where people had been digging clay. There were kaolin mines not far distant but these were a simple "scrape off the topsoil and dig" affair. Cones of piled-up clay were already eroded to look as if they had been there for centuries. Sheep wandered over one working, almost the same colour as the clay and puzzled by the lack of food.

An hour and a half brought me to a building, the bar-restaurant of the Laguna Grande. A gibbet stood before it, hung with block and tackle for butchering animals. A brown old woman was methodically sweeping the gravel outside the door with the dust blowing everywhere. The task was like painting the Forth Bridge — except that the paint ran off as soon as you applied it.

There were only two farms between there and Las Chapas, which turned out not so much to be situated on a crossroads as to *be* the crossroads. I had covered sixty-five kilometres in two and a half hours, but the road ahead was no less interminable. To my left, nothing was visible except two purple hints of hilltops rising above the horizon. To my right, a distant range of white cliffs probably marked the line of the river. Every time my road headed up over a brow, I had no doubt but that I would find exactly the same long straight ahead. With the land around so low and unchanging and the road so swift the piffling apex of each rise felt like riding off into the sky.

Nor had I company: the sun had come out and sent all the wild creatures to siesta. I had not seen even a sheep for a long time. The sun raised a heat haze on the far end of the road, so that the sky came flowing down the road like a river, with the three or four cars an hour appearing to be afloat. When the power lines from the Florentino Ameghino dam swung in beside me, they were comforting, because they gave me a scale which was otherwise totally absent from the landscape. Without them, there was only "here" and "somewhere far off".

An hour and a half later I came to another bar, a tiny place with a vine growing round it and flowers. I did not stop — I was racing for the sea. The expectation that Trelew would contain a tolerable hotel might also have had something to do with my enthusiasm. Yet when a bored farmer in a pickup truck pulled up beside me and offered me a lift in the back, I refused. I would not have the chance of pedalling to Trelew taken away from me. In any case, it was almost quarter to three — the time I had set myself for lunch.

Strangely, just at that moment, there was a white gate and a sign for El Refugio — though the establishment itself had taken refuge down a track. I had reached the one landmark left on the road. I would stop as soon as I found a good place to sit down. There was an old tyre to sit on, but someone had thrown rubbish around it, and I saw no reason why I should be compelled to be intimate with litter when I was surrounded by empty desert. So I rode on. Here was a stone — no, hardly more than a pebble, the wrong shape and too small. There was a bank of what was almost grass; but it was not different enough from the desert to make any real difference. If I walked away from the road, the desert would be the same. So where was a good place? No spot was different from any other. In the end I settled down among the dust and stones.

I was dizzy with the sudden halt, and could hardly untie the knot in the polythene bag, my hands were so sore with gripping the handlebars on rough roads. My lunch had come with me all the way from Esquel — stale bread, a piece of salami of questionable quality, some anonymous cheese and coarse apples, eaten among the dust and stones of Patagonia.

I experienced a curious sensation: and it was not only that I had stopped, while the road was still moving. It was a sensation of understanding. All my way, I had seen poor folk sitting in the dust before their despised houses, like figures in a landscape. Now, I was one of those figures. We would have sat more comfortably, in a better place, if we could; but we could not, so we made the best of it. I understood that because I was used to something different and more expensive, my standards were not necessarily better.

I understood, further, how grudgingly a vast country is tamed. How people are accidental heroes, and reluctant pioneers; how uncomfortable it is to set about converting a country and have to live in it at the same time; how you lack the time, the strength, the money, ever to achieve what you know you should achieve. The land is too big: people are too small. There are two thousand years of working lives missing.

I understood something of the balance between what you bring with you to a new land and what you lose. How the small, significant refinements drift away and are lost: how the very things that had charmed me in the middle-class folk I had met — the love of Europe, the relics of its customs, the old world civilization — these were among the things that held Argentina back. They should have thrown them away. Knowing that, in their shoes, I would not have done it either, I learnt a little humility outside the gate of El Refugio.

I threw the bio-degradable cheese over my shoulder, in the hope that it might attract a *pudu*. It did not. The only thing that appeared was one solitary ant. I threw it some bits of apple. The first bit landed behind — it ignored it: the second to one side: the third bit too far away: the fourth in front of it. It still ignored it. My relationship with the wild creatures of Patagonia remained distant.

It was time to go — and exceedingly difficult getting up, since my legs seemed to have turned to water. Having looked at the map and tightened up the horn, which was almost falling off, I set foot to pedal and went my way, leaving behind me a little circle of rejected pieces of apple and a few scratches in the dust.

A range of greyish-white cliffs had arisen in the distance, and my road was heading towards them. Like me, how many tired travellers must have watched those cliffs grow in size, and known that somewhere near was comfort and — in their case — home. But how slowly they grew — and suddenly, how tired I was of the plain! I was fed up with the sand, fed up with the bushes, fed up with the long, straight road.

The change I craved came as I neared Dolavon. I was plainly approaching civilization; there were more cars and only one bullet hole in the sign for the imminent petrol station. It was more than civilization, it was a fleshpot: there were tearooms, the Draig Goch Casa de Té, whose sign had a red Welsh dragon on it. A little while after, a farm gate that I passed had a tyre sunk into the sand before it with the caption "Hyde Park".

The road humped and bumped its way along to join the white hills I had been anticipating so long. But I forgave it every jolt of its villainous surface, for there, in the evening sun, opened the valley of Chubut — lines of poplars as windbreaks, golden fields, and there were even trees that were not poplars, and they were green. After the barrenness of the plain, the impression of fruitfulness was extraordinary. I had not seen so many trees all my way from Esquel. They were like an enigmatic population in the valley, standing and watching me come in.

There was something that looked like a haystack and, on closer inspection, it was. Next to it was a little house with eaves and gables, as if it was a Welsh house, and a tiled roof with chimneys. A field was incredibly green — I had not seen a green like that, I thought, since I had left England. The secret was a swirling, splashing irrigation canal, with ducks on it. Bordered by tamarisk and willow, with clean, fat cows in a field, it was a picture of prosperity and good husbandry on the very edge of the desert — to my left was nothing but sand and scrub. Now I realized what I had missed on the plains. They lacked that flowing line of foliage which lends movement, grace and height to a landscape. Even here the plains were not far off: the sand came right up to the very threshold of the terraces — and many times a sandy field growing nothing but dry thorn-bushes separated me from the fields and trees beyond.

In one respect at least it was like the Welsh valleys. But for being white, the clay hills looked like nothing so much as pit-heaps. Just before the boundary of Gaimán, I passed a one-man brickfield, with ziggurats of bricks stacked up ready for firing, and heaps of brushwood to put in the arched tunnels beneath them.

Leaving Gaimán, I climbed away from the fertile part

of the valley, in which the trees were beginning to lose their colour with distance and the evening light in which the setting sun was turning everything golden. The blue sky and its thin feathers of white cloud were luminous. The moon became ever clearer in the sky: and, as I rode, the falling sun threw my shadow longer and longer across the desert bushes, making me almost thin.

Hardly a dozen kilometres from Trelew, the horrors of Argentine traffic returned, with heavy lorries thundering past inches away. There was more litter, with plastic scraps and old bags caught in the desert scrub transfigured against light into a garden of flapping flowers. The familiar dust-cloud of Argentine towns raised itself along the road, and made the vision of Trelew appear ghostly.

There was a whole mixture of strange smells as I came in through the industrial outskirts — dung from a slaughterhouse, gases from a chemical plant, hot metal. Within the nimbus of the dust-cloud were unfamiliar lights — the flashings of an acetylene torch in a garage, the streetlights already glowing, bright children's clothes fluorescing in the blue dusk. I came into the bustling centre past poor breeze-block homes cheek by jowl with each other. Engines roared, children yelled, a car backfired like a cannon shot. A loudspeaker van hectored me with the praises of some politician.

After so long in the desert, my senses were raw. I felt like a small animal suddenly let loose in a cattle market. Even the pedestrians were terrifying. An old lady almost hurled herself under my wheels. A young woman tried to push me aside by crossing the road at the same time that I was coming past. Dust was so dense in the biggest plaza, that I could hardly see the statues in the middle.

When I arrived at my hotel, the receptionists were much impressed. "Las Plumas?" they said twice, and *"En bicycletta?"*, twice. It was very gratifying to an extremely unathletic cyclist who had just set himself a new record of 186 kilometres in one day. The bathroom had gold taps and everything else to match — and that was even more pleasing.

I dreamt of endless roads and repeated red hills.

# CHAPTER
# EIGHT

# Cwm Hyfrwd

## *Gaimán, Trelew and Rawson*

"That looks like a grand new building," I said tentatively to the waiter at breakfast, with the object of discovering the future of a particularly ugly and skeletal tower block across the road. The waiter said it was the subject of a lawsuit, and had been like that for ten years. Generally, Trelew had an unfinished air to it, as if it had been so busy growing that it had not had time to tidy up after itself.

There were some good things in it: a modern church on the outskirts with a fairy-tale spire seeking heaven in a wonderful sweep; the odd, red-brick Welsh chapel and the Welsh cultural centre; and in the main plaza, surrounded by oleander and lilac, a delightful period bandstand that is a fretwork artist's heaven. But Trelew was apt to run out of road surface and pavement too often and rather too carelessly for a town of its size. As in many another town in Argentina, you could see the gap between private enterprise and public life. (It was the same sort of gap that has developed in Britain — but at home there had been time to pave the streets first.)

Trelew was now the town that mattered in the place that was the first Welsh colony in Patagonia: they called it "beautiful valley", *cwm hyfrwd*. Gaimán, which had once been the principal town, was hardly more than a village beside it. Rawson, the old provincial capital with the government offices and the gaol, still kept its status, but was losing importance — and there was a growing tendency for the bureaucrats to commute to it from Trelew. The same sort of power shift had happened in the second Welsh colony in the mountains from which I had come; there, the original settlement of Trevelin had become far smaller than the neighbouring Esquel.

The Welsh had arrived in Patagonia in the winter of 1865 — one hundred and eighty-four of them in the sailing-ship *Mimosa*. They landed at Puerto Madryn, which is now an important town in the bay of the Valdes Peninsula, but found life hard and water short. In search of a river, they moved south for some sixty-five kilometres — the men on foot, the women by small boat. At last they came to the mouth of the Chubut river (where Rawson is now), settled the valley and founded Gaimán.

Thus the artery of Welsh colonization was the Chubut river, Gaimán the heart; but it was not until a generation later that the new, adventurous blood of Patagonia went exploring west toward the Andes in search of gold — it being the time of the Klondike. They found some, but not enough to be useful; their real discovery was the fertile valley in which the settlement of Trevelin grew. They say that, when the first Welsh expedition came to Trevelin valley, they looked down and saw that their horses' hooves were red with the juice of wild strawberries. The strawberries have gone now, for sheep have eaten them, but the country around has something of the same plenteousness about it, being verdant everywhere.

**230**

It was in Trevelin that I met Federico Green, before I ever made my way across the Patagonian desert. They called him the Red Fox, and I'm sure he deserved it. He was old and genial, with a sandy, Welsh moustache, a stick to walk with and *bombachas*: but he was like strong wire — a spare patriarch looking out across his domain, part of the land they call "the Welsh farms". His house was on a hillside by a brook which drove the turbine which was his power before the electricity came and the sawmill he built himself out of bits of an old Chevrolet. Almost everything around him was something he had built, imported or preserved.

"All the timber has been brought down and cut here, the bricks have been burnt here, the stones have been gathered here," he told me in English that had an inherited Welsh accent. "The grass on the lawn is from up north. My apples are native apples — there are many varieties, so you have to choose your tree. I found this one because I noticed the peons eating the fruit. They are small, but juicy, very tasty — and they keep till the next spring. It's a healthy tree: other apple trees have pests, but this has none."

He had left ancient trees on his lawn when he built the house as a reminder of the original landscape. "I take good care that they stay here; for, about the house, most people chop them down. I believe we should grow many more trees. All that is to be seen from here, a hundred years ago was forest. We are spoiling the country, and I'm afraid we're going to make a desert of it. The good soil is going away. People just don't care enough."

The house was dominated by a shining aerial array, which stretched almost from one edge of the roof to the other and sent a thick cable down to feed the transmitter-receiver in the kitchen and to curl like a thick black serpent round the cornice of the living-room to the other set. Radio is widely used in a land which has both wide open spaces and poor telephones, and its practical use was to contact his sheep farm in Paso de Indios; but Federico Green was an enthusiastic ham of thirty years' standing, during most of which time, he had been calling Cardiff religiously every Sunday for a chat in Welsh. He gave me a card with his call sign LUI WHG and a red Welsh dragon in the corner, and red figures tumbled over each other on the display as he called up Wales, to show me. Then they talked about the weather. It seemed a great expense of technology to do so, but he said it was a typical subject, along with gossip about friends and what was in the news. He found that he was usually keener on Welsh affairs than Geoff who answered. It seemed that radio hams and Welsh fundamentalists were a different breed. So, for that matter, were the rest of the Argentines.

"We brought Christianity to Patagonia — that's why Patagonia is different from the north," said Federico Green, dismissing the Catholic church at a stroke. "We're not so Latinized you know — more open to things. We receive newspapers from England, from North America, which the Argentines up north don't do. That makes a big difference, you know. Just look around here . . ."

There were books in Spanish, English and French. The room was panelled, with stone flags before the fire, brass candlesticks on the mantelpiece and a Welsh motto over it. The radio sat on a Welsh dresser, below a barometer from Holyhead. The piano, covered with a green cloth, had a Welsh china figure on top; among the books were *A History of Caerphilly, The Lace of Corabeg, The Welsh Bible* and *The Oxford Book of Welsh Verse*. Proudly displayed on its own stand was a tea towel with the legend "Welsh Castles". When his children were at home, he had enforced a strict rule that only Welsh was to be spoken in the house.

He told me of his own childhood. As a baby he went over the desert in the wagons, but the first journey he could remember was in a convoy of three of the first Patagonian cars, throwing stones into the water at every river crossing to test if it was shallow enough to ford. That was in 1918, when he was five and already fatherless. As he said, "They died young in those days.

"My father came here from London. Originally he was from — well I couldn't exactly say a Welsh family, for he came from Chester — but my grandfather drowned in the River Dee, which is a Welsh river. And so I suppose the family came from Wales originally, and moved to Chester," Federico Green said, with more patriotic enthusiasm than strict geographical accuracy.

The other side of the family was thoroughly Welsh. One grandfather had been the first teacher and registrar for the colonists who came with the *Mimosa*.

"There was a great outflow of people from the British Isles — Irish, Scots and the rest of them. Things were very hard in Wales, but the Welsh that moved out wanted to keep their identity. They were looking for a country where only the Welsh would go. First they asked for a large territory in the United States, later they thought about Africa and Australia. In the end, they decided on a country where there was no population; and they came to Patagonia, which the Argentine government was anxious to develop.

"Amongst them came a tailor, and he wanted to be the first in everything. He jumped out before all the rest and put his foot on the shore: and he wanted to be the first arriving at the river. He was my grandmother's boyfriend, and the second day he put his invitation to her. "Come with me to see the land — we'll see if we can see the river up there."

"But she had come as a help to Lewis Jones's family, and she told him, 'I can't, I've got to do the washing.' And that was the last time they saw him — he went out, got lost and never came back. Many, many years later they found his skeleton, not far from the sea-shore."

His voice was musical and swayed easily, like the sea: there was centuries of Welsh in it, the rhythms of the Authorized Version and the confidence of a man who knows what he is, where his place is — and that he is in it. What he said was an article of faith. A ritual story, like a bard — the voice of an elder of his tribe, and one not to be replaced when he was gone.

"Most of them were miners — they knew nothing about the land. They had two working bullocks; they tied them to a cart, but they were never able to get them to walk. They didn't know how to live. They sowed their seed in the land as it was — and it didn't rain. They tried a second season, and they were ready to take themselves out of the place and go look for a new country, when the Argentine government gave them a grant of food and animals, and asked them to stay for one more year."

"It must have been a great shock to come to a dry place from Wales," said I, cynically, thinking of holidays I had spent there.

But Federico Green went on, "Amongst them were Aaron Jenkins and his wife. And Aaron Jenkins said, 'It's no good sowing here: I'll throw down some seed to satisfy the government, and we're going off.' So he sowed their wheat in a clear low place. Well, it happened that they did have an early rain that year, and wheat grew up. Very nice. But then there was a drought. On Sunday morning they went to have a look again at their crop, which was in very poor condition; then Mrs Jenkins noticed that the river was flowing full. And she told her husband, 'Why don't we bring the water from the river?' And they went back home.

"I suppose, since it was Sunday morning, they did not work that day. But they did it on Monday; came along with spades, made a ditch and irrigated the wheat — twice, I understand."

It seemed courageously naïve. Federico went on: "They did not know where they came from, nor the climate, the animals, not even the way to hunt. Once they found that way of cultivating their wheat, there was no problem, but they took two years or more to find it out. It was the Indians who taught them to use the *boleadoras*, the native system of hunting. That saved them.

"The Indians in this part of the country were usually nomads who went down to the coast in the winter. They were Tehuelches — very tall and heavy-set, giants almost — a very happy people, always disposed to have a joke and a laugh. They received the Welsh with great friendship and helped them in every way."

"That wasn't the usual story between Indians and settlers," I said.

"In South America it was the only time it happened. But you must see that the Welsh came here as true Christians. They came with their Bibles, and not with rifles.

"The Tehuelche was a very primitive man: he just lived for the day. He didn't even keep food from one day to the other. He would get up in the morning and go out to hunt — and if he didn't catch anything that day, he didn't eat. His breakfast was the first animal he killed."

"You'd need to be tough to endure that," I said.

"They took everything for granted — they'd arrive at a house, go in and help themselves. But they were exactly the same with their own things. You could go into their camp and help yourself to anything you needed from it. That was their custom. So when you saw them coming, you'd keep most of the valuable things out of sight. They were very fond of bread — *barra*, as a Welshman calls it. They'd come along and ask for *"poco barra, poco barra"*. They'd give you a horse in exchange for a loaf. They did it pleasantly, and once that horse was given, it was given. That was the end of it.

"They were very, very friendly — they helped the Welsh an awful lot, and the Welsh helped them. They used to take Indians into their own families. My mother used to tell me about one they had, a big fellow, and when he and my mother went to school, two miles away, he would carry her on his shoulders. She used to say, 'My pony!' His descendants used to work for me — and that big body is still in the family.

"My mother took young Tehuelches into our home, so I was brought up with them. They learned Welsh very quickly. There are still people of Indian blood who speak it — one woman here in Trevelin, she's married to a Spaniard, so they don't speak Welsh in the home, but she talks Welsh with me.

"They were too confident, you know, the Tehuelches. So they fell right in when the soldiers came and took them off. That finished them off as a pure tribe. They died, almost all of them. They couldn't adapt to civilized foods — and measles, and those kinds of things that the white man brought. It finished them. And the same happened in Tierra del Fuego, with the Onas, their relatives."

"They sound like noble savages," I said.

"Noble. Noble," said Federico Green, and thought for a moment. "Yes, they were great men."

By the 1880s, when the Welsh went over the desert to find Trevelin valley, the community at Gaimán was well established. The dream of a Welsh community, master of its own destiny, had come true: Welsh was not only the language of everyday life and government, but they were printing Welsh books for the schoolchildren.

A town council was elected every year and special assemblies held when there was something particularly important to discuss; the colonists ran a jury system, and every man took his turn as the special constable, which was not usually an onerous job, though Aaron Jenkins the irrigator was stabbed to death taking a prisoner down to Rawson, having unwisely loosened his bonds.

"A great loss to the colony," said a local headmistress to me, as if it were yesterday. "A good farmer, and a poet too." Simple people though many of the original colonists were, Welsh culture was important to them. In her school too, it seemed to be surviving. That day her children were holding their own eisteddfod, even though the school could not afford a piano to accompany them.

I was shocked at that — for in my privileged existence I had been unable to imagine a reasonably sized secondary school without one. But that was before I met Clwdwyn Apaeron Jones, the director of the first Patagonian Music

School, with instrumental teachers who flew from Buenos Aires once a week. He told me that the ever-declining austral (now down to less than a third of its value when I came to Argentina, less then six weeks before) made everything from the international world of music prohibitively expensive — especially with import tax. Most of his violinists had no instruments of their own, he said; the school could not teach the flute, clarinet or bassoon because there were none, but there were two cellos and a trumpet. I had already seen the local harp, which was an exhibit in the Gaimán museum — though I heard later that one girl from Rawson was studying the harp elsewhere. Clwdwyn told me that his piano class had now progressed to advanced studies, but he did not expect to see anything like a local orchestra in his lifetime. Indeed, many of his music students had never heard a live orchestra at all.

"But do orchestras never come here?" I asked.

He replied, "Oh yes, we had a visit from the Sinfonia of Buenos Aires about ten years ago, and the Camerata of Bariloche has been here twice."

"I can't see how musical culture can survive in such circumstances — let alone Welsh culture," I said.

"Choirs are cheap," he said. (He was a choral conductor and bard himself.) The problem was that there were no Welsh schools, so Welsh was learned at home — and when Welsh was no longer spoken there, it was bound to die out eventually.

"I remember when I was a little boy, everything in the eisteddfod was in Welsh," he said. "Now it's mostly in Spanish — otherwise we wouldn't have enough entries for the competitions."

It was growing thinner with time, but the Welsh cultural

tradition seemed to me to be far from geriatric. There were choirs and regular eisteddfods everywhere; and though these might be specially significant to older people, two of the three eisteddfods on while I was there were for children, and the busiest organizers of the big event at Trelew were bright young women.

The Trelew eisteddfod was too large for the Welsh cultural centre, and had to be held in the indoor sports stadium, with basketball goals pushed to either side of the stage and used as stands for spotlamps, with ivy twined round them. Every institutional chair in Trelew seemed to have been brought in, including kiddy chairs from the schools.

A side room housed a small arts and crafts exhibition, with drawings, wood carvings, knitting (three pullovers), doilies and tapestries of bluebirds, horses, winsome dogs and a telephone — a strange subject, possibly occasioned by the fact that in Argentina the making of a telephone call can be a mystic and romantic process, in the course of which you may form many new human relationships, but experience a deep feeling of loss of the one you were hoping for.

The eisteddfod took all day. In the afternoon there were rather a lot of elderly folk among the arrivals, and a good third of the seats were unfilled. However, that still meant an audience of something not too far below a thousand, and by evening the hall would be packed. Some of the girls were part-singing in the street as they came in.

Bright choir championship shields shared the front of the stage with the flower arranging competition: pink gladioli in a basket, chysanthemums and a white rabbit, roses with privet, red carnations adorning a blue and white stuffed dog with a glassy blue stare, cute pink tongue and false eyelashes, sitting on a plastic doily. (Perhaps as a consequence of the Welsh tea, which is an extremely substantial feature of local life, the doily still occupies a place of honour in this part of the world.) The other place of honour went to a venerable upright piano by Spaethe — a maker unknown to me — which provided accompaniments for the solo singing competitions with varying degrees of accuracy.

A prayer said in quiet voices preceded the Argentine national anthem, which was something of a surprise to me. Even the introduction was exceedingly involved, necessitating much running and finger-work on the part of the pianist. From the audience it demanded a wide vocal range, as it was operatic in style, with reminiscences of Handel, Mozart and Beethoven and something very like a Rossini coda at the end. However, everyone seemed to know it and sang it proudly.

The Argentine flag and Welsh dragon shared the backdrop; and one of the most charming things about the event was the easy mixture of Latin and Welsh. (There was nothing Indian in the performance arts, though one of the local dignitaries introduced during the day was a romantic-looking man in black *bombachas*, a brilliant blue folk-weave sash and a poncho slung over one shoulder, who was announced as a representative of the Mapuche-Tehuelche community.)

An elderly man and a white-haired woman performed "La Condición", a handkerchief dance from Buenos Aires, with great poise. ("La Condición" refers to the condition of relationship between man and woman: theirs was one of grace and tender formality.) A choir from Esquel began a

Welsh hymn in a whisper of harmony, swelled to fullness, and died away to nothing. A Spanish folk group with guitars kept the same dynamic throughout, as is often the way with folk groups. An old choral conductor introduced a choir with an impassioned speech and a light in his eyes, and hung on every note thereafter. And so through all the possible permutations of vocal performance — recitation, solo song, duo, vocal quartet, chamber choir, big choir.

Through it all, the judges sat a few rows back at a table with a rich cerise cloth and clashing orange table-lamps, and struggled with the public address system, like judges everywhere.

There was not one, but two bardic ceremonies — Welsh in the afternoon and Spanish in the evening, for poems in the respective languages. The ceremony for the Argentine bard — a blonde in a green dress looking plump and happy — struck more fire; but there was a special intimacy in the Welsh bardic ceremony in the afternoon, though it was not Welsh exclusively, being interrupted by a Spanish instruction *"Toca la trompeta, por favor"* to the trumpeter. They called for the bard the first time. No response: below the stage a little blonde tot in white with pink ribbons swung from side to side as she waited to usher the winner to the bardic chair. On stage, six skinny little girls in skimpy green tunics waited to dance. The second call, the second fanfare, and someone was on their feet in the audience — a smiling woman in a quiet dress. Somehow, the staged delay had not generated a feeling of excitement, so much as affection. We were all glad for her, and through her for the poet she represented. For, alas, only one local woman was qualified to compete in Welsh — she had already been bard four or five times. The eisteddfod competition was open internationally, and the smiling woman — Laura Henry, a teacher — was the proxy for a poet in Wales itself.

They sheathed the sword in peace; the skimpy green girls did springtime steps and brought flowers to Laura in her bardic chair; a Spanish-looking soprano sang the eisteddfod song, with more than one old woman in the audience mouthing the Welsh along with her. Ceremonies often make those who take part into figureheads: this one showed you that ordinary people had depths.

Then, and not only then, many of the faces in the audience seemed aglow. They were in communion with a culture which was both theirs and from a land far away — and a spirit had arrived that was at once unifying, peaceful and intense.

At tea, I found myself sitting next to the Welsh bard, in a school hall where trestle tables of cakes were laid out beneath a gigantic patriotic mural of General San Martín and Simon Bolívar doing brave deeds on the battlefield. Laura was a woman in the prime of life who was no less engaging as a teacher than she had been as a bard, but she made me stumble along in my broken Spanish for ten minutes before admitting that she spoke English. (There is a minor tradition in Patagonia of making sure that English visitors should realize that they cannot impose their own language there, as they did in Wales; but this was the only time I met it.) Not only did Laura speak English, but had lived in Wales. She had been married to a Welshman there, though when he died she had chosen to return to Patagonia with her young daughter.

"It was a shame in Wales in the beginning," said the bard, who had gone there with her head full of ancient castles and green fields. "I thought everybody would speak

Welsh there and I was surprised to hear so much English. Welsh is the language I was taught first; I don't feel it's foreign."

"Why come back to Patagonia then?"

"I was born in this country — this is my place. It's something in the heart. My daughter can speak Welsh, and I think it's all-important for her to be brought up with it, but I don't want her to lose any of Argentina or Argentina's language either."

"Is there really hope for the future of the Welsh in Argentina?" I asked her.

"Well, it was said long ago that there was no hope for the Welsh language, but it's still spoken. I don't know how much hope there is in Wales itself, so why shouldn't there be some hope here? And if it dies — well, it's natural."

Though the eisteddfod took a day, Welshness went on all weekend, though emphasis shifted to the more traditional town of Gaimán, with official singing in chapel, and unofficial at the celebration lunch — based, of course, on asado. Here older folk took up the traditional Welsh songs, of which they knew the chorus but were less fluent in verses, and young people burst out even more spontaneously into sambas. A century in Argentina and an intermingling with other nationalities seemed to have done nothing but good to the Welsh character — keeping the stability, but adding a social easiness and sparkle.

Many of the houses in Gaimán are old — some built in a Spanish style but more are Welsh. The very first permanent house, which was being used as a store shed when I saw it, was a traditional Welsh long-house, built in stone. Generally, faded red brick is the hallmark of the Patagonian Welsh houses, quite often with ornamental gables, like Edwardian railway station buildings. You can see that there is something there that is not Argentine, but — like the people — the character of the houses is different from their counterparts in the dour valleys of South Wales, being easier and more colonial.

It is also exceeding well supplied with chapels — for, in addition to the Catholics (whose church here is unwontedly cottagey and chapel-like itself), there are Jehovah's Witnesses, Seventh Day Adventists, Pentecostalists, Plymouth Brethren, Mormons, Methodists and Charismatics, who are rather similar to the Pentecostalists.

Gaimán also has tea houses. The Patagonian Welsh tea has no fruitcake or cucumber sandwiches — and you will sigh in vain for a selection of Indian and China blends — but there is good tea, grown in the north of Argentina, home baking and much enthusiasm to make up for it. The Welsh tea has a great sense of its own importance, and the rest of Argentina looks upon it as no less exotic than we think the Japanese tea ceremony.

The ritual of the Welsh Tea Ceremony is performed in a place kept sacred for that purpose, whose name is always written in at least two languages in order to inspire respect — as in the Plas y Coed Casa de Té in Gaimán, where I enjoyed a particularly fine service, with Martha Rees officiating, and a number of unidentified acolytes in the kitchen. The tea house was in a typically Welsh setting — a cottage garden containing fine roses, dahlias and a palm tree. Over the gate was the Ikon of the Red Dragon, which is particularly holy in association with teatime, and only equalled in significance by the Sign of the Steaming Teapot and the Symbol of the Ineffable Cup and Saucer.

On entering the Sacred Red Dragon Tea House, it

was immediately clear that the rituals of the place were being performed to an exceedingly high standard, being if anything more elaborate than those of Wales itself. Initiation in the Art of Slicing Bread and Butter Extremely Thin had been most conscientiously performed, as had been the Raising of the Scone, and the Inititation in the Rite of Pot-Warming.

Martha was dressed in a seemly frilly apron, and when she approached me with the Catechism of the Cakes, I saw at once from the twinkle in her eye that we were equally fervent in our attachment to the cult. There were slightly fewer than a dozen different varieties, including *torta gallesa* (Welsh Cake, rather like a gingerbread with a smattering of fruit) and Patagonian Cream Tart, which is so delicious that it is now making converts in Wales itself.

We had some conversation about the *dulce de leche* heresy, to which she was an adherent — but only, fortunately, to the extent of one or two items on the plate. I departed very satisfied with my ritual observance. Later, it was revealed to me that a lot of the *torta gallesa* that the tourists buy is actually made in a factory owned by a Spanish Argentine, but I am convinced that this did not apply to the Plas y Coed Casa de Té, where everything was so good, it had to be home-made.

Gaimán is on the line between nothingness and fertility. In the plaza willows trail in the stream beside an old water-wheel in the swirling canal. There are palms, lilac bushes and the most beautiful roses — Gaimán seems to have something in the air that keeps blooms perfect. Yet sandhills rise directly from the back gardens on the northern edge of town. Within a couple of metres of each other you have flowers and a green lawn, low scrub and desert.

Albina Zampini's house was like that, on a corner of the street called "Miguel D. Jones" after one of the founding fathers. It was a converted shop, smart and white, and its single storey and the desert over the back wall were deceptive. Inside, it breathed tranquillity and knowledge, with shelf upon shelf of books: Albina's husband was a professor of philosophy. The furniture was antique — elegant sofas and chairs and an enormous French commode along one wall, portly, polished and gilt at the edges. A Do-It-Yourself sofa with ambitions to be a *chaise-longue* had been made by Albina's grandfather: it had a cupboard in the bottom, in which, she said, she kept her treasures. From it Albina took four folders of drawings and spread them out on the old shop counter, even though she was in a hurry to get to chapel for the last singing of the eisteddfod weekend.

The folders contained a fashion serial 1859-1939, one hundred drawings of dresses and one hat. It was also a social history. Albina had begun by drawing some of the clothes in old photographs from the Esquel museum out of interest, carried on with them when she was laid up with a broken leg, then thought it would be interesting to find out who the people were, so had gone on to collect information about them.

"This is Mrs Lewis Jones — who came here in 1865 — in her wedding dress, with her Bible in her hand," Albina began. "Anne Thomas, Mrs William Malifant, when she was fifteen and made her own dress. Anne Harrison's wedding gown when she was twenty-three years old and got married in Wales."

They were accomplished line drawings but most of them

had no faces, which gave them an eerie, almost totemic quality. Albina herself had a beautiful ageing face like a kind bird; hands that fluttered in expostulation like wings; and a singing, gentle voice. Her eyes were bad: she still taught art at a local school, but she handled these drawings as if they were her last.

"Mary Humphreys at eighteen, the first white girl born here. Eluned Morgan at eighteen, when she cut her hair without anybody's permission."

I was surprised at the minute detail of the memory — gossip that had lasted a century. "You remember such small things as someone cutting their hair without permission, how many years ago?"

"Their descendants said so, and they probably say the truth. Why would they lie? She wrote four books and never got married. Doesn't she look beautiful? This is her sister Myfanwy Jones, Mrs Llwyd ap Iwan — her husband was killed by some of Butch Cassidy's gang."

"These long-dead people — you talk of them almost as if they're friends," I said.

"Well, are they dead?" asked Albina calmly. "All their descendants are friends of ours; the children I teach are descendants. We never regard these people as dead. There's something about them that I regard with respect. They lived in places terribly lonely. Think how women like to make themselves beautiful, look after their hands and hair and have a lovely dress — I think that belongs to a woman, doesn't it, because that's the way we've been made? Yet they had to live in very hard circumstances. The river here that looks so peaceful — in summer it was half dry, and they had no clear water; then in the winter it rose up in flood, and some of them lost their homes and everything.

"When I first drew these pictures and then found out who they were, there have been times when I was crying at night about some problem they had in the past, because I thought they had probably been very lonely. I felt respect for them because they stayed here. My own mother, she longed to go back to Wales."

"I wonder what the Welsh have given to Argentina?" I said.

"Probably a mildness of character; and, behind that mildness, strength to go on. And I feel there is some kindness. Didn't you feel that yesterday when you were at the eisteddfod?"

"But what should I tell people about Patagonia?" I asked her.

"Tell them to come here, and they'll find by their own experience what Patagonia is. Our authors who've written about this place, they've all given their testimony — and, I would say, truthful testimony. But the people nowadays who come here and stay about a fortnight — I never feel they really know the place well enough to be able to write about it."

She went off to Bethel chapel for the congregational singing; and, later on, I looked in too. The chapel had a planked ceiling of dark wood and dark pews — all crowded with people of all ages, with others standing at the back. It was lit with hanging lights — some chandeliers, some electrified oil lamps — that all had glass shades, which gave them a brilliance as if a celestial presence had consented to come to earth and hang around on the end of a wire.

The choir was ranked up before the congregation, facing them frankly. (I wondered to myself whether the Anglican habit of placing the choir to one side might be one of the things contributing to the special English talent for hypocrisy.) There was a harmonium, or something electronic sounding like one, and a vocal quartet. It was not the most wonderful of quartets, but the singing as a whole was powerful and moving. It was a place for singing as a whole.

In the pews, in the choir were faces I now knew, that had come to know me. Unassuming intimacy filled the place, and a sense of a community concentrating on something very important to it — part pleasure, part artistic experience, part communal rite — that had to do with the past, the present and the future.

There is a great deal of public patriotism in Argentina, with most of the great men and public figures of its history remembered as statues or street names in every town in the country. For myself, I think it healthier to use less rhetoric and a more appropriate distribution of gratitude as an acknowledgement to the fact that countries may be changed by heroes, but are made great by everyday people. That quite humble Victorian chapel was such an acknowledgement; whatever Christian message it contained, it was also a cathedral to the common man and woman. In that, it had what the rest of Argentina lacked. It was stable, united and determined to work for its own salvation. But though it was a part, it could not stand for the whole of that chaotic country. For that, I came upon a more fitting symbol.

It was the only castle in Gaimán. Not that it was the ordinary sort of castle, for its garden contained a re-creation of the Alhambra made out of substandard tights; a petrified forest; a re-creation of Picasso's "Guernica" ("Guernica II") on the wall of the courtyard where Señora Alonso dried her washing; and a religious sculpture made out of car scrap.

249

This was El Desafio, "The Challenge": and the man who issued it was the husband of Señora Alonso.

Joaquín Alonso was seventy and had one of those faces that is all enthusiasm, nose and eyes. He was an artist, joker and iconoclast: a generalissimo of junk. In the great football game that was Argentina, his logic was perpetually offside, but he knew where the goals were. He had been in the army for many years, and had also run a firm of door-to-door collectors and salesmen. Then he had retired, taken over the site of a burnt-out house, and begun to create his Challenge.

El Desafio was a kind of anti-theme park, though it had plenty of themes on it, being plastered with notices containing Señor Alonso's philosophical observations and witticisms. The white castle was a façade on his bungalow. He was making a Zodiac before it, so that visitors could have their pictures taken with their sign. It would be in trees or flowers, he had not decided which; he had had a heavy time planting bulbs recently.

*"Hay tulipanes, hay lilios, hay narcissos, hay anenomios!"* Señor Alonso pointed out, proudly, adding that the ugly bit was where the Council was putting in pipes. He had been working on his art-park eight hours a day, for nine years. Not for him the Patagonian pace of life (which even has its own verb, *patagonisar*, to amble like a Patagonian, to take things slowly). Work was his vice, his addiction, he said.

He was a self-taught artist, and said that he had been a friend of Quinquela Martin, the famous Argentine painter of La Boca in Buenos Aires. He had asked Quinquela Martin what he thought of Patagonia, and Quinquela had replied that Patagonia was wonderful but very grey: "You have to give colours to it," he said. So Señor Alonso painted murals — 130 of them in the coastal city of Comodoro Rivadavia, where he had lived during his working life.

We walked in the garden in Señor Alonso's arcades of tights, rejects from a local factory, strung in complex patterns between poles. "Adoración", a statue of a woman praying, had been made out of scrap by a car mechanic friend, now dead, in whose memory it was. There was a throne set high, for people to feel important in; and a hundred thousand beer bottles edging the paths (the smaller sort of beer bottle, because the larger ones carried a deposit).

Señor Alonso showed me the petrified forest. It was not a very big forest. Ignorant people might even have thought it to be no more than the stumps of a few poplars that had been rather carelessly cut down. "That is to say, it is a forest that will be petrified in eight million years," Señor Alonso explained.

"But why have you made it out of such perishable materials?"

"Like everything else, it will disappear. A few years after I am dead, there will be nothing left. The Seven Wonders of the World have all disappeared, and this one will disappear too — so I call it the Eighth Wonder of the World. This is a park for people without money in a country without money."

There was a mottling of grey cloud across the sky as I set out from Trelew on my last day's journey to the sea — past children huddled in the corner of a plot of waste ground, past buildings half-completed, over gravel roads with the dust clouds already rising from them.

After my experience at El Desafio I found myself looking

at these things with new eyes. There I had seen a man building himself a special and original place out of rubbish and ingenuity. Now, I thought that the disorder around me might not be a sign of prosperity, but at least it was a sign of life — from which one day something new might rise.

On the outskirts of Trelew I came to a scrapyard of the municipal roads department. Like strange metal animals, worn-out road machines slumbered in drizzle. Some were so old, they had been made to be pulled by horses. I saw them not as melancholy, but triumphant: their day was done, but it had been a good day's work. They had built Argentina's roads — and my roads.

The road to Rawson was a moderately busy and not very beautiful one. On my right, the desert landscape had returned: on my left were the prosperous river banks with their fields and poplars. As I rode, the rain stopped, and the sun tried to break through.

Rawson offered me a zoo and amusement park, but I was too near journey's end to pause. Over the muddy river, past the white and green spired church I came, and not a glance but for the murals along the walls. Someone with a liking for big muscles had done heroic workers for a hundred metres on end. One entire side of a large building was covered with a classical painting of General San Matín and his officers. Below it, with nothing to do but look at me, was a small dark boy.

I was through the town, and travelling by the river, which had lost every feature it had ever had and was simply water flowing through flatness. By it was a small assembly of white birds, which I suddenly realized were seagulls, for I had forgotten that there were such things, let alone what they looked like. Ahead was a not unfamiliar fuzz of seaside houses along the skyline. There were estates of new houses unfinished; even the old ones were shut up, as it was out of season. I came down to the front at Playa Union, which was empty, quite deserted, with a rusting white flagpole and a few tamarisk trees.

And in front of me was the Atlantic. I approached it. It was grey, cold and rolling; and smelt like the Atlantic. But looking out from Patagonia it was difficult to believe that this was the same ocean that slapped the shores of Sidmouth.

# THE NORTH-WEST

# CHAPTER
# NINE

# Plaza

## *Salta and Cafayate*

It was four months later. Argentina was in love with a new Peronist president, and they were enjoying an economic honeymoon together with that very same austral, which had been forty to the dollar when I first came, now fairly stable for a few weeks at 635. It was windy and cold at one end of Argentina's 3500 kilometre length, in Tierra del Fuego and by the glaciers of Lago Argentino; tropical at the other, in the jungles of Missiones and by the falls of Iguazú. Bikeless — for I was intending to write, not travel — I flew up to the north-west, where spring was coming, and settled myself in Salta.

Salta is not only a city but a province — and the last one in the north-west, but for Jujuy, which lies on the border of Bolivia. The old Inca road over the Andes went through here; and along it colonial Argentina transported goods on the backs of Salta mules through Bolivia and Peru to and from the port of Lima, through which the bureaucratic Spanish power decided that the plunder of Latin America should be shipped to Spain. Salta is not only historic but has kept its past — the colonnaded colonial-style buildings and the patrician families to go with them — so that it feels quite different from Córdoba, the pampa, or anywhere else I went in Argentina.

Salta is on the edge of a plain; and on the edge of Salta is the Cerro San Bernado, the conical hill that takes its name from the convent that was one of the first important buildings in Salta — and which had previously chosen that name out of a hat. To the passer-by the convent presents itself as an imposing white-walled building in the colonial style with an eighteenth-century main entrance magnificently carved by Indians: but its outward appearance is quite immaterial to the nuns, who are a closed order. Salta has religion like it has tradition, both acutely and anciently; and General Martín Miguel de Guémes is still the most important man in town, even though he died in 1821.

Just below the Cerro San Bernado, Guémes sits atop his charger on his monument, a rough monolith of grey stone the height of a house. On the eve of 17 June, the day he died from a royalist bullet, the people of Salta eat, drink and sing in his honour, and a guard of gauchos stands all night beneath him — inheritors of the tradition of his gaucho freedom-fighters who used guerrilla tactics to great effect against the Spanish royalist troops in the years of conflict that followed Argentina's assumption of independence in 1810. A romantic figure in every sense, he is remembered every time a gaucho dons the Salta poncho — red, with bands of mourning black. Nor are there any prouder-looking gauchos than those of the north-west — especially when wearing their traditional *guardamontes*, stiff rawhide shields against thorns, that stand out from the horse's side like wings.

From the monument, the street called General Martín Miguel de Guémes leads into town. Where other roads may have to make do with dust or pot-holes, this one is lined with flowering trees set in lawns, and the council is growing sweet peas on the traffic island. The houses are not doing a very good job at concealing their affluence. One is in Moorish style, with blue and white tiles and a minaret; another has its swimming pool visible. There is a good selection of discreet bars to the windows, double garages and balconies dripping flowers on to the exotic plants in the gardens below. In the centre of the street is a thirty-foot cross, presumably to strengthen the connection between God and Mammon. They are "traditional families" who live here in the scent of cut grass and roses — and also families who are engaged in becoming traditional by means of a sufficient application of australs.

If you had followed the General Martín Miguel de Guémes into town that spring morning, the August after I had ridden across Patagonia, you would have found me sitting at a café table on the main plaza, the Plaza 9 de Julio.

That morning in Salta was sallow, the hills farther off like ghosts in the hazy air. The Cerro San Bernado, being nearer, managed a clear outline, edged in yellow dawn. The dust cloud hanging over the outer city had spent the night in a vain attempt to settle, only to be stirred up by the buzzing cars and squawling motorbikes for another day. For me, the sun came into the plaza along with a tray of freshly squeezed orange juice, fragrant coffee and *medialunas* — rather solid croissants — from the Victoria Plaza Hotel.

All Argentine towns are proud of their plaza, but Salta has more reason than most. Except where the white cathedral spreads its steps, all the side pavements are under colonnades. The old town hall, with white arches and belltower, fronts the cathedral with its twin towers and blue dome. Those two buildings and General San Martín were the most enduring things in the square, apart from the hole.

The hole was a large round hole in the pavement, full of wires, in front of the women's committee offices — "La Secretaria de la Mujer, distrito Salta" — on the corner of Belgrano street (Manuel Belgrano was another of the founding fathers of independent Argentina). The hole opened up every morning like a shop, along with a cupboard full of more wires, also belonging to the telephone company. One engineer would go down the hole, another stand at the cupboard and they clipped, snipped and put back together again all morning; communicating or failing to communicate with utter devotion to the powers of tiny currents of electricity until it was time for lunch. And siesta. Every day. The tale of human misery and frustration on the other end of the wires was untold, but so it tends to be with Argentine telephones, which — like the railways — were once run by the British, and seem to have changed hands minus the proper instructions for working them.

In the central garden of the plaza, as in plaza upon plaza throughout the country, General San Martín was mounted on the horse which carried him across the Andes to victory against the Spanish royal power in 1817; and a plate on him saying, "Hear the sacred cry of Liberty! Liberty! Liberty!" He was grander and much more important than the hole, but not so revealing about the plaza, which was made up of little things and unflamboyant happenings that at first went unnoticed. I could see them around me as I looked up from my work at the café table. If I stayed there all day the waiters had no objection, any more than to the saleswoman doing her accounts three tables down.

In fact, I had no choice but to look up, given the succession of poor folk — old and young, but mostly children — who came begging and selling round the plaza with a not-quite regularity that defied analysis. The more I met, the more I thought that I was not really looking at them as I ought. Occupied with the brief embarrassment as I got out my money, I had been ignoring them as individuals. So I began to watch them and I began to watch the plaza.

Most, though not quite all, of the plaza poor have the jet-black hair that is the sign of Indian blood somewhere in them. There are beggars, who may be rather casual or much in earnest, like one shuffling old man who cannot manage many yards at a stretch and to whom the younger beggars sometimes give alms. The occasional petty hawker, like the cheerful huckster selling rough wooden boxes of Jujuy strawberries or the ageing, unsuccessful man with leather bags, spends as little time in the plaza as possible — unlike the myriad shoeshine boys and the newspaper sellers. It is to be wondered at how a country that habitually turns its attention away from the television as soon as the news comes on, can possibly consume so many newspapers. I can count six newspaper and magazine kiosks in the square, plus the quantities of people who seem to spend the day carrying bundles of newspapers from one place to another. Some individual paper sellers only carry one newspaper which, from its dog-ears, is probably recycled.

One paper seller with a gold earring seems to have a whole family of sellers associated with her, and to depend in her turn on the girl at the corner kiosk, who in the hierarchy of these things ranks as a considerable capitalist. Wearing thick socks and an anorak in the blazing sun, dangling a specimen newspaper in her outstretched hand, the old woman is toothless and constantly chewing without putting anything between her gums; but she has liquid brown eyes looking out from their hollows, seeing far beyond the plaza; and when she passes close to, I see that her face is not so old, after all. She has a cheerfulness in her poverty that is typical of Salta, where a good many people are very poor but do not seem to have been required to lose their dignity because of it. For instance, there is a pair of rather happy-looking tramps, a couple who never beg but come to get water at the plaza tap and lie comfortably in the sun with a bottle between them. I can hardly see the woman's face, she is so slumped: but he is in his prime — lean and sunburnt, with a blue knitted cap and trousers rolled to the knee, so that he looks like a corsair.

Having returned her papers to the corner capitalist, the old paper-woman takes her break at one of the tables before the Hotel Salta, the most prestigious hotel in town, with two dark-haired girls, a dark-haired boy and a large ice-cream, which they all share — passing it round with scrupulous equality. The white-coated waiter leaves them to it and vanishes into the hotel without disdain, for the waiters and prosperous street-sellers treat the poor almost like fellow professionals, providing change for them and behaving charitably, as long as it does not interfere with the custom.

Change is a perpetual problem, for Argentina's raging inflation means there are never enough of the right notes. In Salta, a lot of the money given away is not national currency at all, but *bonos*, provincial bonds printed to raise money for local government projects — useless outside the province and not always acceptable within it. People are always rushing out to ask for change, even stopping complete strangers in the street. The people who have the biggest problem are people like me: I need lots of small notes to give away, and nobody gives me any. On top of all this, there is a great deal of interchanging of bank-notes for its own sake among the plaza poor. They are always folding them, unfolding and swapping them — though they get no richer because of it.

As I sit there writing and watching, one hundred australs is the going rate for the sort of inconsequential tip that can be easily extracted. It is the equivalent of about fifteen cents US, and the fact that it was worth sixteen times as much when I first came to Argentina five months before, is ancient history now. As a comparison, it is one-fifth of the fee for thoroughly cleaning a car inside and out. However, when the children with Indian hair and ragged clothes run down the arcades to the established citizens at the café tables, crying, *"Cien australes, cien australes"*, it is not always money that changes hands. If you have the bowls of peanuts and crisps that are the standard accompaniments to a beer, or an unfinished tray of *picadas* (titbits), it is acceptable to offer them to a child who — depending on the vibes of the situation — will either take one or two politely, or scoop up the lot into paper napkins and carry them off down the road, munching. A strict rule among beggars is never take anything until you have asked for it and got the all-clear. Today a beggar asked for bread and received the contents of the breadbasket. This, I think, is frowned on by the waiters, since the basket commonly provides much more bread and grisini than people can eat, and these are passed on to future customers. I have seen a child sat at a table and fed an entire meal by tourists, but the poverty does not usually appear as an undernourished look in the children, as much as in the adults.

There is also the technique of putting down a holy picture about double the size of a postage stamp on the table, returning later to pick up picture and/or money. For is it not written: "*Cast Ye your Holy Picture upon the Café Table, and It shall be Returned to You Again, Yea, Plus a Few Extra Australs. For Behold, not Even a True Believer Knoweth What to do with An Holy Picture Double the Size of a Postage Stamp, and Willingly Will He pay to Get Rid Of It*"? It is a method common elsewhere, but less so in the Plaza 9 de Julio, probably because the cathedral is just across the square, and the most religiously inclined beggars tend to hang out there, especially when the Festival of the Lord and Virgin of the Miracle is approaching.

Both the cathedral and the wedding-cake church of San Francisco, a block or two away, date their present buildings from the later years of the last century. The church boasts what is said to be the tallest church tower in Latin America. However, in the ecclesiastical stakes, the cathedral is two heads in front, thanks to El Señor y Virgen del Milagro.

No one who has heard the story of the origins of Lujan will be surprised to hear that the holy lady and gentleman ended up at Salta in 1692 by chance — or, as it is sometimes called, divine intervention. In a glorious prophecy of the future condition of the Argentine postal system, two large boxes containing the images were dispatched from Spain to the cathedral at Córdoba, but got lost and ended up in Peru, where the men of Salta discovered them and brought them back. While they were in Salta there was an earthquake; people paraded the images through the streets, and the earthquake immediately stopped. The Córdoba authorities were so impressed that they agreed to the holy objects remaining in Salta as a tribute to the miracle, since when El Señor y Virgen have been attracting crowds of up to 80,000 to their two-week festival at the beginning of September, extra priests being drafted in from all over Argentina to cope with the rush of confessions.

The first Saturday morning I sat in the plaza, I heard a distant repetition of music — and down the street came a procession, in honour of the Virgen de Copa Cabana. She was a doll with a blank where a face should be, dressed in a white ballgown. Adorned with locks of human hair and a crown like a beer-bottle opener, she was carried shoulder-high among bright banners and serious Indian faces to the sound of trumpets — to be precise, two trumpets, one cornet and something that looked as if it might grow up to be a tuba, all of whom alternated the same short tune over and over again to the rhythm of a thin drummer with a fat bass drum and a fat drummer with a thin side drum.

It was early in the year, as yet a grudging spring — the plane leaves small and emerging drily as dull green pastel. But already the sun was hot: a little girl in the procession had pulled her anorak over her head to ward off the glare, and the fat drummer had to keep his rhythm going one-handed while he wiped the sweat from his forehead.

With the exception of one obligatory Salta gaucho, trudging along behind in his red and black poncho, most of the people in the procession came from the local Bolivian community — the border is less than 300 kilometres north of Salta. What came into that comfortable, European-style plaza was a minor invasion from an older, more native Latin America. The young girl dancers at the head of the procession wore the Bolivian bowler hat along with lots of frills and vividly coloured short skirts, which they twirled demurely above two pairs of knickers for extra decorum.

Apart from the hat and the olive skins, they could have led a parade anywhere, but the youths who followed were a different matter, for they had about them that ritual masochism which comes to the surface at festivals from Mexico downwards. It was masochism in frills; they wore ruffled sleeves of tulle and sequined catsuits of red, black and blue. But they were strong and swarthy, stamping their feet, flinging their arms to heaven, doing Cossack kicks, exorting each other to ever greater efforts, their faces streaming with sweat and contorted with the effort of something that was more like a penance than a dance. Leaping, twisting, shivering their arms like demented snakes, the boys blew whistles that shrieked through the music and the traffic queue, piling up behind and growling past when it would — ancient pickup trucks that looked as if they needed a lift themselves, buses boasting chrome that was brilliant in patches and pop-baroque sign-writing, scooters laden with Saturday-morning vegetables to the point of extreme wobbliness.

The procession had its own retinue of decrepit vehicles, pickups behind with anything that could possibly be festive tied to the bonnets and roofs. Toys and dolls were prominent — Dumbo the stuffed elephant rolling his eyes and leaning drunkenly on one bonnet, a dumb blonde doll in a picture hat obstructing the driver's vision on another; a rather grubby Pink Panther; a model galleon sailing proudly on the roof of a pickup truck. Several cars had the family silver especially well tied on, supplemented by a few prized consumer goods and tapestries in gaudy Indian weaves. Last came a station wagon that had been grand when it was new, long ago, with a four-foot giant panda on the bonnet accompanied by a little panda, both wearing the miserable expression of one who has good reason to believe that his stuffing is coming out. The engine, spluttering in sympathy, soon gave up: pandas, station wagon and all were left stranded at the kerb as the procession swept on. Someone threw confetti, which the dancers tossed off in their movement, but it crowned the musicians with a snow of blue, white and pink spangles.

Such was the observance of the Bolivians, but by the side of the paved road south I met Miguel Fontt, whose kingdom of heaven was of a different kind. I had hired a car to drive to the wine town of Cafayate, and he came into my life as a gaunt hitchhiker on the edge of the plain, just before the mountains. He was an elderly man carrying an old grey jacket and a rather floppy blue suitcase which, when opened, had almost nothing in it but a bulging, well-worn black briefcase, containing a Bible, tracts and a typed book of hymns he had written himself. We had not gone very far before he started to sing them.

Miguel Fontt came from Mar del Plata, and his background was mostly Spanish, with a tincture of French. He had worked in films when he was young, he said. I was politely incredulous. Yes, he had danced in them. Then he had been a businessman, then a waiter in a bar in Buenos Aires. That was a hard life. He had been ill — the ears, the head, the eyes, the stomach, the heart, the feet (he patted each in turn with enthusiasm for their awful condition); he had suffered from seven separate, chronic and awful illnesses. Till one day there came to him a revelation — like Paul on the road to Damascus. A voice told him to leave his wife and four children, and become a missionary. Immediately his illnesses disappeared. In the last thirty years as a Pentecostal evangelist he had only seen his children three times.

"I made a song about how awful you feel without God — that's me, when I was ill," said Miguel Fontt. He sang it, in penetrating tones. "And that's another thing — before I was converted I couldn't sing at all!"

He had travelled in Uruguay, Paraguay and Brazil — he had no home of any kind, he said. He had been in Chile: that was a paradise, though the poverty was even worse than here. There they had a very fine fruit, like sausages, but with cream inside — called *cogiles*. That was indeed Eden, I said. It was fruit he meant, not sausages? Yes, fruit.

"*Cogiles*, like *copigo*, but *copigo* aren't good. But *cogile* — what a tree! They are delicious. In Chile you get up in the morning — and till the time you go to sleep in the evening, there is no need to feel hungry. You find grapes, apples, pears, plums; you find *coges*, you find *copigo*, you find *diguena, quidena*. You need no more. Oooh, yai, yai, yai! *Cogile* are in November, December. Fruit of the field. *Rico, muy rico*."

He was an enthusiast for life. Everything to him was *rico* (delicious) or *lindo* (a word Argentines use constantly to approve everything of any charm, interest or attraction — a passionate equivalent of the English use of "nice"). He sang, "As the flowers of the field, Man needs Christ." He amplified, "He is the Lord. I repeat, the Lord is Jesus. As the flowers need sun, so we need Jesus." He went back to singing:

> As sheep need a shepherd,
> So we need,

We need,
O! O! Señor,
We need Him.

I wondered how I might take his photograph without giving offence, but when I stopped to take a picture of some exotic blossom, he made no objection to being included. At the next halt, he bounded down the rocks to the river and I had to shout at him to dissuade him from attempting a six-foot jump to pose on an island in the middle. Instead, he climbed a large boulder and raised his arms to heaven. When I had taken the picture, he bounded up the bank again and pointed to a tree.

"Here are leaves to eat." He nibbled something non-existent, then tore off a handful from a willow-like bush and munched them. "This is the *dulce* — the sweet. There is an *amargo*, a bitter kind, too."

I tried it — the leaves were indeed sweet and spicy.

"And this is for tea. *Lindo, los vegetales*. Veg-eta-belles! *Lindo*. I am not a vegetarian, but vegetarians eat nothing else. They come upon a vegetable and they say, '*Lindo!*'"

"I see."

"How lucky is Man, with so many good things!"

We drove on, with him singing. There are two roads from Salta to Cafayate, each quite different from the other. Mine plunged through gorges and wound among great red cliffs. In the company of the evangelist it took on a biblical quality: it was a desert in which a holy man might be tempted. One of the most extraordinary canyons was the Garganta del Diavolo, a dramatically narrow fissure climbing up from a sandy floor with a twisted tree to a far-above patch of sky. In "The Devil's Throat" stood Miguel Fontt and had his picture taken, for he had got the idea that I was an enthusiastic photographer of evangelists, and was, therefore, equally enthusiastic himself.

At the boundary of Cafayate, there were three black crosses set above the road. Up the bank he went, for he had the joy of the truly innocent. I have scarcely ever met anyone so endearing. The crosses were old wooden things, stark against the sky. He stood beneath, raised his arms like Moses calling the flood; and, for a moment, was one with his symbols. Now the road followed a river winding in streamlets through its flood plain. The arid landscape was full of colour — white edges to the water, grey pebbles, yellow grasses and a fringe of vivid green trees beyond. There were red rocks, black rocks, rocks bleached by the sun on the mountain. We passed obelisks and columns of rock, cliff ramparts; dead black trees like stumps of rotting teeth studding dunes of intensely white sand that flashed with flakes of mica and blew in clouds across the road. At last we came to the valley and, beneath an avenue of bare but splendid trees, to Cafayate.

Miguel Fontt insisted on being dropped on the outskirts of town. But before he went, he put into my hand an obscure and greeny photograph of himself preaching to remember him by, and said grace for the fellowship of the journey.

"Read the Bible, read the Bible," he abjured, as I drove off.

As I went to bed that night in my single-storey hotel, I wondered if anyone in the town had woken up a Catholic and tonight was going to sleep a Protestant because of the evangelist.

"Evangelists have just begun to come here, but we don't

see them on the plaza. We don't like them very much: they stay on the edge of town," Martha told me. She was a robust, smiling teacher of English, the daughter of the landlady of my hotel, which was on the plaza where the evangelists feared to tread. We sat beneath the hotel colonnade drinking coffee, while a street-sweeper brushed the kerb with a *palmeira* — a besom of a single palm-frond — and the morning sun glittered in the showers from sprinklers on the plaza lawns. Cafayate is quite a small town, but the plaza seemed larger because of the low buildings around it, dominated by the creamy-yellow church.

"When I was in England, I went to the Anglican church, not the Catholic one. I only wish we had it here," said Martha. "Our priests are too powerful. There was a casino in Cafayate once, and many people came to the town because of it. The hotels were full, the restaurants full — but then Monsignor went to the government and said the casino should be closed. Lo and behold, it was closed. And still is. The position on contraception here is terrible. I'm a teacher and I see the results — girls of fifteen, fourteen, even twelve, with babies. Of course, abortion is illegal."

In the plaza, a man on a bicycle crossed himself as he passed the church and a priest in brown corduroys, brisk about God's uncompromising errands. Argentine dogs went about their self-important but inessential occupations, tails held high.

"Here is a very calm people," said Martha. "We don't run." The sun beat down, flattening the dogs. "It is a very kind people here. All the same, I wish I was in Europe now. Here, we are going downhill. People come to the door and ask for stale bread, anything — and it's getting worse."

As a teacher of English, after seven years at university

and two years at a language school in Cambridge, she reckoned her daily salary at the price of two packets of cigarettes. It all went to her nanny, whom she paid over the odds. Like most middle-class Argentines she had a maid, which she could afford because her husband was well paid as the chief wine-maker for Etchart, which, with the firm of Michel Torino, is one of the two leading vineyards in Cafayate, and which had won five gold medals at Bordeaux the year before.

In fact, both companies make delicious wines. Etchart's "Cafayate" is a powerful red, quite grand at its best, while Michel Torino's "Cabernet Don David" from the Bodega La Rosa is a smooth Cabernet Sauvignon of European style. Both vineyards produce delicious and evocative whites from the Torrontes grape, which is of Spanish origin, and — certainly at this quality — unique to the region: Etchart's is more sophisticated, Torino's fruitier.

Generally, the taste of Argentine wines is more Italian than French: and so is the general attitude of the consumers, who see wine as something to be drunk rather than revered. (The middle classes, at least, tend to be quite abstemious, and you will often find half-bottles of wine or — even more likely — soft drinks on restaurant tables.) Though wine is also made elsewhere in the foothills of the Andes, notably, in La Rioja — and wine-growing is developing in Rio Negro in the north of Patagonia — the main Argentine production is in the city and province of Mendoza, across the country from Buenos Aires. Mendoza produces everything from vinegar to vintage (as well as olives), including many enjoyable wines and a few that are also distinguished, notably red, rosé and white from the house of Weinert. Though the production of Cafayate and the neighbouring Calchaquí valley is much smaller than Mendoza, the area keeps a reputation for quality, and there a number of interesting wines enjoy the benefits of sun, altitude and the local micro-climate.

I drove out of Cafayate through vineyards in which the vines were grown like flat umbrellas on tall stems, cash providing its own shade. They were leafless as yet, the sandy soil light brown below them and the mountains, hanging above the town, a pale yellow-grey. In that time before the summer rains, the colour was washed out of the landscape by the dryness and the brilliant sun.

Some kilometres further off, at the town of San Carlos, the road turned to dust. For a while the river Calchaquí kept its immediate valley fertile, with some meadows and orchards; but as the road strayed upwards away from it the landscape became bare, thorny and ever more deserted, with cliffs eroded into fantastic sandstone teeth. The few houses I saw were mud-coloured, as if they had been persuaded with difficulty to provide a little temporary accommodation, and were anxious to return to the earth from which they were made.

The road got worse. It careered around cliffs and boulders, over gigantic sand-dunes drained of colour by the white sun. Bits of it dropped off the edges of precipices, other bits jumped up and hit the car sneakily, but hard. It was made of mud, boulders and villainously sharp flints — and it was the flints that worried me.

Sixty kilometres or so into nowhere, there was a flap-flap from the back nearside corner. A puncture. While I was changing the wheel, a pickup drew up. "Problems?" "No!" I said gaily. A VW came along. "Problems?" "No, not at all — just finishing, thanks."

"We've just had two punctures in half an hour," said the VW, and drove on with a second spare on its roof-rack. It was ominous, and in that empty landscape there was no sign of *gomerias*, those tyre-repair shacks found all along most roads, being to the bald tyres of many Argentine cars what meat is to the Argentine stomach: i.e. frequently and profoundly necessary.

Sure enough, some thirty kilometres or so further on, in mid-afternoon, there was a flap-flap from the other back corner. I pulled into the side and meditated. I had never had this problem with a bicycle, but the bike was in Buenos Aires. The map showed a village ahead: there was nothing to do but start walking.

The Calchaquí valley is said to have been populous before the Spaniards came, but for me it was a desert. Nobody was going my way, but I flagged down the first of two car-loads of overheated Argentine tourists travelling in convoy in the other direction — two fat men in front, very red-faced, and two fat women behind, crammed into the back seat as if it were a corset.

On hearing my predicament the women said "Tut-tut" and the men rather less. Had they come from Molinos? "Certainly." Was it far? They failed to take the hint. "Not at all. Twenty kilometres or so." I did my best to look fortunate and they drove on. I had the same conversation with the second car-load, who looked worried at the news of a double set of punctures and drove off hooting at the car in front. I wondered whether they might come back and give me a lift even if it meant booting out mother-in-law into the sun that was frazzling me. But the tooting faded into the distance, and I went on.

I walked a long way. Occasionally there was a mud

ruin. Three swarthy roughs in a pickup came towards me and passed. I waved. They stopped, grudgingly, and were shamed into admitting that Molinos was indeed ahead, and that for all they knew it might even include a *gomeria*. They drove on.

The sun lowered and shone into my face. I took a detour into nowhere, down something that looked as if it was a path, and scrambled up over rocks back to the road at the other end. After some kilometres winding over the sandhills, an old woman carrying a bag approached.

"Is Molinos far?" I asked her.

"Oh yes, yes. A long way on foot. You should go in your car." She grinned encouragingly, but without many teeth. I said I had one, but it had broken down. "Oh yes, very far, and there are hills." I left her before she could go into detail about how the nearest *gomeria* was a hundred miles away, the repairman was ill, and had run out of rubber solution.

I trod on. Waves of scent wafted from the yellow *churqui* thorn trees on the verge, with their brilliant mimosa-like blossom. Waves of dust wafted from the road. No cars passed.

The road neared the river again; there were more mud houses and an agreeable smallholder leaning on his garden gate. "Los Molinos? Oh yes, there is everything at Los Molinos — hotel, *gomeria*, everything." To him it was Paris, Rome, Vienna all rolled into one.

After fourteen kilometres I came to Los Molinos in the dusk: the *gomeria* man was part time, had almost run out of petrol with the nearest filling station fifty-five kilometres away at Cachi, and was out. Fortunately, there was also the promised hotel.

It was not until the next morning that I was able to persuade the *gomeria* man into action with the offer of a supply of petrol from my tank. We banged along in his old Fiat, which had most of the dashboard hanging out on its wires. Did many tourists have problems with their tyres? Yes. Did he have problems with his tyres? No. Why? No idea: it was just something that happened to tourists.

When we got there, the *gomeria* man worked with the minimum of tools. He broke the seal of the first tyre by driving over it: and of the second, by putting it under the rear jacking point and jacking the car up on it. Then he found the leak by listening, checked that there was no second puncture in a drainage ditch nearby, and repaired the inner tube and pumped the tyre up with a footpump. The second tyre had had the valve ripped off, so he sold me his spare tube, which was several sizes bigger than mine. The punctures were not flints but thorns. He warned me to drive in the middle of the road, for the *espinas* were on the edges.

North of Los Molinos, the road wound along the hills beside the river valley, with more red-mud houses following the brown irrigation ditch from which they drew their water. For all their poverty, the huts kept their pretensions to the colonial style of architecture: along their fronts attempts had been made at constructing colonnades, with mud columns shaped according to the skill and perseverance of the sculptor — some clean-cut with neo-classical pediments, others bodges of vagueness. I still saw the odd patch of vines, and fields ready for the local cash crop, chilli peppers; but the road never seemed to tire of going upwards, and after Cachi, whose pleasant plaza was full of the sound of water (a mountain stream ran down its gutter), the road went higher still, among the peaks themselves, the vast, implacable, unforgettable Andes.

My way ran parallel with the Chilean border a couple of hundred kilometres away — and I saw from the map that, in all that space, there were salt flats and mountains but no more than two roads. It was beautiful and desolate. The *cardón* cactus dotting the slopes like spiny hat-stands made it more desolate still: there is nothing in the world as lonely as a hat-stand without hats, even in the Andes. The *cardón* is protected in the national parks, but you can still buy boxes and other things made of it. I have even seen a dinner table. The church at Cachi is partly built of it, for it grows four or five metres high. The wood is unmistakable, being deathly white and full of holes, like timber lace.

Travel north and up to San Antonio de los Cobres and you cross the single-track railway line to Chile, to whose construction a young Marshal Tito is supposed to have contributed. Going so high is like the body growing old. As the landscape grows scrawny, the coverings that were once so thick reduce to patches — in all the vast panorama of crag and desert there are only a few blades of grass, a hollow of icy snow, a few wizened bushes, a tiny distant valley trying hard to be green and managing a bilious yellow. There is the odd mine and oil well here, a few hamlets along the railway, a footpath with an unguessable destination and the occasional, lonely stone stock-pen with its archaeological collection of ruined walls. It is all part of the area's majesty, but it also means people: when the tourist *Train to the Clouds* comes to the end of its outward journey at the alarming Viaducto la Polvorilla (over 4000 metres up), thirty or forty children with bleating infants in their arms come crowding in for a tourist photograph and

277

*cien australes*; there are boys of seven or eight, shivering in tracksuits and holding out all they have to sell — a box of stones; and weather-beaten women bedecked with woollen and alpaca sweaters as if they were a washing line, offering little knitted llamas, gloves, bootees. The tourists are like lords for ten minutes, dismissing with a wave of the hand, buying cheaply with another. No time to appraise the goods or the work that has gone into them — just a ten-minute intrusion of frenzy into a world where there is hardly any meaningful time at all among the biting winds and the dust devils.

Also, you often see a patch of ground that is stony and far too small, with rickety goal posts, but is a football pitch nevertheless. Some pitches must be relics of the men who built the railway half a century and more ago, with only ghosts to play on them; for the others, you can only wish them a full team and someone to play against once in a while.

Further north still, towards the borders of Bolivia, the land is less barren and sometimes lower, but the people of the *puna* or *altiplano* still chew coca leaves and drink coca tea as an antidote to altitude. The Coyas, who are among those living here, are rather small and dark and have a taste for clothes in very bright, pure hues. As I drove along the largely deserted Pan-American Highway up the broad flood-plain of the Río Grande, a brilliant pin-head of colour in the distance would turn out to be a brown-cloaked horseman, who could easily have been from the borders of Mongolia; a blue and scarlet shepherdess with a few sheep or goats; or a woman with a green poncho and an Andean hat, carrying a load of leeks on her back, so that the leaves looked as if they were part of the decoration of her clothes. The frequent vividness of the dress echoes a colour sense that is already in the landscape itself. The towering rock faces may contain light greys, smoky greens, ochres, reds; over them the mountain skies are a blue so deep and transparent that it would be an artist's fantasy elsewhere; the earth is leached brown and the river holds pools of white light; the weeping willows are a green as vivid and clear as the sound of a single trumpet. (More than that, they move as if they were full of weasels. I never understood Kenneth Grahame's title until I saw the spring willows of Purmamarca, with their feeling of small animals disturbed within.)

But the greatest wonder of these high Andes is when the chasms and cliffs are gone, leaving an elemental landscape — earth and sky, hills, stones, sun, wind. The vegetation looks like spindly heathers, tufts among the stones, but everything close to is made irrelevant by the vast scale of mountains sweeping down like lawns, their contours like the folds of a giant inflatable in the last stages of an interestingly uneven collapse. With the sheen of distance on them, the Andes have a smoothness, as if made of suede, and cry out to be stroked.

"I was very fond of the wind. Sometimes it was so strong, you could hardly breathe against it: but I love it and I dream of it."

Carlos Hugo Aparicio was a plumping, genial man of energy, with a shining scalp from either side of which tufts of white hair waved out like the wings of Mercury. He had something of the housemaster in his manner, and something of the professor too as we talked in his book-lined study in the Salta library, which he superintended as well as being the author of three books of poetry, a novel and short stories. A light that had been white in the street came yellow through the brown curtains — an even yellower one fell from the table lamp warming the papers on his desk. The room had large round brown chairs and sofas: and the man himself was brown — in clothes and in skin — like some earth spirit come up from the dusty land. So he had: his childhood had been spent in La Quiaca, on the Bolivian border, where his father was a customs man; and which he described to me:

"We had a bridge between Argentina and Bolivia. It was crowded every minute of the day. The place was always full of wind and people. There I was a child, not yet seven years old — unable to write or read, but listening to the tangos on the radio from Buenos Aires. My mother loved them — and they fascinated me. Sadness, nostalgia, homesickness — the tango has everything about us. In a sense we *are* the tango: it is our human music, let's say.

"I wanted to know Buenos Aires. Well, what I had was school and football. I loved football and I loved to study. I wrote my first poems at seven, though I didn't know they were poems then: a song to my mother and one to the flag. I was a patriot then. I loved my flag and my national anthem; I most patriotically hated the Bolivian people. I had an aunt living across the border, and I cried when I had to go and see her. Now, first of all, I love mankind.

"I used to dress myself up in my best clothes and go to the station to wait for the trains from the south. They brought me everything that I loved best — books, magazines, records — oh, and the noise, and the feeling of distance!"

Salta is known for its poetry and music. Apart from dead writers like Juan Carlos Davalos and Manuel Castillo,

Señor Aparicio told me that he could easily muster a hundred young poets in their twenties and gave me a slim collection of local work that included forty living poets who were more established. The strength of the tradition is founded in the *copla*, a verse form of four eight-syllable lines which arrived from Spain via Peru in the earliest years of Argentine colonisation. Some songs dating back to those times are still sung. Others inspired a revolution in Argentine popular music in the Fifties and Sixties. The *copla* unites popular and intellectual poetry, Señor Aparicio thought, more closely than anywhere else. "The poorer people worship their poets and musicians," he told me.

"My father was a gendarme, and he wrote *coplas*," he told me. "At every party, carnival, religious feast; in pain, or in joy, they sing *coplas*. All human destiny is there, in those four-line verses. My God! I envy them."

The *copla* is primarily music for special occasions, but singer-poets and folk groups also perform in the *peñas* of Salta and its northern neighbour, Jujuy. *Peñas* are a mixture of nightclub and restaurant, folk club and drinking place, something that has hardly been seen in England since the music-hall was developing in the days of the young Victoria. Their artists are important enough for a number of them to have received special attention from the authorities during the military persecution, which in traditionally-minded Salta was particularly bad. The most notorious case was that of the leading singer, Cagrune, shot as he rode his horse from Jujuy to Salta; but a number of musicians and poets had to escape as best they could. Aparicio quoted me the words of the musician Atahualpa Upanki, who lives in France: "I think, therefore I am exiled."

"We have never been free. I feel that," said Aparicio. "You don't see military people in the street nowadays. They are very unpopular indeed. If they did go about like anyone else, there could be a battle. There is a deep-seated feeling that most of them are guilty of many deaths."

He had been on the blacklist himself, but had escaped trouble. Now there were other things to worry about.

"Our economic situation now is terrible," said Aparicio. "Lately, the poetry of social conscience has come to the fore. The poet is one more citizen, so it must." And he read me one of his poems that he had translated that day, to the shoe-shine boys of the plaza:

> Shoemaker, make the shoes of soft light
> For a child that went to school shoeless,
> Longing in tears for mine.
> And so longing for my sweets, my trousers, my
>     overcoat —
> Mum, don't look at my eyes,
> Instead, look at these boys.
> Shoemaker, shoemaker, all your work is worth
>     nothing
> If you don't make shoes for this poor, poor kid.

Sitting at my table on the plaza, I have been granted immunity by the shoe-shine boys, on account of wearing sandals. All except the smallest walk with their heads askew, so as to spy out the prospects under the tables; each one has the same home-made wooden box to carry his brushes, rags and tins: otherwise they are various.

One round-cheeked boy has a dirty face, bottom hanging out of his jeans, and the sleeves of his once off-white pullover in tatters. A tiny one with whom I am getting quite friendly, since he comes to see my computer when he has nothing better to do, has *scolar* written across his box: and if he only had a brush-up himself and a school uniform could easily pass for the first-form swot.

Another could be the Head Boy. He is a trim teenager with a brisk manner, who tells me that there is an Association of Shoe-shine Boys. It has a President, and he himself is the Honorary Secretary. There are some 2000 shoe-shine boys in the city as a whole, aged seven and upwards, and they have to belong to the Association, which is seven months old and has a monthly membership subscription equivalent to about five shines. (What they get for a shine is up to the customer, but it is usually the magic *cien australes* or a bit more.) He is such a neat, determined young man that I ask him what he is going to do with his life. He says he is going to be a militar.

There may be six to a dozen or more boys prowling the plaza at once, and small demand for their services; but I saw one lad strike lucky with a man with an insignificant sandy moustache eroding at the edges. While his shoes were being done, the customer stared into the distance like Columbus discovering America, with never a glance down except when required to transfer the other shoe to the footstool. Not only did he get his shoes cleaned but he also enjoyed a brief moment as monarch, with a subject at his feet.

The boy went to it with a vigour, born not only of a desire for money but of relief from boredom (with brushes, with hands, with bits of rag and strips of old jeans), until the dusty shoes shone like a pair straight from the shop in Buenos Aires, which is the eternal home and Mecca

of everything a fine shoe ought to be. For his work —
which was excellent — the boy got the equivalent of his
*cien australes* in the local *bonos*, and took them off to a
trio of other shoeshine boys in the shade at the corner of
the colonnade. There they crouched comparing notes and
making noises like owls, with their hands.

The shadows were longer, and the traffic was beginning
to increase. Among the cars were Mercedes, BMWs and
some splendid period pieces. Taking a stroll to Salta's
best delicatessen, I saw that a bottle of an obscure brand
of imported Scotch cost about 700 shoe-shines, $110.

Ignoring a poster for "An Evening of Folklore by the
Circle of Sub-officers of the Police Federation of Argentina"
at the Cultural Centre, I made my way to the corner of the
plaza, to be welcomed at the office of the Salta women's
committee, La Secretaria de la Mujer.

The director looked rather different from most of the
feminists I was used to, being a theatrical blonde with
green eye-shadow turned up at the corners and silver
nails: and the striking thing about her and her friends
was not their power of attack, but warmth of personality.
They were the nicest possible people, but it seemed that in
Argentina the fight for women's rights was, as yet, hardly
on the agenda. There were women's committees like theirs
in some other provinces, but by no means all, they said.
Politics in Argentina meant politics for men; their aim was
to integrate women into this, get them out of the house into
work, and get them to educate their sons. They were not sure
of their precise membership in Salta but they estimated three
to five hundred women or so; and they showed me neatly
drawn charts of their twenty-five sub-groups and twelve

sub-committees. They could not remember the name of whatever Latin-American international movement it was that they were affiliated to, but Margarita could.

Margarita came over. She was a different creature from the others, older than them, short and fat, and with features that looked as if they had been applied in rolls; her woman's rights seems to be fairly intact, since she was president of a bank. In her bag she had a President Menem pocket calendar, which was printed in gold. Looking around I saw that the posters and symbols of the Peronist party were everywhere. It turned out that all the women's committees were Peronist, subscribing to the twenty principles of Peronism.

"Twenty commandments?" I asked them, absent-mindedly gazing out of the window at the crowds before the cathedral.

"Twenty principles of Peronism, formulated by Perón himself."

To my surprise, they had no written version, but they could quote me a couple. The first seemed quite inappropriate: "First the Fatherland, second the Movement — and after that the Men". The second one ran: "For a Peronist there is nothing better than another Peronist."

I was wriggling slightly at that when Margarita was joined by her son, Leonard, who spoke good English. He had something of the same coarseness of feature as his mother, a prize-fighter's nose and hair cut close, like an executioner's cap; but he was pleasant to me and looked me in the eye when I asked him what Peronism stood for.

"Peronism has a human and a Christian philosophy," Leonard replied. "It asks for social justice."

"Then," said I, "since there are so many very poor people in Argentina, and also a lot of people who are exorbitantly rich, you will want to take some money from the rich and give it to the poor?"

"To take money from the rich and give to the poor — that's communism! For the Peronist, when everyone has work, that is social justice. Peronism has three slogans — social justice, political sovereignty and economic independence."

"What if there are two people with different jobs — say, one works in a restaurant as a waiter or washer-up, while the other is the president of a bank?" It was perhaps a tactless comparison. "One is very, very poor and the other very, very rich. Is that social justice?"

"This is a great problem for all countries." He listed a few, including my own — and, to my shame, I could only say that it was getting worse in Britain. "It is an intellectual problem. The difficulty is the different cultural level. The answer is education."

I said, "What does a good Peronist think if he sees a teacher very badly paid?"

"A good Peronist works all his life for his country."

It all seemed to be rather short on self-examination and humility. Yet Peronism had carried all the polls before it, and if Argentina was to have a political hope, this was it. Perhaps it had just been a charismatic and clever presidential candidate the Argentines had been voting for — a god out of the party machine, who would absolve the rank and file from any serious thought or responsibility, and save their world without bothering them too much.

Leonard's mother took out the Menem pin-up masquerading as a calendar. On the wall behind me was a Menem election poster, in which he was riding a white charger. Peróns of every age and every degree of authority, beauty and saintliness looked down upon me, the memorabilia of someone who had worked closely with the top levels of the party. On the table by the door, Evita was ever-young, ever-beautiful, sculpted in extra-white perfection. Beside her, Perón himself was not young, but neither was he old — and he was pristine too, not a dirty finger on him. At their breasts were pink roses.

"What is the relationship of Peronism to the military?"

"A good relation. All the militars are Peronists."

"But not so long ago the military killed and tortured people."

"Not really."

"Real enough."

"Different shoes. There was a dirty war in Argentina — they fought the terrorists. Terrorists, subversives, revolutionaries."

"Are you saying that all of the people who disappeared were terrorists?"

"Yes."

"All of them?"

"Yes." Unequivocally. "The terrorists killed many people."

"But I've heard that people were taken for many reasons, sometimes even because they had the wrong sort of haircut."

"I live in this time and I am free: I am not a terrorist." I could have said that he did not have anything like the wrong sort of haircut. "Ordinary people is free. Terrorists — yes, put in prison and kill."

"But without a trial?"

"In a war there are no courts. It's different, a different situation."

"But if you don't go to court, how can you know if it was right to kill them?"

"Have a trial, no!" (To my astonishment, "No, No!" echoed from the women round the table.) "That was the law. Our constitution is Catholic, and the Catholic law says, 'Thou shalt not kill'. Well, it's a different situation. Mrs Perón was President at this time. The law says, 'Destroy terrorism. No prisoners. Destroy it all.' That was the law, signed by the President. The commanders of the three forces took the law. That is not contrary to human rights."

"So you know of nobody wrongfully arrested in Salta?"

"None. In Salta, no: in Tucumán, yes."

"None?"

"In Salta few, more in Tucumán. But in fighting there is no trial, and the law says 'no terrorists'. The militar is a soldier — he takes orders. He can't think, he can't discuss orders."

His mother broke in, "In fighting, no prisoners. Is all dead."

I thought of the bereft mothers parading another plaza in Buenos Aires; of a girl piecing together the bones of innocents in an attempt to discover which innocents they were; and I could go on no longer, without being discourteous. I returned to the original subject I had meant to discuss, aware of the fact that the women had been rather quiet since he started talking — probably because he was the English-speaker, but . . .

"What do you think of the position of women in Argentina?"

"Women are not going to equal the men in Salta. In Argentina as a whole there are women with power. Ninety per cent of this society is macho. But ten per cent of the women is more great than ninety per cent of the men." The women laughed — in fact, I would almost swear that they cooed slightly.

But Leonard and his mother were fidgeting. It was clear that they were in a hurry to go. He was celebrating something. I caught the word *"cumpleaños"*.

"Happy birthday," I said.

Back on the plaza, the shoe-shine boys were deep into a discussion of a new kind of polish out of a bottle, which they squeezed on to their fingers in minute quantities and compared professionally. None of their own shoes were capable of much beautification. They all wore sneakers, often in the last stages of dilapidation. The little one who liked computers came and sat beside me. Yes, he did go to school, he said, but only in the mornings.

A clown in costume passed, selling red roses. In the gardens the swings squeaked to and fro, and birds flew in and out of the bandstand roof. Lying among their bundles, the plaza tramps came to the end of their bottle. Tenderly the man put a cigarette in the woman's mouth and helped her to her feet. Then they, the bottle and the bundles left the plaza, almost entering the grandiose mouth of the Hotel Salta by accident, and wandered off in search of fortune.

That evening the festival of El Señor y Virgen del Milagro began, with loudspeakers in the square relaying the services from the cathedral, shining with gold decoration and brilliantly lit with a prodigal expenditure of religious electricity. Inside it was a mutter of prayer, amplified priestly voices and pre-recorded music — and one woman crawling up the aisle on her knees through a forest of legs.

For her it was a holy offering to God, for me a perversion of humanity.

In the square, dark-haired children tended trays of red toffee-apples. The hot-peanut men had steam whistles on their barrows that drowned the squeals from the swings; and the cathedral not only bonged its great bell, but tinged its illuminated clock. Over the loudspeakers a soprano slid on and off her notes in a wail of devotion.

Will-o'-the-wisp in the dusk were glass-enclosed popcorn stands, with flames inside — each a peripatetic gas stove inside a conservatory. Within, the hills of popcorn were snow-white, almost like relics themselves.

By the telephone hole, which was shut up for the night, I was accosted by a middle-aged, middle-class man with thinning hair, in a state of fury over the latest descent of the austral. *"La Argentina — no America Latina, America latrina!* The other countries are the same. Paraguay has a dictator — that's better, there's no inflation there. What's inflation with you? Five per cent? Here it's that every day.

"Here, he who doesn't work, lives: he who works doesn't. Employees are in a terrible way. And look at *los diputados, los senadores* — a million a month, when other people were earning twenty or thirty thousand. And the national politicians more. *Ladrones*, sons of whores, idiots — that's our government. Crooked as they come — gangsters, the lot of them."

"It may be difficult to be free," I suggested, "but it's better than a military regime, surely?"

"I never had any trouble with them. Never. We've been going down for forty years, and they think inflation can be cured in months. That's the future —" He made a gesture with his hand like someone falling off a mountain.

"What do you do?" I asked him.

"Me? Nothing. I live off commission." Another member of the middle classes came along, and they went off together.

Above the plaza the weather was turning, and clouds hid the stars. There were crowds before the cathedral, moving in and out, standing meekly before it with their prayer books. In the tower, a man struck the great bell with a hammer in time to their penitence. A few spots of rain began to fall.

# APPENDIX

# Cycling and Travelling in Argentina

By this time it should be fairly clear that I find Argentina a wonderful country with wonderful people. When I was there it was also cheap; and hotels and their more economical equivalents, *residencials*, are usually of a reasonable standard. *The South American Handbook* is the best accompaniment to a journey, and the *Insight Guides* to the country as a whole and to Buenos Aires are excellent as background reading. Spring starts in the north-west in mid-August, and progressively later as you go south. Depending on where you are, most leaves are off the trees at the beginning of May.

The most important information for cyclists is the prevailing wind — which is westerly from the Andes to the Atlantic. The calmest period in Patagonia is autumn, but even then you should be extremely wary of planning a route in the other direction. The road surface is another thing that can make the difference between happiness and misery. There is a good number of paved roads, but unpaved ones can be extremely bad, especially if they have not been recently maintained; and they can make progress very slow. Heat can be a problem: and it can be cold in the mountains. Buenos Aires is a pig to cycle in.

Distances between accommodation can be greater than is comfortable for touring: since I travelled with a companion in a car when I was working on the research for the two television programmes, I was able to do some stretches in more than one stage, returning next morning to the end of the previous day's ride. Without this, or local hospitality, a tent is a necessity in some parts. There are a few camp sites, and there is no shortage of space in any case.

Argentine maps are not the most informative in the world, often because there is not a great deal to put on them. The Argentine automobile association, ACA, publish a set which mark their garages (some of whose excellent facilities are restricted to members, including members of other international motoring organizations), but which have no contours. There are a couple of other sets available commercially in Buenos Aires, but I was not able to find any large-scale maps of the kind I normally like to use for cycling, outside the possession of the army.

For the record, my first trip, Lujan to Córdoba was about 844 km (525 miles), though I actually rode only about 750 km (465 miles). The second trip to the sea was about 950 km (590 miles), of which I cycled 875 km (545 miles). The longest day's journey was 186 km (116 miles); and the total distance cycled 1625 km (1010 miles). From Córdoba to my starting point on the Road of the Seven Lakes, about 150 km (93 miles) beyond San Martín de Los Andes, was 1653 km (1027 miles).

# INDEX

Pargoment, Juanita de, 30-1
*parrilla* (grill), 20-2, 65, 68
Partido de San Antonio de Areco, 56
Paso de Indios, 211-12, 232
Patagonia, xiii, 3, 145-253, 292
Patagonian Music School, 237-8
*pato* (game on horseback), 98, 99
*payadores* (gaucho singers), 69
*peñas* (nightclub), 281
Pergamino, 89, 91-4
Perón, Eva, 45, 137, 285, 288
Perón, Isabel, 148
Perón, President Juan Domingo, 45, 74, 78-9, 101, 137, 139, 148, 199, 285, 286
Peronism, 121, 284-9
Peru, 257, 264, 281
*picadas* (bar snacks), 8
*piché* (armadillo), 203
Pigafeta, Francesco, 146
Plate, river, 9
Playa Union, 253
Las Plumas, 216-17, 219-21, 228
poetry, 280-2
police, 25, 54, 56-7, 169
polo, 97, 99
*porteños* (inhabitants of Buenos Aires), 9-10, 18, 20, 29
La Posta de Figeroa inn, 74
*pudu* (tiny deer), 221, 225
Puerto Madryn, 230
*pulpería* Los Ombues, 74, 75-8

La Quiaca, 280
Quichaura, river, 207
Quilmes orphanage, 10-14

rabbit, plastic, 124, 127
radio ham, 231-2
railways, xvi, 75, 79, 89, 96, 120, 189, 191, 193-201, 277;
    Buenos Aires underground, 6
Rawson, 230, 238, 252
Rees, Martha, 244
El Refugio, 221, 223, 225
Los Repollos, 171
ribbon cake, 87
Río Grande, 278
Río Negro, 147, 180, 272
Río Villegas, 168
La Rioja, 272
Road of the Seven Lakes, 146, 150, 154, 293
roads, building and mending, 55, 169, 171, 186, 252;
    roadman, 195-201;
    rough, 164, 170-1, 189, 292
Rosario, 80
roses and rose hips, wild, 155, 156-7, 165, 182
Rowan, Brian and Mari, 176-8, 179-81
Las Ruinas, 215
Rumboll, Bill, 158
Rumboll, Mrs Hilda, 158-60
Rumboll, Maurice, 159

**LARGE PRINT**

ISIS publish a wide range of books in large print, from fiction to biography. A full list of titles is available free of charge from the address below. Alternatively, contact your local library for details of their collection of ISIS books.

Details of ISIS unabridged audio books are also available.

Any suggestions for books you would like to see in large print or audio are always welcome.

**ISIS**
**55 St Thomas' Street**
**Oxford OX1 1JG**
**(0865) 250333**